QUESTIONS

AND

REFORM JEWISH ANSWERS

NEW AMERICAN REFORM RESPONSA

by Walter Jacob

OTHER BOOKS OF INTEREST TO THE READER

Walter Jacob CONTEMPORARY AMERICAN REFORM RESPONSA, Central Conference of American Rabbis, (1983) 322 pp.

Walter Jacob AMERICAN REFORM RESPONSA, Central Conference of American Rabbis, (1983) 561 pp.

Elliot L. Stevens RABBINIC AUTHORITY, Central Conference of American Rabbis, (1982) 184 pp.

Simeon J. Maslin GATES OF MITZVAH, Central Conference of American Rabbis, (1979) 166 pp.

Peter S. Knobel GATES OF THE SEASONS, Central Conference of American Rabbis, (1983) 208 pp.

Solomon B. Freehof NEW REFORM RESPONSA, Hebrew Union College, (1981) 282 pp.

Solomon B. Freehof TODAY'S REFORM RESPONSA, Hebrew Union College, (1990) 165 pp.

Walter Jacob THE PITTSBURGH PLATFORM IN RETROSPECT - With the Proceedings of 1885, Rodef Shalom, (1985) 123 pp.

Walter Jacob and Moshe Zemer DYNAMIC HALAKHAH Institute of Progressive Halakhah, (1991) 148 pp.

Available through the Central Conference of American Rabbis, 192 Lexington Avenue, New York, New York 10016

QUESTIONS AND REFORM JEWISH ANSWERS

NEW AMERICAN REFORM RESPONSA

by Walter Jacob

Central Conference of American Rabbis
5752 New York 1992

Library of Congress Cataloging-in-Publication Data

Jacob, Walter, 1930 -
    Questions and Reform Jewish Answers : new American Reform
responsa / by Walter Jacob
       p.   cm.
Companion volume to: Contemporary American Reform responsa.
1987. Companion volume to: American Reform responsa. 1983.
Includes index to three volumes.
ISBN 0-88123-017-0 : $ 24.00
1. Reform Judaism - Customs and practices.   2. Responsa -
1800 - 3. Jewish Law - Reform Judaism. I. Central Conference of
American Rabbis. II. Title
BM197.J34 1992   92-3271
296.1'8-dc20   CIP

Dedicated to

KATE STERN

for her love and devotion to three generations

Contents

Shabbat

Holidays

YOREH DEAH

Medicine

Funeral - Burial - Tombstone

EVEN HAEZER

HOSHEN MISHPAT

Preface

This volume, published by the Central Conference of American Rabbis, has benefitted from a gift of the Rodef Shalom Congregation of Pittsburgh, Pennsylvania. I am very grateful to the Congregation for its generous support. I want to express thanks to Elliot Stevens for his advice. The typescript for this volume has been done with much devotion by Barbara Bailey, my special thanks to her; she was aided by Robert Goldman and Svetlana Gyeguzyina to whom I am grateful.

All of the responsa in this volume were written by the author; responsa marked with an * were circulated to the Responsa Committee for their reaction and comments or discussed at meetings. Some of the comments by my colleagues have been incorporated in those responsa. Their names are listed in the appropriate *Yearbooks* and I am most grateful to them for their suggestions.

Several of the responsa printed in this volume have appeared previously in the *Yearbook of the Central Conference of American Rabbis* and in the *Journal of Reform Judaism*. They are now reprinted with the permission of the Central Conference.

I am especially thankful to my dear wife, Irene for her patience through some exceptionally full years and to my sons Kenney and Daniel who have watched this book grow.

December 1991
Tevet 5752

Introduction

Setting Limits in Reform Judaism

Responsa by their very nature expand the parameters of the *halakhah* and set limits to what is permissible and what is prohibited. That has been the path since the beginning in *Gaonic* times. Questions which elicited brief or lengthy answers have dealt with very specific matters but cumulatively have covered entire areas and in this way established new boundaries for the *halakhah*.

This has been the effort of my responsa and those of my predecessors. Of course, as we turn to *halakhah* and Reform Judaism at the end of the twentieth century, the issues which this form of Jewish expression, raises are quite different from those anticipated in 1907, when the Responsa Committee was established under the chairmanship of Kaufmann Kohler. Yet the differences may not be as great as they might initially appear.

If the Responsa Committee was to help graduating students from Hebrew Union College defend their Reform positions through references to traditional text, then the work of the committee lay in the defining of perimeters within the larger context of the more than a thousand years of responsa literature. The early questions and their answers indicate that this, indeed, seems to have been the intention. When new ground was broke and matters discussed which had previously not been raised, the responsa set boundaries and provided guidance. This was equally true of the handful of American Reform responsa written before the creation of the committee such as Schlessinger's *Cremation from a Jewish Point of View* (1891) or Isaac Mayer Wise's on *Circumcision of Adult Proselytes* (1893). In the early years of the committee most concerns were ritual and the responsa dealt primarily with the practices of Judaism and their expression in the Reform Jewish community.

None of the early chairmen collected their responsa, and so they never provided an overview or introduction to what they were doing. Therefore, we do not know their philosophy of responsa or *halakhah*. We can obtain that, in part, through an analysis of the responsa, but we must remember that their intent may have been slightly different than what their efforts produced.

Matters became different with Solomon B. Freehof whose eight volumes of responsa were each provided with an introduction which provided the developing *halakhic* philosophy of the author. His general view may be best summarized through the well known statement that the responsa should provide "guidance not governance." Solomon B. Freehof began his series on responsa volumes with the opening sentence "Reform Judaism is strong in ethical idealism but weak in legal discipline" (*Reform Responsa*, 1960). This echoed the statement by Kaufmann Kohler in 1906 that it was the intent of the committee "to bring about some order within Reform Jewish practices and to provide ready access for those who sought answers in rabbinic matters" but, of course, Freehof carried it much further. Now, three decades later in the nineteen nineties, we may well ask whether the time for a more concerted effort of *halakhic* discipline has not arrived or is overdue.

A great deal has happened in the last decades which has moved us toward *halakhah*. Fine volumes as *Gates of Mitzvah* (1979) edited by Simeon and J. Maslin, and *Gates of the Season* (1983) edited by Peter S. Knobel, have used terminology which would have been avoided in an earlier age. They continually state

INTRODUCTION

"it is a *Mitzvah*...." and simply list *mitzvot* which are considered significant for Reform Jews. Without clearly defining the nature of the obligation or the source of the obligation, they nevertheless state the obligation. This means that a pattern of life has been provided for Reform Jews; it is consistent and gives ongoing guidance at least in the cycle of festivals and the path of life from birth to death.

The somewhat earlier *Shabbat Manual*, edited by W. Gunther Plaut, provided similar guidance for the observance of *shabbat*. It was not specific when it dealt with work prohibited or permitted on *shabbat*, but concentrated on an outline of ritual observance; it stimulated individuals to think about their life style and the mood of *shabbat*.

These books, strangely enough, were a product of the sixties and seventies which led to the *Gates of Prayer* (1975) with its excessively large choice of services and its inability to provide a standard service. These decades also gave us the "Centenary Statement" which restated in the underlying principles of Reform Judaism in a way which took into account the post-Holocaust world as well as the State of Israel. However, in matters of *halakhah* it did not move very far.

If it was possible despite the turmoil of the sixties and seventies within and outside the Jewish world to produce books which dealt with *mitzvot* and tried to set a pattern for Reform Judaism, then it should be easier for us in the nineteen nineties to move along the same path. We must now ask ourselves how should this proceed.

We will always want the Conference to make policy decisions on major issues such as patrilineal descent, the status of women, *gerut*, *gittin*, homosexuality and lesbianism, etc. They will need be resolved thorough careful debate preceeded by thorough committee work.

The annual resolutions of the Conference provide us with a moral and ethical basis for action and *mitzvot*. They successfully treat the specific problems of our age.

These methods are not practical for the hundreds of issues of daily conduct which continually arise. Answers for them should be given through codes of conduct. We need volumes like the *Gates of Mitzvot* and *Gates of the Season* for professional and business ethics, not *musar*, but *halakhah*. Such guides may not initially attain an ideal level or win instant acceptance, but they will set standards and provide goals for our lives. Neither the *Shulhan Arukh* nor its predecessors won immediate or universal acceptance, but they provided patterns which could be modified. That tradition remained remarkably flexible till the rabbinic leadership was frightened by the Enlightenment and refused to make further adjustments.

New problems will always be discussed by our Responsa Committee. This committee instead of dealing with broad general issues has limited itself to specific questions. Precedence, both traditional and Reform, has played a major role as have the scientific and sociological data of our age. This has been the traditional way of writing responsa throughout the centuries. We differ from our predecessors as we consciously acknowledge the various factors and influences. The responsa represent the decision of the Conference whether written by the chairperson or the entire committee.

Our broader concern with *halakhah* has led to the establishment of the Freehof Institute of Progressive *halakhah*. This international body, led professionally by Moshe Zemer and of which I am chairman, deals with a wide range of *halakhic* matters, both

INTRODUCTION

the underlying principles and the practical concerns on an international basis. We encompass the Reform Jewish communities of the United States, Israel, Europe, as well as the other continents. Although this Institute has just gotten underway, the initial volume, *Dynamic Jewish Law* (1991), has provided some substantive essays and a basis for future discussion.

Responsa represent individual decisions in very limited areas, but cumulatively they cover a broad range. So, for example, the medical responsa written by Solomon B. Freehof and me provide a good indication of the Reform Jewish attitude toward most modern medical issues. The same would be true in virtually every field which has been covered in depth. Responsa, therefore, are a cumulative way for providing Reform *halakhah*.

As we proceed along these *halakhic* lines, many legitimate issues must be raised. We must concern ourselves with personal autonomy. We are not certain about the nature of God, the source of the *mitzvot*. In other words, whose *mitzvot* are we dealing with? In addition, we must define the *mitzvah*. How obligatory can it be within the framework of Reform Judaism? We must establish a relationship with the other *halakhic* systems, Orthodox and Conservative as well as other ideologies.

We must be willing to give up a certain amount of autonomy to eliminate anarchy. We have already surrendered considerable autonomy quietly. We gave up our congregational prayer books at the turn of the century in favor of the *Union Prayer Book*. Any congregation which wished to continue it's own prayer book could do so, but eventually all adopted a common book and we have continued along this path with successive editions. Within the prayerbook a greater or smaller number of alternative services have been provided, in some editions with strong ideological differences, in others with relatively minor distinctions. In this way

xxiii

we have solved the problem of autonomy versus the interests of the community. For us, at the end of the twentieth century the vigor of the community is more important than autonomy.

There are many areas of observance in which we have taken a similar path over the decades, sometimes through gentle persuasion and at other times unconsciously. Neither rabbis nor congregants have been coerced, yet a pattern of uniformity in many areas has emerged.

We must assure the rights of individuals to differ and to take us along still uncharted paths. That is not only important for us as individuals, but also vital to the Reform Jewish movement. We shall always be open to new ideas.

In the struggle between guidance and governance the latter must be our path. Guidance no longer fits our mood. It was appropriate thirty years ago, but we have outgrown it and need governance. This means that we will adopt measurable standards. Individuals who wish to remain outside this system will need to work out a rationale for their actions rather than hide behind vague feelings of autonomy. Too often the specifics of our religious life have been lost through inertia and an unwillingness to take Reform Judaism seriously cloaked behind autonomy.

When we ask about the essential nature of the commandment and its source, we stand close to some traditional lines of reasoning. We along with many earlier Reform thinkers would say that the source is Divine, however, mediated through millennia of human voices. The Divine element may sometimes be a difficult to recognize, but we should generally be able to see it in the underlying premise of a commandment. We recognize that there are commandments provided by tradition, for which we see no Divine basis, so we exclude these from our list or understand them as *minhag* (custom). This view may seem presumptuous to the Orthodox, but fits into our framework and our understanding of the historic development of Judaism.

We should not and need not deal with the nature of God and the way in which the commandments were given. Such theological debates are fascinating and are important in their own way, but they have rarely played a significant role in the development of the *halakhah*. Maimonides alone provided a theological framework at the beginning of his *Mishneh Torah*. All other codifiers, respondents and commentators developed their theology as they wrote. It was implicit, but not stated explicitly. It may not always have been totally consistent, but this did not disturb them and it should not bother us. We have never given theology a primary place in our religious development and need not do so as we develop *halakhah*.

The responsa in this volume bring the total number of responsa which I have published to five-hundred and five. If these are added to the four-hundred and thirty-three of Solomon B. Freehof then we have a total of slightly less than one-thousand Reform responsa. We must add to them *halakhic* letters and many answers given in a summary less formal way. Solomon B. Freehof's *halakhic* correspondence extends to hundreds of letters. My unpublished responsa, *halakhic* correspondence, as well as notes of brief answers number more than a thousand. So, together we have probably dealt with more than three thousand questions in the last thirty-five years in addition to the responsa of our predecessors. There is, therefore, a good beginning for a Reform *halakhah* which can make general statements on a large number of business, medical, interreligious, ethical and ritual issues for Reform Jews. It is time to place them into a form which will appropriately govern us and set standards for our lives.

QUESTIONS AND REFORM JEWISH ANSWERS

We, at this juncture in Reform Jewish history, must set boundaries and can only do so by establishing clear *halakhic* parameters in every area of life. Judaism demands a path of life; it is our task to define that path clearly. Thereby we may help our people live a life which is authentically Jewish and modern. The responsa in this collection represent another step in this direction.

Orah Hayim

1. QUALIFICATIONS FOR A CANTOR *

QUESTION: A young man has shown an interest in the cantorial position of the congregation. He has a good voice, fine character and knows Jewish music. His general Jewish knowledge is limited and he knows no Hebrew. Our services contain a fair amount of Hebrew and, of course, he would represent Judaism in the general community. Is it appropriate to engage him with the title of cantor? (Rabbi Robert A. Seigel, Charlotte NC)

ANSWER: The term *hazan* was used in the *Talmud* to designate a number of different positions not all related to the service. The synagogue *hazan* looked after the lights of the synagogues, cared for the *Torah* scrolls, sounded a horn or trumpet to announce the beginning of *shabbat* and holidays, and guided visitors in the synagogues of Jerusalem (*J* Maaseh Sheni 56a; *M* Sotah 7.7 f; *J* Meg IV l5b, 75b; *M* Sotah VII 21d; *Tos* Bik 2.10). At times the *hazan* seems to have also been a teacher, a *sheliah tzibur* and a *darshan* especially in smaller congregations (*J* Yeb 13a; *Midrash Rabbah* Gen 81). In the *Saboraic* or *Gaonic* period when services presumably became more complex, the *hazan* became the permanent *sheliah tzibur* (*Sofrim* 10.7 ll.3), so it was possible for Amram Gaon to state that a congregation should find a qualified *sheliah tzibur* for itself (*Theshuvot Hagaonim* (ed) Blick #84; Solomon ben Aderet *Responsa* I #450, 691). In later centuries *hazanim* frequently led services especially in the larger congregations.

The qualifications for those who lead the prayers whether paid or voluntary are basically the same. They were originally outlined by the *Mishnah* which demanded maturity, knowledge of the Hebrew prayers, a family with children and enough need to be able to pray sincerely (*M* Taanit 2.1). In the *Talmudic* discussion of this verse, Judah Ben Ilai added a number of other stipulations which required good character from youth onward, a pleasant voice and that he be a farmer dependent upon the rain for which he would, among other things, pray. He was also to possess a thorough knowledge of the entire Bible which included the *Torah*, the prophets and writings, along with mastery of the *midrashic* and legal literature and, of course, the liturgy (*M* Taanit 16a). Some of the medieval authors emphasized other characteristics so, for example, Maimonides stressed modesty, probity, good deeds within and outside the city and if possible good lineage (*Responsa* (ed) Freiman #86). On the other hand, Meir of Rothenburg argued for life experiences which would enable him to pray with real feelings (*Responsa* #137), while Solomon ben Aderet emphasized a feeling of the reverence and awe in the presence of God (*Responsa* I 215). These and other sources both ancient and modern as summarized in the *Tur* and *Shulhan Arukh* (Orah Hayim 53) dealt with the spiritual, moral and educational qualifications of a *hazan*. Although scholarship was desirable, personal character was more important. Naturally a pleasing voice and the ability to give meaning to the prayers was always considered important (*Ibid*). However, even those who felt that the cantor need not be excessively learned or an expert in the Bible and the later legal literature, insisted on sufficient knowledge of Hebrew to understand all the prayers and to chant the *Torah* without difficulty (*Tur* and *Shulhan Arukh* Orah Hayim 53 and commentaries).

The main problem connected with *hazanim* in the *halakhic* literature dealt with moral issues, styles of music and liturgical innovations. The qualifications mentioned above were accepted in all periods of Jewish history.

Although many of our prayers are in English, a large

number are recited in Hebrew and these are increasing. Furthermore, as a representative of the congregation in the larger community, an adequate knowledge of Hebrew and of all areas of Jewish studies is necessary. It may be possible to engage the individual in question as a cantorial soloist and encourage him to acquire sufficient knowledge to become a *hazan* and to enter that honored profession. We should remember that in modern times professional education which meets certain standards has become required. There are also professional associations which have established standards. Congregations should be encouraged to seek such standards in a candidate. The congregation may wish to provide some scholarship incentives to this able young man.

February 1988

2. A CANTOR MARRIED TO A CONVERT

QUESTION: A congregation has asked whether it is appropriate for a cantor, who leads the congregation regularly in worship, to be married to a convert? (Mary Greenwald, New York NY)

ANSWER: When a person has been converted to Judaism and has joined us, then there is no difference between that individual and a person born as a Jew. Neither the cantor nor the rabbi are prohibited from marrying a convert. Only *kohanim* in the Orthodox tradition are prohibited from marrying someone who has converted (*M* Kid 4.5; Kid 77b ff; *Shulhan Arukh* Even Haezer 7.21). Although if such a marriage occurs, the couple is not forced to separate. These prohibitions are not valid for us as Reform Jews. There are no other restrictions on marrying a convert.

June 1989

3. THE REBBE'S PICTURE

QUESTION: The Lubavitch group has placed many advertisements with large pictures of it's rebbe. Is this in keeping with Jewish tradition? Does not Jewish tradition frown upon a display of any image? Does this include such photographs? (Rabbi Amiel Wohl, New Rochelle NY)

ANSWER: Although portraits have rarely survived the Middle Ages we have a picture of what is assumed to be Maimonides, now unfortunately found on the label of an indifferent kosher wine. We possess portraits of various other figures, for example, Manneseh ben Israel, several paintings by Rembrandt of Jews who did not seem to hesitate about sitting for him, etc. In more recent times various Orthodox authorities have been reluctant about photographs so for example, the Hungarian custom of placing photographs on the tombstone of a deceased has been denounced (Greenwald *Kol Bo al Avelut* pp 380 ff). Similarly Jacob Emden felt it was wrong to have a portrait done. We can see that in the last centuries there was some reluctance to move in the direction of portraits, but it was usually overcome in favor of a picture as long as it did not appear in the synagogue. Two dimensional pictures as well as portrait busts were permitted in the older tradition, we as

4

Reform Jews have no objections to them even in the synagogue (S. B. Freehof *Modern Reform Responsa #33*).

We should remember, however, that with the Lubavitch Rebbe we have an additional problem of adoration verging on idolatry. This is an issue which should be appropriately addressed by that group and by their Orthodox colleagues as such adulation is not appropriate within the Jewish tradition and approaches *avodah zarah*.

December 1989

4. A SERVICE WITH LESS THAN A *MINYAN*

QUESTION: May we conduct a service at home with less than a *minyan*? (James Harrison, Memphis TN)

ANSWER: We seek a *minyan* for all public services, but we have not seen this as an absolute requirement. We should make every effort to obtain the ten individuals for services at the house of mourning, at a *berit*, etc., of course, in keeping with our Reform tradition that both men and women are counted in this quorum.

Under unusual circumstances the service may be conducted with less than a *minyan*, for example an early *Talmudic* tradition indicated that even seven men were enough (*Mas Soferim* 10.6; *Tos* to Meg 23b). This was based on a verse in Judges 5.2 which contains precisely seven words. This tradition was generally not followed and these sources were not mentioned again.

Discussed at greater length, both in the *Talmud* and later tradition, were situations in which nine people were present, but a tenth could simply not be found. Under those emergency conditions one *Talmudic* authority, Rab Huna, decided that the ark with the *Torah* could be considered the tenth person, but as other authorities felt that this was improper they discussed whether it would be possible to free a slave in order to obtain a *minyan* (Ber 47b).

Much later Rabenu Tam indicated that a small child still in it's cradle or a child carrying a *humash* would be included in the number necessary for a *minyan* (Isaac of Vienna *Or Zeruah* 196; *Mahzor Vitri* #82). Joseph Caro mentioned the custom but discouraged it while Isserles felt that one could be more permissive in this matter (*Shulhan Arukh* Orah Hayim 55.4).

We can see that there were situations in which communities had great difficulty assembling a *minyan*; the discussions dealt with public services. When this occurred authorities were willing to be lenient. We, however, in most communities should simply make a more vigorous effort and assemble the necessary *minyan*, if it is at all possible, for a service whether public or private.

June 1989

5. A FIXED SERVICE TIME

QUESTION: Should Friday evening or other religious services occur only at a fixed time or can they fluctuate according to the needs and desires of the congregation? My congregation would like to have some services on Friday evening at 7:00, others at 8:00 or 8:30. (Allen Roth, New York NY)

ANSWER: You are perfectly correct that traditional Judaism demands that worship be conducted at a regular time. The *Talmudic* injunction to set a "fixed time for services", as well as the commandment of worshipping with the congregation (*Shulhan Arukh* Orah Hayim 90.19), refer to the *mitzvah* of setting aside a definite time each day for prayer and that prayer was to be from the heart (*M* Pirqei Avot 2.13). Ideally, of course, a person should pray throughout the day (Ber 21a).

There has been considerable discussion about the exact times for prayer so the *Talmud* (Berakhot) began its discussion of prayer with the question, "At what time do we recite the *shema*." We learn from the discussion which followed that the morning prayers could be recited from sunrise until one-third of the day has passed. While the afternoon prayer, *minhah,* may be recited from noon until sunset (Ber 25b; *Shulhan Arukh* Orah Hayim 233.1 ff). As a matter of convenience the *minhah* prayers have often been said just before the evening prayers so that it would not be necessary for the congregation to gather again. The evening services should be conducted any time after three stars appear in the heavens (*Shulhan Arukh* Orah Hayim 235.1). However, tradition has been lenient with the evening prayers; they may be recited from sunset onward (*Shulhan Arukh* Orah Hayim 233.1), preferably before midnight, but actually until dawn (Ber 2a; *Shulhan Arukh* Orah Hayim 235.3). All of this shows that the tradition had no fixed times for prayers but set them into a general portion of the day. As those segments were determined by sunrise and sunset, the actual time varied seasonally. In an earlier period, when life was governed principally by the beginning and end of the day, this *de facto* provided a "set time". Nowadays, of course, when we are governed by clocks, Orthodox services are linked to the beginning

7

and end of day in accordance with stipulated times which change weekly; this has been precisely noted for each time zone. There is, therefore, no obligation in tradition to set a constantly fixed time for a service.

We should consider the practical implications of moving the time when the congregation worships and try to avoid confusion. There would be nothing wrong with having one service a month at a different time than the other services, but from a practical point of view it would be wise to fix the schedule and remain with it, i.e. an earlier service on the first or second Friday of each month, etc. Such changes should be made for good and valid reasons, as the inclusion of young children in services, or provisions for a more traditional segment of the community which wishes to worship before sundown.

December 1988

6. SYNAGOGUE HONORS *

QUESTION: Does a family have the right to claim certain synagogue honors for itself? May these honors be inherited from one generation to the next?

A number of years ago, when honors were sold, a certain member always held the honor of opening and standing before the ark at *Neilah* on Yom Kippur. When he died, his son-in-law claimed this as his right. (The rightful "heir" presumably acquiesced). It was conceded to be his "*hazaqah*."

Following the death of this son-in-law the remaining daughter's husband assumed this role. He has claimed this as a

8

tradition which the congregation must respect, and that a descendant of this particular family has the claim to this honor in perpetuity. Is there an inherent right to such honors? What are the limits? (Rabbi Albert A. Goldman, Washington PA)

ANSWER: The principle of *hazaqah* has been applied to various assets (movable and immovable). It has also been applied to synagogue honors (*Shulhan Arukh* Hoshen Mishpat 162.7). Some discussions concerned specific synagogue seats and the length of time necessary to make a claim to a seat permanent. Three years of uninterrupted synagogue attendance was deemed necessary to fulfill the obligation although occasionally an absence was excused due to mourning or illness (Solomon ben Aderet *Responsa* I 943; *Bet Habehirah* B B 29a; *Bet Yosef* to *Tur* Hoshen Mishpat 140.16; 141.2, etc). Some of the responsa have dealt with other synagogue honors which were inherited from one generation to the next. Usually this was only possible for the founders of the synagogue. In other words, through their action to establish the original synagogue they had certain rights which could be given to their heirs (*Shulhan Arukh* Hoshen Mishpat 162.7; see also *Pithei Teshuvah*). It was, however, generally not practical to follow this custom with synagogue seats or honors as income for the maintenance of the synagogue was related to them. Therefore, the heirs were provided the opportunity of acquiring such honors by making substantial contributions to retain them.

We must make a distinction between honors acquired through a financial contribution and those bestowed by the congregation in recognition of distinguished service or scholarship. The latter depended entirely on the will of the congregation which could grant them and revoke them.

There is a great deal of local *minhag* involved in all such matters, but one can say with the exception noted above, honors or special places in the synagogue cannot be inherited in perpetuity. Additional exceptions may, of course, be created through documents which may grant such honors in perpetuity (E. Margolis *Shaarei Efraim* Shaar 1, 2 f).

The local *minhagim* are intended to strengthen the congregation and to assure peaceful relationships within the congregation. In this instance, therefore, it would be wise to place a good bit of emphasis on those factors. Many synagogue honors are available during the High Holidays; furthermore, it would be quite possible for more than one person to open and close the ark during the *Neilah* service. This should make it possible to reach an accommodation which preserves the honor of the family and the rights of the congregation.

June 1987

7. HEBREW OR ENGLISH AT AN ISRAELI SERVICE

QUESTION: My family and I spend a part of each year in Israel. Although we are beginning to feel at home with spoken Hebrew, it remains rather basic, and we feel ill at ease in the Liberal Jewish services which we have attended. We would like to establish a service which will use English. That effort has been discouraged by various individuals who felt that this was inappropriate in Israel, and that it would hurt the Liberal movement in Israel. May we use a service which contains a considerable amount of English in Israel? (Norman Miller, Tel Aviv Israel)

10

ORAH HAYIM

ANSWER: Problems with the lack of familiarity with Hebrew are very ancient. Ezra already had to explain the *Torah* to the exiles who returned from Babylonia (Neh 8.7). Subsequently the *Torah* and other sections of the Bible were translated into Aramaic as well as Greek, so that they could be properly understood.

We find some discussion of the language to be used in prayers both in the *Mishnah* and the *Talmud*. Permission to recite the basic prayers in the vernacular was granted quite early (*M* Sotah 7.1; 32b ff). Such decisions in favor of the vernacular were carried into all the great codifications of Jewish law (*Yad* Hil Qeriat Shema 2.10; *Tur* and *Shulhan Arukh* Orah Hayim 62; 101). In addition to this, of course, many devotional volumes and books of women's prayers were written in the vernacular throughout the Middle Ages (Solomon B. Freehof "Devotional Literature in the Vernacular" *Central Conference of American Rabbis Yearbook* Vol 33 pp 380 ff). Reform prayerbooks began to use the vernacular in Europe and in the United States. The earliest such liturgy is the Charleston, South Carolina prayerbook of 1824. We have continued to use the vernacular alongside Hebrew in lands throughout the world. The amount of Hebrew in our services has varied from one locale to another, but we have always retained enough Hebrew to continue a strong bond with the tradition, and enough vernaculer to enable our congregants to understand the prayers and to recite them with appropriate devotion and not by rote. This should also be the goal of your services in Israel.

During this period when English remains your primary tongue and, therefore, the local Liberal services are not meaningful, there is nothing wrong with starting another service for your family and friends which follows the American *minhag* and contains some English. We should remember that *minhagim* connected with ritual, poetry, melodies and language were often continued by immigrants

11

or long term visitors in the land in which they found themselves. Since the first century, synagogues in Israel were identified as Babylonian which meant that they followed Babylonian rites and possibly some Aramaic. Later, of course, many Aramaic prayers were added to all services. In the Middle Ages the immigration of *Sephardim* to *Ashkenzi* lands led to debates and acrimony as local congregations sought to impose a single *minhag* on all Jews in their locale (David Cohen of Corfu *Responsa* #11; Moses of Trani *Responsa* Vol I #307; etc). Such efforts to establish uniformity inevitably failed. In the United States, each group which arrived brought its own *minhagim* and these included variations in liturgy and melodies.

There would be nothing improper about establishing a *minyan* which will have a service partially in English for the benefit of your friends and family.

January 1991

8. OLD AND NEW CUSTOMS

QUESTION: My Reform Congregation has introduced a wide variety of rituals which the previous generation did not use. Some members of the older generation feel that this casts aspersions on their practice of Judaism. Need they adopt the new rituals and practices if they do not feel comfortable with them? (Florence Stern, Buffalo NY)

ANSWER: *Minhagim* have changed continually through our history. Customs were dropped by congregations when they were no longer considered appropriate while others were adopted. We find reflections of this in discussions about the use of *piyutim*, other prayers, melodies, opening the ark, etc. in synagogue services. Some have always insisted that *minhagim* be continued while others felt that change was appropriate. When the community made a decision nothing prevented individuals from continuing in the older manner; it became problematic only when such an individual led the public service. In some communities the congregation was tolerant and permitted such variations and in others it refused to ask such people who were unwilling to follow the new *minhagim* to lead services (*Tur* and *Shulhan Arukh* Orah Hayim 68 and commentaries; *Yad* Hil Tefilah 1.9; Isaac Unna "Über den Minhag" *Jeshurun* Vol 10 pp 463 ff; L. Zunz *Die Ritus* pp 21 ff; H. J. Zimmels *Ashkenazim and Sephardim* pp 99 ff; I. Elbogen *Der Jüdische Gottesdienst* pp 9 ff; Samuel de Medina *Responsa* Orah Hayim #35; Hayim Halberstam *Divrei Hayim* II 8; Eliezer Deutsch *Peri Hasadeh* #35; Moses Sofer *Hatam Sofer* Orah Hayim #15,16; Joseph Saul Nathanson *Shoel Umeshiv* III 1 #247; Jacob Ettlinger *Binyan Zion* #122; L. Löw *Ben Hanania* Vol 9 pp 381 ff; Joseph David Azulai *Yosef Ometz* #20).

Customs were questioned most frequently when the nature of the community itself changed; this was usually due to the arrival of newcomers who brought their own *minhagim* and sought to establish them in the synagogue which they found. Normally the original inhabitants succeeded in defending their customs against the new settlers and this invariably led to the establishment of a second synagogue.

In our Reform communities a change in mood has led to the reestablishment of certain *minhagim* while others have been dropped. We should permit the older generation to continue in their fashion both publicly and privately. Neither way is "right"; both the old and the new represent noble paths of religious expression. For example, it is our custom now to recite the *Torah* blessings in Hebrew, but if an older member recites them in English it is perfectly acceptable.   In periods of transition, unnecessary strife may result unless tolerance and understanding is shown by both generations. We should make the changes which express our mood while continuing to recognize the validity of practices of a former generation.

December 1990

9. CONGREGATION AND *TALLIT*

QUESTION: Should a Reform Congregation provide a *tallit* for all worshippers? Up to the present time it has been the custom for the rabbis and cantor, as well as anyone involved in the *Torah* service to wear a *tallit* We have also encouraged the congregation to wear a *tallit* at the *Kol Nidrei* service.

Although traditionally the *tallit* is worn only during daytime services, would it be appropriate for congregants to wear a *tallit* on Friday evening as we customarily read the *Torah* on that evening? May the *tallit* reflect some individuality? (Robert Strauss, Oklahoma City OK)

ANSWER: The *tallit* and the *tzitzit* represent the rabbinic interpretation of a Biblical commandment (Nu 25.38 ff). This was originally fulfilled through the wearing of the four cornered garment with *tzitzit* (fringes) at all times as a constant reminder of

14

the obligation to perform the commandments. When styles changed, the *tallit* became an additional garment worn beneath other garments and so it remains as the *tallit qatan* worn by many traditional Jews. This is worn throughout the day.

The *Talmud* (Men 43a) debated whether women are obligated to wear *tzitzit*. Rab Judah felt that the obligation rested upon them as did other earlier teachers while Rab Simeon declared them exempt as this was a positive commandment which depended upon a fixed time. In other words, one was obligated to recite a special blessing in the morning when the *tallit* was donned. It has been the general Orthodox practice to exclude women from this commandment (*Shulhan Arukh* Orah Hayim 8.6).

The *tallit* worn during services grew out of the same custom as the *tallit qatan*. It is generally worn at all morning services and in the Orthodox tradition by all males even those below the age of *Bar Mitzvah* (*Shulhan Arukh* Orah Hayim 17.3). There are, however, other traditions which state that it is worn only after *Bar Mitzvah* (*Tur* and *Shulhan Arukh* Orah Hayim and commentaries) or only after the male has married.

A *tallit* is also required, according to tradition, for those who participate in the *Torah* service (*Shulhan Arukh* Orah Hayim 14.3). This would be true whenever the *Torah* is read. It is likewise worn at the *Kol Nidrei* service to demonstrate the great significance of this service. Traditional Jews will try to begin to wear the *tallit* before it is dark so that the appropriate blessing can be said while it is still daylight. Otherwise they don it without any blessing (*Levush* Orah Hayim 619.1).

The wearing of a *tallit* during morning services is an option for us. There is a provision for this in the *Gates of Prayer* where the appropriate benedictions may be found. Furthermore, it should be worn by all those who participate in the *Torah* service if that is the

15

custom of the congregation. This means both the *shabbat* morning *Torah* readings as well as any *Torah* readings which may take place during the evening and if the *Torah* is read during *shabbat minhah*. This is in keeping with the traditional moods and we should encourage it wherever it is appropriate. As a number of worshippers may come to the synagogue without a *tallit* or may be a guest in the city, the congregation may want to provide them with a *tallit*. I am sure that most individuals will, however, bring their own.

We would, of course, make no distinction between men and women in this obligation so both men and women of all ages who wish to wear a *tallit* during the morning service should do so. If it is customary to wear a *tallit* during the *Torah* service then this should also be equally obligatory for men and women. As a wide variety of woven and decorative *tallisim* have become available in the last decades, it should be easy to find an attractive *tallit* and to express one's individuality through it.

April 1988

10. A MULTICOLORED *TALLIT*

QUESTION: May a *tallit* be woven of many different colors? Are there restrictions on the material which may be used? Who should wear it? (Patricia Levinson, Rochester NY)

ANSWER: The *tallit* and the *tzitzit* represent the rabbinic interpretation of a Biblical commandment (Nu 25.38 ff). This was originally fulfilled through the wearing of the four cornered garment with *tzitzit* (fringes) at all times as a constant reminder of the obligation to perform the commandments. When styles changed the *tallit* became an additional garment worn beneath other garments and so it remains as the *tallit qatan* worn by many traditional Jews. This is worn throughout the day.

The *Talmud* (Men 43a) debated whether women were obligated to wear *tzitzit*. Rab Judah felt that the obligation rested upon them as did other earlier teachers, while Rab Simeon declared them exempt as this is a positive commandment which depended upon a fixed time, as the wearer was obligated to recite a special blessing in the morning when the *tallit* is donned. It has been the general Orthodox practice to exclude women from this commandment (*Shulhan Arukh* Orah Hayim 8.6).

The *tallit* worn during services stemmed from the same commandment as the *tallit qatan*. It is generally worn at all morning services and in the Orthodox tradition by all males even those below the age of *Bar Mitzvah* (*Shulhan Arukh* Orah Hayim 17.3). There are, however, other traditions which state that it is worn only after *Bar Mitzvah* (*Tur* and *Shulhan Arukh* Orah Hayim and commentaries) or only after the male has married.

A *tallit* is also required, according to tradition, for those who participate in the *Torah* service (*Shulhan Arukh* Orah Hayim 14.3). This would be true whenever the *Torah* is read. It is likewise worn at the *Kol Nidrei* service to demonstrate the great significance of this service. Traditional Jews will don the *tallit* before it is dark, so that the appropriate blessing can be said while it is still daylight. Otherwise, they wear it without any blessing (*Levush* Orah Hayim 619.1).

There were discussions about the way in which the *tallit* was worn and its length (BB 57b). Some have suggested that it be folded double over the shoulders (Shab 147a; Men 41a; *Yalqut* Psalm 103).

The color was guided by the Hebrew term *tekhelet* normally translated as blue or a bluish purple, however, in the *Talmudic* period it was decided that blue need not be used in order to fulfill the obligation of this commandment (Men 38a ff). That was the pattern followed by the later codes (*Yad* Hil Tzitzit; *Shulhan Arukh* Orah Hayim 8ff). Normally the stripes on the *tallit* are black or blue, occasionally it has been decorated in addition with a silver embroidery (S. Z. Ariel *Meir Netiv* p 212). The *tallit* itself should be made of wool or silk (*Shulhan Arukh* Orah Hayim 9.2f). It may be woven of other material as along as it is consistent throughout. Nothing has been said in the literature about the color of the material, although the traditional *tallit* is white or a shade close to white. I have not been able to find any prohibition which deals with a colored *tallit*, and so it would be appropriate to use such a *tallit* at a synagogue service at the appropriate times.

October 1989

11. *TALLIT* AT AN INTER-FAITH SERVICE

QUESTION: May a *tallit* be worn generally on other interfaith religious occasions when Christian religious leaders appear in their vestments? (Rabbi E. L. Sapinsley, Bluefield WV)

ANSWER: The origins of the *tallit* and the times when it was originally worn are no longer clear. Some scholars speculate that this was the daily garment worn by all Jews and designated them specifically as Jews (See the previous responsa). In the *Talmud* we learn of the *tallit* worn by scholars (Men 41a, Shab 147a; B B 57b,

98a, etc.). In later tradition the *tallit* came to be worn by adult males during morning services, by those participating in the *Torah* service and at the *Kol Nidrei* service on *Yom Kippur*. Those who led services always wore a *tallit* (*Shulhan Arukh* Orah Hayim, 8-24). The *Zohar* gave a special status to the *tallit* and felt that it brought the worshipper closer to God particularly as it created a feeling of awe (*Zohar* Toledot p 141a).

In many of our Reform congregations the *tallit* is not generally used by the congregation, but is worn by the rabbi or cantor who leads the services. There is nothing in the tradition which deals with the wearing of the *tallit* outside the synagogue, although it seems that in the *Talmudic* and *Gaonic* period scholars wore the *tallit* as a kind of an academic robe throughout the day (*Siddur Rav Amram Gaon* p 2a). Furthermore, we should note that a *tallit qatan* is worn by all traditional Jews throughout the day, although it is generally invisible. In an earlier age the *tallit qatan* was worn above the other normal garments.

For us as Reform Jews the *tallit* has become a vestment of the rabbi or leader of the religious service. It is not mandatory but customary. In other words, prayers recited even by the leader of the congregation without a *tallit* are considered valid.

Although the *tzitzit* of a *tallit* are considered to possess a degree of holiness and should therefore be treated reverently when discarded if they are frayed, the garment is not sacred in any way. Nothing would preclude wearing it outside of a specific Jewish setting. A *tallit* may therefore be worn during interfaith occasions if it is felt that this will add to the dignity of the occasion. It is, however, in no way necessary.

May 1988

12. *KIPPOT* FOR WOMEN AND MEN

QUESTION: What is the origin of the covering the head for women and men? May women wear *kippot* as a sign of equality or would tradition prohibit this as imitation of masculine garb? How did the practice of wearing *kippot* develop? What is the Reform view? (Aaron Phillips, Cleveland OH)

ANSWER: Tradition stated that any woman who wore her hair loose and uncovered was considered a virgin (*Sifrei* #11); if a married woman exposed her hair in this way she was considered a loose woman. A married woman either had to cut her hair very closely or had to cover it in some manner. Any married woman who left her hair uncovered provided grounds for divorce and forfeited the money and property of her dowry (*M* Ket 7.6; 72a). Furthermore, all women were to cover their hair during the reading of the *shema* (Ber 24a; *Shulhan Arukh* Orah Hayim 75.1 ff; *Sheelat Yaavetz* Vol 1 #9; Vol 2 #718). This in essence meant that women were required to cover their hair in the synagogue whether single or married; this has also been discussed in the next responsum.

We can see that the wearing of a covering over the hair for married women is very old and has generally been followed by traditional Jews through the ages. Women, both married and unmarried, are required to cover their hair. As styles of hats, scarfs, and other head gear have varied according to fashion through the ages, it would be difficult to accuse women of imitating masculine garb through any head covering.

We Reform Jews would object vigorously to this requirement for women which places them in an inferior position and sees them primarily in a sexual role. As Reform Judaism has stressed the equality of men and women, we would reject this path of tradition. Reform Jewish practice does not require women to cover their hair within or outside the synagogue.

A number of women do, however, wish to keep their head covered during worship in the same manner as men, and do so as another symbol of the equality between men and women.

Let us now inquire into the origin of this custom of head covering for men. An excellent essay on this subject has been written by Jacob Z. Lauterbach (*Studies in Jewish Law, Custom, and Folklore* pp 225 ff). He demonstrated that there was no Biblical or rabbinic basis for this custom. In fact the priest in the ancient temple performed their ritual with bare head (Yoma 25a), and individuals covered their head principally when they were in mourning (M K 15a, 24a). A statement from the age of the Maccabees indicated that the pious of that period objected to a regulation of Antiochus Epiphanes which forced individuals to wear hats (II Macc 4.12); Paul registered the same custom of bareheaded worship in the Jewish communities which he visited two centuries later (I Corinth 11.4-7). In late tractate *Sofrim* the text specifically indicated that the *shema* may be recited bare headed (14.5 see also Ber 60b). In Babylonia, however, it became a sign of respect to cover one's head in the presence of a scholar. In other words, precisely the reverse of the Biblical and modern Reform custom (Kid 33a). Various historians have assumed that this practice was later adopted by the synagogue and may have been borrowed by the Babylonian Jews from their Persian neighbors (J. Z. Lauterbach *Op Cit* 232).

As Jewish communities of the Mediterranean were influenced by Babylonian custom during the hegemony of the Islamic empires, authorities in these areas insisted on a head covering during worship. On the other hand, communities influenced by Palestinian custom as those of France, Germany and Italy worshipped with uncovered heads (*Or Zarua* 2.43; Solomon Luria *Responsa* #72; Isserles to *Tur* Orah Hayim 282.3 in which he argued against the custom). This custom of covering head eventually spread and became standard in Germany and Central Europe from the thirteenth century onward although we still find some discussion of this matter later.

The most radical element of the Reform movement in the nineteenth century called for the removal of all head covering during worship as this was seen as a general sign of politeness. This was intended to distinguish Reform Jews from the rest of the Jewish community and so became a symbol for this group. This practice, however, was not followed by continental European Reform Congregations with one exception; it became standard only in the United States. There has been a trend now toward wearing a head covering in some American Reform congregations and among individuals in others as a symbol of *kelal yisrael*. This is appropriate especially as the Reform movement is well established in the United States; it does not need an obvious symbol in order to distinguish it from the remainder of the Jewish community. The historical studies have made it clear that prayer both bareheaded and with head covering have a strong basis in Judaism so both should be permitted without argument.

As women seek to express their equality with men in a wide variety of ways there is nothing wrong with their adopting a head covering for this reason. Nor would we consider this a violation of the Biblical commandment against women wearing the clothing of men (Deut 2.5). In summary then, if a woman wishes to wear a *kippah* or any other head covering in order to indicate a mood of worship akin to men it would be appropriate for her to do so in a Reform setting.

February 1990

13. WOMEN WITH HEADS COVERED IN THE SYNAGOGUE

QUESTION: In my synagogue, which is a little more traditional, it is customary for women to wear hats and to have their hair covered during services; is a wig sufficient? What is the traditional basis for this? Does the custom have ancient roots? (Richard Bernstein, Miami FL)

ANSWER: Various periods in history have considered different portions of the female body as sexually enticing. Hair was certainly considered so in the *Talmudic* period, and it was to be covered for that reason among married women (*M* Ket 2.1; 72a; Yeb 114b; Ber 24a; I Cor 11.5). Maimonides insisted on hair covering for married and unmarried women in public places (*Yad* Hil Issurei Biah 21.17). The matter has been discussed at considerable length through responsa as well as other classical sources. A full summary has been provided by Samuel Krauss "The Jewish Rite of Covering the Head" (*Hebrew Union College Annual* 19 pp 121 ff; and J. Z. Lauterbach (*Studies in Jewish Law, Custom, and Folklore* pp 225 ff and *Otzar Haposqim* Vol 9). We, of course, are concerned primarily with the question of whether prayer may be conducted when a woman's head, married or unmarried, is not covered. Caro definitely felt that it was necessary for all women to cover their head during prayer (*Shulhan Arukh* Orah Hayim 75.2); yet unmarried virgins who customarily go bareheaded could do so in the synagogue also. In a later age when uncovered hair became the general custom of society, it was no longer considered necessary for women to cover their hair. Hair in those societies had lost its sexual overtones (Y. Hayim *Sefer Huqei Hanashim* 17.1; *Masat Mosheh* Even Haezer 21.5; *Sefer Eleh Hamitzvot* Mitzvah #262). Among the Orthodox this represents a minority view; the majority continue to agree with Caro (Moses Feinstein *Igrot Mosheh* Even Haezer 1:53; Y. Weinberg *Seridei Esh* 3.30; E. Waldenberg *Tzitz Eliezer* Vol 7 48:3; etc).

In modern times traditional authorities have reached a somewhat different conclusion. Women had changed their mode of dress, and so women's hair was generally now not covered, and this, therefore, no longer constituted a barrier against prayer in a synagogue (*Arukh Hashulhan* Orah Hayim 75.8). These and other modern authorities as well as those of the last century realized that many women who were forced to cover their hair did so with a wig, which in some instances was more beautiful than their original hair, and so made them more rather than less enticing. This was precisely what the original prohibition intended to combat.

The traditional statements therefore are clear. The hair of married women, possibly unmarried women, must be covered during public prayer. A wig is generally also considered sufficient covering outside the synagogue, but not within, mainly as a matter of *marit ayin*. However, some modern Orthodox authorities have given way to the widespread custom of Orthodox women not having their hair covered and have permitted this in the synagogue.

Our Reform view is different. We do not see uncovered hair as likely to distract and be sexually arousing. The question of a wig would not arise. Women may worship in our synagogue with hair covered or uncovered, as they wish.

August 1990

14. PRAYER MOTIONS

QUESTION: Some congregants have asked about certain body motions made during various parts of the service. For example, raising one's eyes during the recital of the *qedushah* or rising on one's toes on that occasion. What is the origin of these customs? (Joseph Lieberman, Pittsburgh PA)

ANSWER: Most customs of this nature seem to have an origin in the mystical literature. The *minhag* of raising the eyes to heaven may have expressed a desire to rise to the level of the heavenly host during worship. This verse, of course, reminds us of the prophet Isaiah (6.3). Among *Sephardim* it was customary to turn the eyes downward during the recital of this prayer. These and other movements may represent an effort to encourage greater inner concentration (*Tur* Orah Hayim 125 and commentaries; *Hamanhig* #52). They generally were created by mystics and their source may be found in various Kabbalistic books. In later generations the origin of the customs was forgotten and they remained as they do now among many traditional Jews. There is no reason for us, however, to follow these customs.

August 1989

15. A TELEVISED JEWISH SERVICE IN A HOSPITAL

QUESTION: A neighboring hospital which does not have a Jewish chaplain has decided to make televised *shabbat* and holiday services available to Jewish patients. The services would be provided on a cable channel and be transmitted several times on the appropriate day. Is it permissible to provide a religious service in this fashion to bedridden patients? May a morning service be shown at another time of the day? (Karen Halperin, Boston MA)

ANSWER: A public service requires a *minyan*, but that is not possible for those who are ill and who may pray individually, they should be encouraged to do so. We may properly consider the service broadcast over the cable network as a stimulus to individual prayer. Those who are capable of participating in prayer at the same time as the broadcasts occur should do so with their own prayerbook, and perhaps with members of the family present to be part of that private service. Certainly such prayer would be much enhanced by being part of a larger group through television. Furthermore, for those individuals who are very ill and therefore unable to use a prayerbook, a broadcast service may lead them to direct their thoughts toward prayer.

Previously such services could only be broadcast directly from a synagogue and there were Orthodox objections which dealt with the *shabbat* prohibitions (*Mishpetei Uziel* Orah Hayim #5, 21). We, however, are dealing with a prerecorded and presumably abridged service and in any case we as Reform Jews would have no objection to recording such a service on *shabbat* or on the holidays. The Orthodox could record such a service on another day when there would be no objection.

As far as broadcasting the service a number of times in the day, we should ask the hospital to limit the broadcast of a morning service to the morning hours. It should be possible for almost all the patients to listen to a complete service during that time, and therefore to have a feeling that they are participating in a service at the appropriate time of the day. The broadcast of such services should be encouraged as a way of enabling Jewish patients who are seriously ill to participate in religious services.

October 1989

16. INCENSE

QUESTION: A group of Jews interested in meditation wish to use incense as part of their service. Their liturgy is normative Jewish. In place of a sermon, they meditate and feel that incense might help them and be appropriate as it was used in ancient times. (Norman Cohen, San Jose CA)

ANSWER: Incense was used continuously in the worship in the Bible. We find lengthy descriptions and they even provide details of precise mixtures of the ingredients. This material was further expanded subsequently in the *Mishnah* and the *Talmud*. A good deal of modern work in studying the plant material has been done. However, the interest in incense and its use ended with the Temple. This was a form of worship which was related to the sacrifices and therefore could not be replicated in the synagogue except through readings, and these occurred in various points of the service particularly at the Friday Evening service. In other words, this along with all other matters associated with the Temple was limited to Temple worship and not considered transferable.

There is nothing which would prohibit the use of incense for this Jewish meditation group as long as they made no effort to copy the ritual of the ancient Temple, but simply did whatever they felt appropriate for their meditation. This might be considered as imitation of the Gentile community as incense continues to be used in Catholic Christians as well as oriental religious services. We should therefore be cautious and look closely at the motivation of this group. Although we would not recommend the use of incense, there is no impediment to its use by this group.

October 1990

17. ALL NIGHT VIGILS

QUESTION: A peace organization has held a series of all night vigils through the years as a way of calling attention to the war in Afghanistan, nuclear disarmament and the mistreatment of prisoners in various lands. Is there a Jewish basis for a vigil? (Flo Levi, Houston TX)

ANSWER: Various pietists movements in Judaism have used the vigil to increase the devotion of their followers. Such vigils have been incorporated into the regular liturgy so, for example, *selihot* services are held from the Sunday before *Rosh Hashanah* (or the entire month of *Elul* among *Sephardim*) and during the interval between *Rosh Hashanah* and *Yom Kippur* either before dawn or late at night (*Shulhan Arukh* Orah Hayim 619.6). In the United States

28

it has become customary to have such a *selihot* service after midnight on the Saturday night before *Rosh Hashanah*. That service often lasts into the early morning hours (*Shulhan Arukh* Orah Hayim 581.1). This represents an effort to create a mood of repentance. A large number of special prayers and poems have been composed for these occasions; these *selihot* also appear in the regular liturgy. Some traditions encouraged the people to pray throughout the night of *Yom Kippur*.

The commemoration of the destruction of the Temple on *Tisha B'av* is often continuous throughout the night with *kinot*, *Lamentations* and other appropriate readings.

In a totally different mood the evening of *Shevuot* is celebrated through all night reading and study of *Tikun Leil Shevuot* composed of verses from each *parashah*, all books of the Bible, and verses from each tractate of the *Mishnah*. As the ancient Israelites had prepared themselves for the giving of the law in Sinai, so pietists did the same within their circles (*Zohar* Emor 98a; *Shulhan Arukh* Orah Hayim 494). There were also local events which have been commemorated through all night vigils.

During times of communal troubles communities have become involved through fasting and special vigils (*Yad* Hil Taaniyot 1.4; *Shulhan Arukh* Orah Hayim 576). There is a Biblical origin for this custom as the people were called upon to fast in times of unusual danger (Joel 2.15, Jonah 3.9, Esther 4.3, Nehemiah 9.1). We can see from this that vigils as well as fasting continue to be very much part of our life when we have dealt with communal danger. The components are prayer, study and when appropriate also fasting.

29

When such issues involve the broader community, Jews may, of course, join their Gentile neighbors in an effort to deal with the communal crisis. It would be appropriate for us to follow this pattern in our own time when the community wishes to use this format. We should add the Jewish element of study to the vigil.

January 1991

18. POPULAR ISRAELI SONG IN THE SYNAGOGUE

QUESTION: A youngster in our community has brought an Israeli melody back from a visit to Israel. The words which usually accompany it are rather wild, however, he has successfully set a portion of our liturgy to it and it has become popular with our young people. Should this adaption be permitted? (Lloyd Lehman, Los Angeles CA)

ANSWER: The sources of Jewish music are varied. Some of our music may be traced to melodies used in the ancient Temple (E. Werner *The Sacred Bridge: A Voice Still Heard*; A. Z. Idelsohn *Jewish Music*). Other melodies have been composed specifically for liturgical settings by Jewish and Gentile composers. In addition a great deal of music comes from anonymous sources. When musicologists have investigated those sources they found that they have sometimes reflected popular songs of another era. This has included military tunes as well as dance and folk melodies (A. Z. Idelson *Jewish Music* pp 379 ff). The melodies were soon forgotten by the general public, but continued in Jewish liturgical use.

There would be problems in using the melody which you

have described in an Israeli setting. There the association with the profane words would make it objectionable to those acquainted with the song. In our American setting the words are not known, so we are simply left with an appealing melody. The song will probably be quickly forgotten in Israel, and its place taken by other pop tunes. It may, however, survive in its American liturgical setting and so add to our musical heritage.

January 1991

19. A CHRISTIAN COMPOSER OF JEWISH MELODIES

QUESTION: Our organist and choir master is also a composer, and has set a number of pieces to music. The style is modern and has no specific Christian overtones. Is it appropriate to use music by a Christian composer in our services? (Bertram Lefkowitz, Los Angeles CA)

ANSWER: Synagogue melodies fall under the rubric of *minhagim* and vary greatly between *Ashkenazim* and *Sephardim* as well as within each community. There are traditional modes for the *Yamim Naroim*, and other festivals, as well as special *shabbat* services during the year (E. Werner *The Sacred Bridge: A Song Remembered*; A. Z. Idelsohn *Jewish Music*). The local *minhag* is considered binding in matters of melodies (Eruvin 20b; *Shulhan Arukh* Yoreh Deah 376.4). The distinction among communities has been studied (H. J. Zimmels *Ashkenazim and Sephardim* as well as numerous *Sefer Minhagim*).

In addition to the anonymous pieces borrowed through the centuries from the secular or Christian environment, we have in the

31

last century also incorporated tunes by known Christian composers into our services. Sometimes pieces which were particularly appealing by classical composers such as Mozart or Schubert have been used for liturgical texts. On other occasions Christian organists or choir masters wrote music for Jewish worship. Such settings may be found in the *Union Hymnal* (1918, 1934), and also in other publications of the nineteenth and twentieth century. We have welcomed this music as it has added to the slender musical heritage which has been preserved from the past. Frequently these composers have written in traditional modes or in a manner reminiscent of them, and so their music has enhanced our attachment to our musical traditions. The music of this composer should be used in our services.

January 1991

20. HEBREW TRANSLITERATIONS AND JEWISH MELODIES

QUESTION: Some individuals have objected to the use of transliterations with Hebrew melodies. It is commonly used and allows the text to match the musical notation. Should the melody simply be printed in reverse with the Hebrew text to avoid this problem? (Fran Aaronson, St. Louis MO)

ANSWER: I do not know why anyone would object to transliteration as it simply means using another set of letters to spell out the Hebrew words. It has been used since Hellenistic times in an effort to help those whose knowledge of Hebrew was limited.

The modern form of musical notation, in contrast to the cantillation marks, has been used by us only since the nineteenth century. This was part of the expansion of synagogue music beyond the chants and melodies of tradition. It was part of a revolution in synagogue music.

As music is universally written from left to right, it would be confusing to attempt to print it in reverse. There can be no objection to a transliteration especially when this deals with a practical issue and simplifies the use of Hebrew with musical notations. To the best of my knowledge transliterations are used with musical texts in Israel.

January 1991

21. FACING THE ARK

QUESTION: It is our custom when we name a baby to have the rabbi face the ark; the young people and the baby face the congregation. The president of the congregation felt that this should be done. Some members of the congregation asked whether there is any *halakhah* which demands that the rabbi face either the ark or the congregation during such a prayer. Should the rabbi face the congregation during a baby naming, or the ark? (Rabbi Stuart M. Geller, Lynbrook NY)

ANSWER: As all of us know, the general orientation of our services has been toward Jerusalem which has usually been interpreted as having the congregation and any synagogue building face East either during the entire service or certainly during the most important prayers of the service. Therefore, the reader in a traditional synagogue or the cantor who leads the service faces the ark and usually has his back to the congregation. We should, however, note that leaders of the congregation often were seated on the *bemah* facing the congregation. They face the congregation for most of the service with the exception of the *barkhu, amidah,* portions of the *Torah* service, etc. (*Tur* Orah Hayim 150; *Shulhan Arukh* Orah Hayim 1.4). There were also local *minhagim* which demanded that the ark be faced or the ark be opened and this, of course, meant facing it. Such customs varied from one locale to another. Similar *minhagim* have also been established within the Reform movement. For example, in a large number of Reform Synagogues the rabbi or cantor faces the open ark during the *aleinu*. Yet in my congregation that is not the *minhag*. We neither face the ark nor rise.

In the matter of baby naming, there is no tradition at all. Normally this was done during the *Torah* service while the *Torah* was on the reading desk, and therefore the father and the rabbi faced in whichever direction the *Torah* was read according to local *minhag*. In some congregations it was toward the ark and others it was facing the congregation. I have seen both in traditional synagogues as well as Reform synagogues. You must therefore establish a local *minhag* and remain with it. Tradition provides no guidance.

November 1990

22. *ALIYAH* WITH THE HEBREW OR ENGLISH NAME

QUESTION: In my congregation we have recently decided to invite individuals to participate in the *Torah* service by their Hebrew name. This has caused embarrassment among those who do not know their Hebrew name or were never given a Hebrew name. I have hesitated about assigning a name just for the occasion. Should the English name be used if the Hebrew name cannot be remembered or should English names always be used for the sake of consistency? (Norbert Katz, London, England)

ANSWER: When the tradition discussed *Torah* honors and the names of individuals asked to participate, it was principally concerned with the dignity of the individual. If there was a blemish connected with his father, then the shame was avoided by simply mentioning his name alone, or designating him as X, who is the grandson of Z (*Shulhan Arukh* Orah Hayim 139.3; Isserles and commentaries). If the father was unknown or he was a foundling, then the person was designated as the son of Abraham. These discussions inform us that Hebrew names were regularly used in the traditional service, and that the individuals invited to the *Torah* were not to be embarrassed in any way.

The introduction of Hebrew names for *Torah* honors in our Reform services represents a reemphasis on Hebrew names. It creates an additional bond with the Hebrew language. It is, therefore, good and useful. We, however, should also follow the inclination of the *Shulhan Arukh* and earlier sources and not shame the individuals who are going to be honored.

It would probably be best to continue the use of Hebrew names for those who know their Hebrew names, and English names for those who do not. As *Torah* honors are often assigned some days before the service, it may be possible for individuals to rediscover their Hebrew name or if they have none to ask for a Hebrew name. Slowly over the years the use of Hebrew names will become more common and that is a direction in which we should proceed.

May 1989

23. A *KOHEN* AND *TORAH* HONORS

QUESTION: What is the position of a *kohen* among us? As a *kohen* has priority in the *Torah* readings, may he agree to accept a *Torah* honor in another position? (Nora Deutsch, Seattle WA)

ANSWER: Among us as Reform Jews the *kohen* and the Levite possesses no special status and both the honors as well as the disabilities which remain among Orthodox Jews are disregarded by us. However, your congregation seems to be somewhat more traditional and therefore the question.

All of the *kohanim* nowadays are, of course, of doubtful status as no strict genealogies have been maintained. When a priest is called to the *Torah* as the first and receives this honor, it is done as a *minhag* (custom) and not because the individual is entitled to that honor (*Shulhan Arukh* Orah Hayim 457 and commentaries; Ribash *Responsa* #94). As the matter is only a *minhag* the *kohen* may refuse and not ascend to the *Torah* altogether or take a *Torah* honor later, but in a traditional congregation he should at least be offered that honor in order to indicate that no doubt has been cast upon his status,and that the congregation thinks him fit for the honor although he may not wish to accept it.

December 1990

24. NON-JEWISH PARENT AND *HAGBAHAH*

QUESTION: Is it appropriate for a non-Jewish father of a *Bar/Bat Mitzvah* to physically hold the *Torah* for the *hagbahah* while the *Bar/Bat Mitzvah* reads the verse *vezot hatorah...?* (Rabbi Jonathan Stein, Indianapolis IN)

ANSWER: The participation of a non-Jewish parent in the *Bar/Bat Mitzvah* of his/her Jewish child, as well as participation in the other religious festivities of the weekend, have been discussed a number of times although this particular question has not arisen before. Our answer is based on two principles (W. Jacob *Contemporary American Reform Responsa* #160). The essential elements of the service must be conducted by Jews. Non-Jews readily understand this and so there is rarely a problem with the non-Jewish partner.

Equally important, we wish to encourage strong family relationships and have the non-Jew feel at home and at ease during life cycle services. Furthermore, we want the child to understand that the non-Jewish parent can be included in some measure in the joyful festivities of his/her life.

The ceremony of *hagbahah* is part of the *Torah* service and is therefore considered a special honor. It is, however, not one of the traditional *aliyot* which are regularly part of our Saturday morning service, and so we need not be too careful about who receives this honor (*Contemporary American Reform Responsa,* #149). Frequently in smaller traditional synagogues this task is given to a boy not yet *Bar Mitzvah* or boys who are attending services, but would normally not be honored by *aliyot,* etc. This represents an effort to involve a larger number of individuals in the service itself. We could therefore involve the non-Jewish parent in this part of the service especially as that individual need not say anything. We must balance these considerations with *marit ayin* as this is a highly symbolic boundary issue. How will the congregation perceive this individual's participation? Will it blur distinctions which need to be clear?

We have no problems about a non-Jew coming in contact with the *Torah.* Christians, of course, are to be considered monotheist and have been regarded in this fashion for a thousand years (W. Jacob (ed) *American Reform Responsa* #151). We regularly teach Christians *Torah* and have them see and touch the ritual objects of our synagogue in order to understand Judaism better. Of course, participation in the synagogue service is different and should be limited (*Contemporary American Reform Responsa* #160). It is possible to involve a non-Jewish parent in the ceremony of *hagbahah* during her/his child's *Bar/Bat Mitzvah,* but it may in conformity with congregational policy be denied.

February 1989

25. YIDDISH *TORAH* BLESSINGS

QUESTION: Some new Soviet immigrants who have attended services at the synagogue regularly have been given *aliyot* to the *Torah*. Their spoken English is poor, they know very little Hebrew, and they would like to recite the *Torah* blessings in Yiddish. Is that appropriate? (Sidney Kowalsky, Detroit MI)

ANSWER: Prayers in the vernacular have a long tradition among us (W. Jacob *Contemporary American Reform Responsa* #135). It is clear that a large proportion of our people were no longer familiar with Hebrew even in the time of Ezra and Nehemiah (Neh 8.9), so the Scriptural reading had to be translated for them. By the time of the *Mishnah*, the common people no longer used Hebrew, therefore, the *shema, tefilah* and the *birkhat hamazon* were permitted in the vernacular (*M* Sotah 7.1). This, then, also was the later decision of the *Talmud* (Sotah 32b ff); therefore individuals should pray with full knowledge of what they were saying.

A parallel stand was taken by later authorities, so the *Sefer Hassidim* of the eleventh century (#588 and #785) stated that those who did not understand Hebrew should pray in the vernacular. Maimonides provided a similar statement (*Yad* Hil Ber 1.6), while the *Tur* and *Shulhan Arukh* made a distinction between private and public prayers. Private prayers were preferably read in Hebrew, while those in the congregation might be recited in the vernacular. A preference was expressed, but this did not exclude the vernacular in either instance (*Tur* Orah Hayim 101; *Shulhan Arukh* Orah Hayim 101.4). Aaron Chorin, Eliezer Lieberman and others, who defended the changes made by the Reform movement in the last century and its use of the vernacular, however, insisted that a number of prayers should continue to be recited in Hebrew (*Qinat Haemet*; *Or Nogah* Part I). They felt that nothing stood in the way of using the vernacular. *Torah* blessings were among the prayers which could be recited in the vernacular.

I am sure that in your congregation as in most, the prayers before and after the reading of the *Torah* are normally read in Hebrew, but if an individual does not have sufficient mastery of Hebrew we would certainly consider them equally appropriate if read in English. As we are making every effort to encourage Russian Jewish immigrants to become part of synagogue life, we should include them in this part of the service by reading the appropriate prayers in Yiddish, or for that matter in Russian if they do not know Yiddish. At a later stage I am sure they will master Hebrew and continue their participation in synagogue life.

July 1990

26. ORNAMENTAL *TORAH* BINDERS

QUESTION: The congregation some time ago commissioned some ornate hand stitched *Torah* covers and has arranged for *Torah* binders of a similar nature. The binders are beginning to look worn. May they be displayed in a museum? How should we ultimately dispose of them? (Sarah Nemeroff, Rochester NY)

ANSWER: The objects which surround the *Torah* should be beautiful. The *rimonim* and the breastplate have been discussed in detail (*Yad* Hil Sefer Torah 10.4; *Tur* and *Shulhan Arukh* Yoreh Deah 282.16; Orah Hayim 138.18). The *Torah* binders themselves were not discussed, and often consisted simply of a piece of cloth designated for this purpose. However, all objects connected with the *Sefer Torah* possess some of the sanctity of the *Torah*. Anything directly associated with the *Torah* should be buried when it is no longer usable (Meg 26b; *Shulhan Arukh* Orah Hayim 153.2). Of course, the more distant the object, the less the sanctity, so an ark is different than the covering of the *Torah*. When the covering or the binder around the *Torah* are no longer useable they should be buried or used as shrouds for the deceased.

The objects which you have described are now too frail for use as *Torah* binders; they can serve an educational purpose through museum a display. Such a setting also accords them proper reverence. Later they should be buried.

January 1989

27. *WIMPELN*

QUESTION: A family whose grandparents came from Bavaria possesses several *Torah Wimpeln* which were used to bind the *Torah* in the small German community from which the family came. They wish to recreate this custom for their new born son and want to know whether this is appropriate. (Charles Harris, Pittsburgh PA)

ANSWER: The custom of creating a *Torah* binder from the cloth used during the circumcision has a strong tradition in various rural sections of Germany. The oldest known example can be traced to 1685 but the tradition may be older. Such linens would not survive indefinitely so no earlier samples exist. Usually the name of the lad, the date of birth, his parent's name, and the hope "may he live a good life, reach maturity and be blessed with a good marriage" was inscribed. Other statements have also been found on these *Wimpeln*. A sample of such binders has been published by the Judah Magnes Museum (Ruth Eis *Torah Binders*). Some binders were hand painted, others stitched by folk artists, members of the family, or professionals in the community. The binder was then presented in the synagogue when the lad was old enough to participate in a service. I remember presenting such a binder in my father's synagogue in Augsburg at the age of three. The *minhag* usually called for it to be used again at the time of the child's *Bar Mitzvah*, and the *shabbat* immediately before the wedding as well as other personal occasions in the life of the individual.

It would be appropriate to reestablish this custom for this family and others. This will provide a close link with the synagogue throughout their life and the life of the child.

March 1986

28. THE FORM OF THE *YAD*

QUESTION: All of the *Torah* pointers in my congregation are in the form of a hand, sometimes with a ring on the index finger and at other times not. A young silversmith would like to create a *Torah* pointer which is more akin to the branch of a tree, as that would fit with a *Torah* ornament which he is also in the process of creating. Is this permissible? (Fred Danovitz, Washinton DC)

ANSWER: There is nothing in the traditional literature which deals with the *yad* although there is a considerable amount of discussion about the (*rimonim*) *Torah* crowns (*Yad* Hil Sefer Torah 10.4; *Tur* and *Shulhah Arukh* Yoreh Deah 282.16; Orah

Hayim 138.18). The pointer seems to have been incidental and was a practical device to prevent the reader from getting lost in this text with which contains no markings of any kind.

The earliest known pointer comes from Frankfurt in 1570 (Franz Landsberger "The Origin of European Torah Decorations" *Beauty in Holiness* (ed) J. Gutmann p 102 ff). Pointers from succeeding centuries are found in many collections; all examples which I have seen are either in the form of a hand or akin to a scepter. They represented the taste of the particular age and it was the gold or silversmith who determined the design. They were often created by Gentile craftsmen. We should note that a large number of pointers were wooden rather than precious metal.

There would be nothing wrong with designing a pointer in the form of a tree branch and it would be a refreshing change in *Torah* ornamentation. Such a *yad* would be appropriate.

May 1990

29. A METAL *ETZ HAYIM*

QUESTION: May a metal *etz hayim* be used in a *Torah*? An artist would like to use the metal support for decorative crowns as well as a more decorative lower handle for the *Torah*. Is this permissible? (Aaron Cushman, Philadelphia PA)

ANSWER: There is some discussion of the *Torah* vestments and their status, however, even this is limited. There is none at all of the *etz hayim* which is considered one of the appurtenances of the *Torah,* and so possesses the same degree of sacredness as the various coverings or vestments (*Shulhan Arukh* Yoreh Deah 382, 12 ff).

There is no discussion about the material used for the *etz hayim* or how it should be produced. The name itself "tree of life" would indicate that wood has been used. This probably occurred for the very practical reasons that wood was always available. Decorative crowns sometimes made of silver were limited to wealthy congregations. When the *etz hayim* needed to be renewed it occurred without any ritual.

In this period of environmental concern and our desire for a strong link with nature, we may prefer a wooden *etz hayim* as the name indicates. There is no good reason to change the material. Decorations may be applied to the top or the bottom without difficulty and this should be done.

September 1990

30. PROPHETIC SCROLLS

QUESTION: A member of my congregation would like to commission some scrolls which would then be used for the reading of the *Haftarah*. Is there a tradition for reading the *Haftarah* from a scroll? Would it be appropriate to maintain such scrolls in the ark with the *Torah*? (Thomas Shapiro, San Francisco CA)

ANSWER: We, of course, continue to read from the scroll of Esther, the *Megillah*, and the writing of the *Megillah* is governed by rules (*Shulhan Arukh* Orah Hayim 691). The other minor books which may be used in scroll form (Ruth, Song of Songs, Lamentations and Ecclesiastes) are generally read from books and only rarely from a scroll. Certainly there is no mandate to do so.

As the *Haftarah* is chosen from different sections of the prophets for each *shabbat,* we do not have a continuous cycle of readings as with the *Torah.* Having the text available in book form rather than in a scroll makes the process of finding the text and reading it much easier although special scrolls with the *Haftarah* sequence have existed. Perhaps for this practical reason there is little reference in the traditional sources to prophetic readings from a scroll. Clearly at an earlier stage of our history, scrolls of the prophets were used and the most famous of these, the Isaiah scroll, is now in the Shrine of the Book in Jerusalem. Later, the codex form of the book was introduced; it was widely used by the third century but among Jews only in the eighth century.

I do not know of any synagogue that regularly uses scrolls of the prophetic books or the five *megillot,* although several synagogues possess them and keep them in the ark alongside the *Torahs.* There is nothing wrong about commissioning such scrolls to be written, but I do not find much in favor of doing so. It might be better to interest the family in another project which would be more useful to the synagogue.

November 1989

31. ADULT BAR/BAT MITZVAH AND ADULTERY

QUESTION: A woman in her forties has participated in an adult *Bar/Bat Mitzvah* program. The course has almost been completed with the ceremony rapidly approaching. Unfortunately she has established an adulterous relationship. She will, of course, be encouraged to finish the course. Is it possible to have her participate in the *Bat Mitzvah* ceremony under these circumstances? (Sidney Silverman, Long Beach CA)

45

ANSWER: It is good that this woman has taken this course of study and hopefully it will bring her closer to Judaism not only in the formal ritual sense, but to a deeper understanding of the commandments. The ceremony itself bespeaks a willingness on the part of children to accept and live by the commandments of Judaism. This, rather than the brief *haftorah* portion and the family festivities are the primary aim of *Bar/Bat Mitzvah*. It is to be taken very seriously.

For an adult that acceptance has occurred long ago and an adult *Bar/Bat Mitzvah* marks a completion of a course of study and a rededication to the *mitzvot* rather than a change in the pattern of life. This woman can hardly rededicate herself to *mitzvot* and also commit adultery. She should *not* participate in this ceremony.

We must also ask whether we should give an *aliyah* to a known public adulterer. There are some who would argue that being called to the *Torah* is a *mitzvah*, not an honor, and as a *mitzvah* one can not withhold it from anyone. Solomon B. Freehof has demonstrated that the tradition disagreed on this issue with some authorities arguing in each direction. He felt that we should not deprive an individual of the *mitzvah* of reading from the *Torah* unless the person was "notoriously evil" or the honor of the congregation was at stake (S. B. Freehof *Current Reform Responsa* #16). He made this decision as he considered this act as a *mitzvah*. In our modern congregations, especially the larger ones, the *aliyah* is an honor as it is impossible to involve the entire congregation in the *Torah* service even over a period of several years. Individuals are honored for communal leadership, or family and life cycle events through an *aliyah*. This honor should be restricted to those individuals who exemplify Jewish ideals and Jewish morality or at the minimum do not publicly reject a major commandment. I am sure that the woman in question will understand such a decision and finish the course in the spirit which led her to she enroll in it. At some later time when the pattern of her life has changed, she should be called to the *Torah*. This will recognize her study and also her efforts to resolve her marital problems.

February 1989

32. A *BAR MITZVAH* AND HER ESTRANGED MOTHER

QUESTION: A *Bat Mitzvah* candidate is the offspring of a divorced couple. The father has sole custody of the child. He has remarried and the daughter lives with him and his wife. The daughter's natural mother has absolutely no contact with her and the daughter feels estranged from her natural mother.

The natural mother, however, insists that she has a right to share in her daughter's forthcoming *Bat Mitzvah*. This potential participation sorely troubles the child who perceives her mother in negative terms and accuses her of child beating. May the mother be excluded from the *Bat Mitzvah?* Does the mother possess natural, inherent rights to participate? (Rabbi Leonard Poller, Larchmont NY)

ANSWER: The responsibility of children toward their parents has been broadly stated through the commandment: "Honor your father and your mother...." (Ex 20.12) and "You shall each revere his mother and his father..." (Lev 19.3). Furthermore those who cursed their parents could be punished by death (Ex 21.15, 17; "the rebellious son" Deut 21.18ff); statements which later tradition found abhorrent and therefore surrounded with so many obstacles that they could not be carried out (San 88b; *Mekhilta; Sifrei;* see also M. Kasher *Torah Shelemah*).

As these statements were not developed further in the Bible, we must look to the early rabbinic sources. They indicated that the obligation to honor parents rested equally upon sons and daughters (*M* Kid 1.7), but they too did not define it; they, however, removed the death penalty as indicated above. We should note that although Jewish law in this period developed within the Roman sphere, it never gave absolute power to a father over his children. In Roman law this meant complete control throughout the children's lifetime. This included their person, as well as all property (*Institutes of Justinian* Bk I Title ix as quoted in G. Blidstein *Honor Thy Father and Mother* p 175). The *Talmudic* and *Midrashic* literature along with later exegetes and philosophers loosened the bond of obligation between children and parents. Broad general statements about the meaning of the Biblical commandments were made, but the scholars carefully refrained from concrete examples except in peripheral matters of etiquette. The responsa literature, which must by its nature be specific, primarily dealt with obligations during critical periods in the lives of the parents: the duty to ransom them if taken captive and their proper care during debilitating illness or old age. Appropriate support was mandated as a form of honoring parents (W. Jacob *Contemporary American Reform Responsa* #26). On the other hand, parents power over their children was severely restricted even in matters like the choice of a marriage partner; honoring parents did not generally extend so far. (A.H. Freiman *Seder Qidushin Venisuin* pp 12 ff, 66 ff, 138 ff, etc; *Shulhan Arukh* Yoreh Deah 240.25; Isaac b. Sheshet *Responsa* # 127; Simon ben Zemah Duran *Responsa* III 130 sec 5; Ezekiel Landau *Noda Biyehudah* II Even Haezer 45 etc). As children's attitude to parents depend on specific situations, few efforts to generalize were made.

ORAH HAYIM

There is little material about the rights and privileges of parents at the time of *Bar/Bar Mitzvah*, as this ceremony which has become so significant for us was of minor importance in earlier generations. Some historical background of the *Bar/Bat Mitzvah* has been provided in an earlier responsum (W. Jacob (ed) *American Reform Responsa*, #33).

As we turn to the troublesome question which you have asked, we should review the role of the father in the ceremony; for us, of course, the rights of the father and mother are equal. The father's sole obligation during the ceremony was the recitation of the blessing *shepatrani* (Maharil, *Hilhot Qeriat Torah* quoting *Mordecai; Shulhan Arukh* Orah Hayim 225.2 and commentaries). Some authorities were not convinced of the necessity for this prayer and so suggested that it not be recited *beshem umalkhut* (Isserles *Ibid; Sefer Minhagei Habad* Ammud 74). Generally this prayer was recited at the *Bar Mitzvah* in the presence of the son and the *minyan*, but if the father was away or abroad, he could recite it in another synagogue (*Yad Yitzhaq* 3.303; Efros *Responsa* #48). Some also permitted the father to recite the blessing in the same city at another time (*Responsa Maharam Brisk* II 68; *Responsa Tztitz Eliezer* Orah Hayim, 225; Hatam Sofer *Shaar Birkhat Hashahar*). These statements indicated that there was only a vague obligation to recite this prayer.

We should also note that there was no obligation on the part of the father to be called to the *Torah* on the day of his son's *Bar Mitzvah* although it was customary (*Shaarei Efraim* II 2; *Miqraei Qodesh* I 6.31) These citations indicate that tradition considered parental obligations and rights during the *Bar Mitzvah* ceremony as minimal.

49

We are dealing with a somewhat different situation as *Bar/Bat Mitzvah* have assumed a greater significance in our age. We have used this ceremony to stress family ties as demonstrated by the gathering of the entire family for the occasion. We have, however, along with tradition emphasized the child and its maturation. All children must be made aware of the duty to honor and respect their parents. Although this may be difficult in situations of divorce, it is nevertheless necessary. This child should, therefore, be encouraged to establish better relations with her estranged mother now and if that is not possible, later. In a normal divorce the mother would have the right to participate in the ceremony in whatever manner is customary and the rabbi as a neutral party may adjust the participation in order to maintain peaceful relations. Here, however, matters are different as the child seems to have been subjected to unusually bad treatment by her mother. This apparently led the court to give sole custody to the father without visitation rights. This judgement by a neutral outside party combined with the feelings of hostility of the child toward her mother indicate that it would be *inappropriate* for the mother to participate unless some reconciliation has taken place. The natural mother may, of course, attend the service and should be encouraged to do so although a stipulation of good behavior with appropriate safeguards may be set for her attendance.

The father's new wife should not participate in the *Bat Mitzvah* in this case as that might very well be considered an unnecessary irritant. In many other situations the participation of both the new wife, who currently cares for the child, and of the natural mother would be appropriate and welcome by all parties.

April 1988

33. BABY NAMING AND *BAR/BAT MITZVAH*

QUESTION: In our congregation *Bar/Bat Mitzvah* normally participate in the *shabbat Torah* service to the exclusion of everyone else except the members of the family. We also customarily name babies at our *shabbat* morning service. A family would like to schedule a baby naming on a *shabbat* on which a *Bar/Bat Mitzvah* has been scheduled. There would be no possibility of moving it to a *shabbat* without *Bar/Bat Mitzvah* as we have them scheduled for several months ahead. Would the naming of a baby be considered an imposition on the rights of the *Bar/Bat Mitzvah*? (Harold Nobel, St. Louis MO)

ANSWER: There is a good bit of discussion about the rights of various individuals to synagogue honors. Some of these discussions dealt with *Torah* honors (Meg 32a ff; *Shulhan Arukh* Orah Hayim 135 ff). Special rules also developed around the recital of the *qaddish*, especially in those congregations where the mourner felt entitled according to *minhag* to lead the *qaddish* or to recite it alone (*Shulhan Arukh* Yoreh Deah 376.4, Isserles and commentaries). Similar, although somewhat less heated, discussions occured about other synagogues honors which had become associated with synagogue offices or with certain families.

None of these discussions dealt specifically with *Bar/Bat Mitzvah* and its prerogatives as the *minhag* which you described was not known in the past. Traditionally other individuals were also called to the *Torah* when a child was being *Bar/Bat Mitzvah* and the *Bar/Bat Mitzvah* usually read only a concluding section of the *sidrah*. Female babies were traditionally named during the *misheberah* following the *Torah* reading and a blessing was recited for them.

51

QUESTIONS AND REFORM JEWISH ANSWERS

As the naming was not part of the regular liturgy but only by custom associated with the *Torah* service, so for us it is not absolutely essential that an *aliyah* be given to the parents. The baby may be named during another part of the service and the parents as well as the child (if that is the custom) could be brought to the pulpit at that time. This might be a way of avoiding the conflict.

It would, however, also be perfectly legitimate to insist that the parents of the child and the baby (if that is the custom) come to the pulpit during the *Torah* service as the *Bar/Bat Mitzvah* is be part of a public service in which the entire congregation has rights. It is the purpose of the *Bar/Bat Mitzvah* to indicate that the individual is now a member of a larger congregation with all the privileges, rights, and duties. One of those duties surely is consideration for other individuals at their time of personal joy. This would include a baby naming on the day of a *Bar/Bat Mitzvah*. Such a stand would reinforce the public nature of the *shabbat* service; it is not a private gathering which happens to take place in the synagogue. If a number of babies are to be named on a given *shabbat* and that can not be avoided, then it might be wise to scatter the baby namings throughout the service so that each family will feel that they are being given due honor.

June 1989

34. CONFIRMATION AND *BAR/BAT MITZVAH**

QUESTION: Our congregation has had a long history of *Bar/Bat Mitzvah* and not a great deal of emphasis has been placed on Confirmation. Should this be stressed by me as Religious School principal? What is the purpose of Confirmation today? (Sarah Klein, Newark NJ)

52

ANSWER: When Confirmation was established by Israel Jacobson in Seesen, Germany in 1810 in his pioneering school and synagogue it intended to accomplish two purposes: (a) It recognized the need to educate beyond twelve or thirteen the traditional age of maturity for girls and boys, and (b) it demonstrated the equality of men and women in the synagogue. Through the years Confirmation has continued to play a significant role in Reform Jewish life serving to stress both purposes. Slowly the age of Confirmation has been moved to sixteen or seventeen; in some congregations it is the equivalent of high school graduation. At that age a different understanding of Judaism has been acquired especially when compared to thirteen.

As the emphasis on *Bar/Bat Mitzvah* continues to be linguistic despite efforts in other directions, it limits Jewish education. The youngsters in order to do their *Bar/Bat Mitzvah* portion will need to study Hebrew and to spend a great deal of time upon that, at the price of other Jewish studies. Ideally that should not be so, but realistically it occurs particularly with youngsters who have some trouble with the Hebrew language.

Confirmation emphasizes a general knowledge of Judaism and so continues to be important alongside *Bar/Bat Mitzvah*. It has not been seen as the Reform equivalent of *Bar/Bat Mitzvah* for some time. Every effort should be made to use Confirmation as a way of attaining a broad Jewish education, ideally to high school graduation. Some congregations as mine in Pittsburgh continue to confirm in the tenth grade, but we encourage our youngsters to follow our high school program and about sixty percent do so. We might, therefore, say that this approach offers youngsters an intermediate goal and, so serves a good educational purpose.

In addition to these purposes, Confirmation has added new meaning to *Shavuot*. This important holiday which celebrates the giving of the Ten Commandments was not widely celebrated by the general Jewish community. Confirmation has brought new spirit to this day and added significance not only for those confirmed but for the entire congregation.

Confirmation has lost significance, but it remains important. As this ceremony has had a good effect on the general observance of *Shavuot* and on the educational pattern of our young people, we should continue to give Confirmation a significant place in our religious calendar.

January 1989

35. *BAR MITZVAH* ON MASSADAH

QUESTION: A family scheduled the *Bar Mitzvah* of their son at the synagogue on Massadah. When they and their guests arrived, they found that another group was using the synagogue for a *Bar Mitzvah* and two others were waiting to have services there. Rather than spend hours waiting for each of the private services to be completed, they decided to have their *Bar Mitzvah* at another spot on Massadah. Is there a special sanctity to the entire area? Would there be an extraordinary sanctity to the synagogue on Massadah? (Dorah Aaronson, Denver CO)

ANSWER: Massadah was the last fortress in the Judean Desert which fell to the Romans three years after the destruction of the Temple. It was turned into a virtually impregnable fortress by Herod with large amounts of grain and water stored there. The

54

garrison remained defiant until the Romans, through a massive effort, raised the level of a neighboring hill and began their attack. At that point the garrison committed suicide rather than fall into the hands of the Romans (Josephus *Bel Jud* 8, 1-7 ff). The site played no subsequent role in Jewish history or in the memory of our people; it became important only with the rise of Zionism and the establishment of Israel. Since then it has been frequently visited by tourists; it has also been used for special ceremonies by various Israeli military units and *Bar/Bat Mitzvah* ceremonies have been held there.

The ruin on Massadah which has been tentatively identified as a synagogue may also be something else (Y. Yadin "The Synagogue at Massadah" *Ancient Synagogues Revealed* (ed) L.I. Levine pp 19 ff; G. Foerster *The Synagogues at Massadah and Herodium* pp 24 ff). The identification remains uncertain. It is based primarily on the orientation of the building and its general design. However, there are no mosaics, inscriptions or decorations which would clearly establish it as a synagogue. It is also possible that the synagogue building was used for a secular purpose during the siege itself.

A *Bar/Bat Mitzvah* on Massadah is intended primarily to celebrate the bond with modern Israel and with our ancient history. Although it is appropriate to celebrate this *Bar Mitzvah* within the ruins of what may have been a synagogue, any other site on that mountaintop would be equally appropriate. After all, any place where ten Jews meet constitutes a synagogue. So the presence of a *minyan* in another location would also serve the purpose.

I faced the same problem when I traveled to Israel with a family which wished to have a *Bat Mitzvah* on Massadah. Although we could have waited for the synagogue to be vacated and then had a very hot service at high noon, we chose instead to select a beautiful shaded spot and have our service there. This was practical and fulfilled the requirements of tradition as well as the family.

June 1989

36. A *BAR MITZVAH* AT HOME *

QUESTION: A child has been incapacitated by a serious accident and will be in a cast at home for more than a year. His *Bar Mitzvah* preparations are well along and the family would like to know whether they can celebrate the *Bar Mitzvah* at home. (Ted Danovitz, San Jose CA)

ANSWER: The traditional *Bar Mitzvah* intended to declare that the young man was part of the adult community; the ceremony sought to involve the young man more seriously in the congregational life. A full discussion of the nature of *Bar Mitzvah* and its meaning for us as Reform Jews has been undertaken earlier (W. Jacob (ed) *American Reform Responsa* #33). *Bar/Bat Mitzvah* entails a considerable period of study and working toward a ceremony which possesses special meaning both in the traditional and comtemporary sense.

It is important to encourage this youngster in every way. He should continue his Jewish education and his involvement in the community. A *Bar Mitzvah* at home during the period of convalescence will encourage him. We should view this *Bar Mitzvah* at home not only in the traditional way, but also as part of the process of healing. We should encourage such a *Bar Mitzvah* ceremony. It should be held in the presence of at least a *minyan* composed of men and women, and the young man should participate in every way physically possible for him.

August 1989

37. *BAR/BAT MITZVAH* INVITATIONS

QUESTION: Some *Bar/Bat Mitzvah* invitations as well as wedding invitations have become unusually extravagant. Their size and gilded lettering seems out of keeping with the ceremony of *Bar/Bat Mitzvah*. What should our attitude be? (Rose Hartz, Pittsburgh, PA)

ANSWER: There are few discussions until recent times of the festivities connected with a *Bar/Bat Mitzvah*. Among the first to deal with them was Solomon Luria (*Yam Shel Shelomo* to B K ch 7 #37). He stated that the festivities provided by the *Ashkenazim* for a *Bar* Mitzvah were to be considered religious occasions (*Seudat Mitzvah*). There are numerous modern authorities who have discussed these celebrations and have tried to keep them within some reasonable bounds, although this has proven to be difficult in contemporary America. We, too, would object to undue emphasis on the social aspect of the *Bar/Bat Mitzvah* at the expense of its religious significance.

Efforts have been made through the centuries to maintain an atmosphere of dignity and simplicity in connection with synagogue life through sumptuary regulation. There were many attempts to keep life cycle rituals such as weddings and funerals within reasonable boundaries (I. Abrahams *Jewish Life in the Middle Ages* pp 144 ff).

Extravagant *Bar/Bat Mitzvah* are a recent addition to Jewish life and reflect the prosperity of the American Jewish community. We should make an effort to maintain simplicity for a variety of reasons: (a) It will encourage emphasis upon the religious service and the education which the child has achieved; (b) it will enable the family, perhaps in honor of the child, to use funds in more appropriate ways such as enhancing the education of the youngster through a trip to Israel, generous gifts to charities, etc.; (c) it will curb social competitiveness and not place an undue burden on less affluent families.

All of this, of course, begins with the invitation. The rabbi, as well as the appropriate committee of the congregation, should make every effort to encourage simplicity here as with all other aspects of the *Bar/Bat Mitzvah*.

March 1988

38. LAY OR RABBINIC SERMON *

QUESTION: In my congregation it has become customary for lay leaders to speak during the interval between formal services on *Yom Kippur*. Some individuals have protested and indicated that it is the rabbis prerogative to give sermons and this should not be assigned to lay people. What is our attitude toward the sermon? (Toby Isaacs, Miami FL)

ANSWER: The sermon has a long and honored history in Jewish tradition. Leopold Zunz traced the sermon most effectively in one of his first historical studies through which the whole scientific study of the Jewish tradition became established (*Die Gottesdienstlichen Vorträge der Juden*). This thorough study dealt with the entire range of Jewish history from the Bible to his own time. It demonstrated that the sermon represented a well established tradition which took different forms in various ages.

Until the thirteenth or fourteenth century when the rabbinate became a profession, in a limited way, it was not possible to speak of a division between rabbis and laity. The rabbi was the most educated Jewish individual of the community, but often followed some other profession. In eighteenth and nineteenth century Eastern Europe, we find a large number of *darshanim* engaged in teaching and preaching who were not rabbis. Some, as Baal Shem Tov and his disciples, were vigorously opposed to the rabbinic tradition. This founder of Hassidism taught through the story and parable; he never claimed to be a rabbi and as his stories indicate, felt that learning was not the way to God. At the same time, within the framework of the *mitnagid* community, the *maggid* and interpreter who traveled from village to village played an important role. The *darshanim* of seventeenth century Poland and Germany served the same purpose (L. Zunz *Ibid* 458 ff).

During this period, the formal sermon was limited to a few occasions in the year and primarily outlined the way in which certain holidays were to be observed. This was in keeping with the judicial role of the rabbi. In addition, there was *pilpul* not expounded at the religious services, but on other occasions in the synagogue. It demonstrated the brilliance of a rabbinic scholar as he intertwined and juxtaposed difficult rabbinic text. This was intellectually stimulating for the elite, but meaningless to others.

The Reform movement reestablished the sermon as an important vehicle for education in the synagogue service (L. Zunz *Ibid* 469). Many of the early Reform leaders who preached were not rabbis, Israel Jacobson among them.

There is no reason to restrict the sermon to rabbis. We should avoid professionalizing Judaism as much as possible; intelligent, thoughtful lay persons with a good Jewish background should be encouraged to present their thoughts. In many congregations like my own we have the custom of asking young leaders of the congregation to speak from the pulpit annually. It is wise to discuss such presentations with the speaker so that the factual data is correct. This will keep the speaker from embarrassing lapses into ignorance.

We will always insist on a complete freedom of the pulpit, a tradition strongly established within the Reform movement. The rabbi must possess the freedom to preach on whatever she/he chooses and so be able to challenge and change the lives of the members. An invitation to the pulpit may be extended by the rabbi and the individuals asked should also have complete freedom of expression.

August 1988

39. THE GOVERNANCE OF A CONGREGATION

QUESTION: My congregation is in the process of revising its constitution. I have been asked what the tradition says about the officers of a congregation or the documents which describe their duties (Karl Harris, Dallas TX).

ANSWER: We should begin by remembering that most Jewish communities in the past were small and so the life of the congregation and the community was one. The head of the community was also responsible for the synagogue.

As we look through the long history of Jewish communal life, we see many forms of governance. In the period of the *gaonim* rabbinic leaders were frequently sent from the great academies to distant places in an effort to provide leadership and to retain control of the community. It seems that the Karaite movement was in part a rebellion against this centralization.

The Genizah material of the tenth to the twelfth century in Fostat revealed a communal structure with an oligarchy; the communal leaders were expected to deal with both the intellectual and economic responsibilities (S. D. Gottein *A Mediterranean Society* Vol 2). In Western Europe at the same time, i. e. the period of the Crusades, leadership was in the hands of the rabbinate along with a communal council (M. Güdemann *Geschichte der Erziehungswesen*; O. Stobbe *Die Juden in Deutschland während des Mittelalters*; I. Abrahams *Jewish Life in the Middle Ages* pp 49 ff; M. Bloch *Das Mosaisch-Talmudische Polizeirecht*; S. Asaf *Batei Hadinim*). A little later, however, it was frequently the Court Jew who was the communal leader. He possessed the connections with the rulers necessary to protect the community. In Eastern Europe of the thirteenth, fourteenth and fifteenth century a semi-democratic series of regional bodies arose (Louis Finkelstein *Jewish Self-Government in the Middle Ages*). We possess a number of documents which dealt with communal governance, but mainly with the relationship to the secular government, charity within the community, sumptuary problems and synagogue ritual regulations. They were not akin to our constitutions and by-laws (Jacob R. Marcus *The Jew in the Medieval World - A Source Book* pp 185 ff, pp 20 ff).

Constitutions of congregations rarely antedate the early nineteenth century. These modern European documents represented an effort by the secular government to control the inner life of the Jewish community, to change the relationship with the Christian community, and to secularize the community. Such documents were viewed with justified suspicion. In some European lands a chief rabbinate was instituted. However, those chief rabbis exercised their authority alongside communal leaders selected by various means. In other lands the powers of the rabbi and the board were defined by the government, often in the framework of parallel legislature affecting Catholic and Protestant bodies. This led to lengthy debates and considerable lobbying, as for example in the Rhineland in 1910 (B. Jacob *Die Stellung des Rabbiners*).

I have said nothing about the democratic system of congregational life which has evolved in the United States and in many Western European lands recently. This reflects the organizational pattern of the surrounding society. The constitutions have become increasingly democratic in an effort to provide an opportunity for leadership to a greater number of individuals. This is especially important in the larger congregations.

The ramification of each section of the constitution as well as the by-laws should be fully understood by the congregation as well as it's professional leadership. Such matters as division of responsibilities, lines of authority, definition of membership are of utmost importance. The model constitutions provided by the Union of American Hebrew Congregations or other bodies may not solve local problems and will often be inappropriate.

Relatively little guidance can be given from the past for our congregational governance. Our democratic system represents a specifically American Jewish contribution to Jewish life.

April 1989

40. UNUSUAL SYNAGOGUE SUPPORT

QUESTION: Our synagogue is located in a resort area. This means that we have a large congregation during three or four months of winter, a somewhat smaller congregation during another six weeks in fall and spring, and a very small congregation the rest of the year. Many of the individuals who worship with us and come to synagogue programs make no financial contribution, while others provide a nominal gift. Most retain their membership in northern cities. As almost none of these individuals are with us for the High Holidays, they feel little responsibility to the congregation although they turn to it for worship as well as attention during times of illness or bereavement. We have, therefore, asked for contributions at each service and passed a basket around the synagogue. We have also instituted a practice of seeking a donation when a name is read for *Yahrzeit* or when a person is invited to the *Torah*. Some have vigorously objected to these efforts. How does tradition view them? (Patricia Rosenthal, Miami Fl)

ANSWER: It is the duty of individuals who settle permanently or temporarily in a community to support it. This *mitzvah* has been established in our tradition. The financial obligation of adult Jews toward religious institutions was first mentioned in the discussion of the ancient half *sheqel* (Ex. 30.11 ff). All men above the age of twenty were obligated to give it, both rich and poor. Later the Diaspora Jewish community provided regular maintenance for the Temple in Jerusalem. When the Temple was destroyed, the Romans sought to divert this financial obligation to the royal treasury, which caused considerable misery. That measure eventually lapsed.

During the Middle Ages a community could force its members through taxation to help maintain the necessary religious institutions (*Shulhan Arukh* Yoreh Deah 256.5; Orah Hayim 150.1). Actually, measures went considerable further and a community which had only ten males could force them all to be present for the High Holidays, so that the community could conduct proper congregational services. Anyone unable to be present had to obtain an appropriate substitute for the *minyan* (*Shulhan Arukh* Orah Hayim 55.20; Solomon ben Aderet *Responsa* V #222; Isaac bar Sheshet *Responsa* I #518 and #531). A community could force an unwilling minority within it to contribute to a synagogue (*Yad* Hil Tefilah 1.1; *Tur* Orah Hayim 10.50). When members sought to escape their obligation it was, in the past, possible to place them under the ban (J. Wiesner *Der Bann*). *Torah* honors and other honors were not accorded to them.

When the Reform movement reorganized the synagogue services, it sought to remove financial considerations from all portions of it along with much else. The custom of seeking gifts for *Torah* honors was also eliminated. We should be very hesitant about reestablishing this custom as it commercialized the central portion of a service. If the honors are distributed on another day before the service then this objection would be removed. Some should always be given to individuals who have made non-financial contributions to the synagogue.

The other matters which you have suggested are somewhat different. The passing of the basket, of course, is taken from the Christian churches around us which regularly have a collection during their service. I can understand people's hesitation and discomfort with this practice (*huqat goyim*). Perhaps it can be done in a somewhat different way by having envelopes available at each seat or giving them to individuals as they come to the service. Something along these lines should be attempted to avoid the overtones of *huqat goyim*.

The reading of *Yahrzeit* names can be limited to those who have made prior arrangements with the Temple office; the contribution can be explained at that time. As people are concerned about *Yahrzeit*, this would probably generate a reasonable income.

In addition, it should be possible to educate the individuals of this holiday community who regularly use the services of the Temple that they have an obligation to support it for themselves and the broader community.

April 1989

41. A CRIMINAL AS A MEMBER OF THE CONGREGATION *

QUESTION: A member of our congregation was (several years ago) convicted of brutally murdering his wife by repeatedly stabbing and drowning her in a bathtub in the presence of one of his children. He is serving a lengthy prison term and shows no remorse as he claims to have acted in self-defense; his children live with members of the congregation and attend our religious school. The man is still listed on the congregations membership roster. May we expel him from membership? (Los Altos CA)

ANSWER: We must ask ourselves about the purpose of expusion from a congregation which is the equivalent of the *herem* or *nidui* in past ages. At times the *herem* was invoked to protect the congregation or to indicate that certain kinds of action were considered reprehensible and would not be condoned by the community. This power was invoked for criminal acts, various types of dubious financial transactions, rebellion against the existing religious or governmental authorities both Jewish and Gentile, or any person whose deeds seriously threatened the community. On other occasions the *herem* or *nidui* was used as a way of punishing an offender and forcing that individual to repent and return to the community. Maimonides listed the twenty-four possible causes for imposing various forms of the ban; they were casually mentioned in the *Talmud* (Ber 19a; *Yad* Hil Talmud Torah 4.14; *Shulhan Arukh* Yoreh Deah 334.43). We should also note that in the last century the *herem* was used in unsuccessful attempts to quell liberal tendencies in various European communities. In other words, this was part of the struggle between Orthodoxy and Reform.

The various forms of exclusion *nidui* and *herem* were imposed for limited periods and seldom permanently. Furthermore, the bans remained in force only as long as the individual did not change his/her ways. The bans meant social and religious ostracism so no one could associate with the individual on a social basis or in business relationships; the individual could not be counted as part of the *minyan* or as part of *mezuman*, his children were not circumcised or married (*Shulhan Arukh* Yoreh Deah 334.10 and Isserles). For most purposes he was treated as a non-Jew (*Shaarei Tzedeq* 4.5). He/she was also excluded from all congregational honors and privileges. As the punishment was so severe some rabbis abstained from using it while others sought to limit its range (Solomon ben Aderet *Responsa* V #238, etc.). The *herem* did not necessarily preclude attendance at services or worshipping with the congregation although it often did. The authorities always hoped that the individual under the ban would repent and this was considered as possible to the very end of life. Even convicted unrepentant murderers, who were executed were buried in the Jewish cemetery albeit in a separate corner; they were considered a part of the community. Burial itself was considered an act of possible repentance; it was mandated in order to show proper respect for the human body (*Semahot* II; San 47a; *Yad* Hil Avel 1.10; *Tur* Yoreh Deah 334; *Shulhan Arukh* Yoreh Deah 333.3). Apostates, who were frequently a thorn in the side of the Jewish community, were also still considered part of the community; they were permitted to be buried in Jewish cemeteries for two reasons: (a) In order to spare the feelings of the surviving Jewish family members. (b) If they died suddenly, on the assumption that they had actually repented just before their death.

Clearly the community does not need to distance itself from this murderer in order to demonstrate abhorrence of his crime. We might, therefore, exclude this individual from membership in order to punish him, but it is doubtful whether this would be an effective tool. We might rather say that given the conditions of modern Jewish life in which a large percentage of individuals remains unaffiliated, we should encourage the affiliation of all Jews with the hope that those who are criminals or on the borderline of legality may be moved toward an ethical and moral life. We would make an exception only for individuals who represent a clear danger to the Jewish community (like Messianic Jews, certain political offenders, etc.). This particular individual can, of course, not attend synagogue services but the fact that he continues to be informed of congregational activities and receives the regular mailings may prompt him in a positive direction.

As an individual who is a criminal and has been convicted, he should be denied all special rights and privileges. He can not claim any of the honors or privileges normally accorded to a member of the congregation (*Shulhan Arukh* Orah Hayim 153.21 and commentaries; *Toldot Adam Vehavah* 23.1). This would include those privileges normally associated with his status as a father. He may, for example, be excluded from participation in any rites or services connected with his children, nor need his name appear in the published directory of the congregation. As we normally exclude members who may be somewhat in arrear in dues payment, we may certainly exclude a member who has committed a serious offense.

This individual should be retained as a member of the congregation with the hope that he will ultimately repent and change his attitude. He may, however, be excluded from all privileges and honors normally due to members of the congregation.

April 1988

42. ADVERTISING AND CONGREGATIONAL FUND RAISING

QUESTION: A catering business has suggested that a portion of its profits would go to the congregation whenever congregants use its services. The caterer would like to mention this in his advertisement. Would this be appropriate? May the congregational bulletins advertise special discounts to members of the congregation? (Rabbi Jonathan S. Woll, Hagerstown MD)

ANSWER: Many methods of fund raising for congregational and charitable purposes have been used through our long history.

It is, of course, most desirable to support a congregation through direct donations and charitable giving has been emphasized by Judaism through the ages (W. Jacob *Contemporary American Reform Responsa* #139, 151). However, simple generosity has often not met our needs and therefore other methods have been used. Gambling in various guises has been suggested, but we have opposed it (W. Jacob (ed) *American Reform Responsa* #167). We have also frowned the sale of tickets for the High Holidays (W. Jacob *Contemporary American Reform Responsa* #150) and reject raising funds through the sale of synagogue honors (*Ibid*).

Advertisements in fund raising programs or in synagogue bulletins are a matter of taste rather than *halakhah*, as nothing wrong or immoral is implied. As the bulletin or program is available to competitors, no endorsement or restriction of trade is involved. In other words, a service is purchased by the advertiser and the synagogue benefits. As the advertiser cannot afford to make an outright donation or does not wish to do so, this provides revenue for the congregation. An advertisement which is in good taste and is acceptable. As everything connected with the synagogue contains an element of the sacred, we should be careful.

Now let us turn to the question of gifts to the congregation from a caterer used by members of the congregation. This presents a combination of advertisement and a gift. It is not appropriate as it may lead into the gray area of unfair competition and the offer of "kickbacks."

When we compare advertisements with some other widely used methods of fund-raising they are, if controlled and kept in good taste, acceptable. It is, of course, preferable to obtain funds through charitable contributions and anonymous gifts.

July 1988

43. HANDICAPPED ACCESS

QUESTION: My synagogue is interested in designing access to the building for the handicapped. We face unusual difficulties because of our landmarks status at Central Synagogue in New York. Although we have engaged an outstanding architect to prepare the plans and supervise the construction, some individuals connected with the historic landmark institutions object to any change in the building. What responsibilities does a synagogue have toward handicapped congregants? What does tradition say about this matter? (Rabbi Stanley M. Davids, New York NY)

ANSWER: The Jewish Biblical tradition, and later rabbinic tradition, dealt primarily with the deaf, the mute, and the blind (Lev. 19.14 ff). Rabbinic literature separated the deaf and mutes from the others as these individuals were considered unable to understand like the insane, and so incapable of participating in general or religious life (Hag 3.5; R H 29a; Eruv 31b; Hul 2a). For the lame no disabilities were indicated except that along with the blind they could not serve as priests (Lev 21.18); neither could anyone else with a permanent blemish. The blind were free from religious obligations (B K 87a; Kid 31a), but according to their ability were permitted to participate and lead services. So a blind *hazan* was permitted to officiate although he was not to read from the *Torah* (Meg 24a; Get 60b; *Yad* Hil Tef 8.12; *Shulhan Arukh* Orah Hayim 53.14; Git 60b). There was no discussion of other physical disabilities as such individuals have been considered part of the general community. They possessed all the rights and obligations of any other Jew including the obligation to pray with a *minyan* in a formal service (*Shulhan Arukh* Orah Hayim 90, 109, etc.; Peter S. Knobel (ed) *Gates of Mitzvah* p 12). No Jew could be excluded from religious service except in those rare occasions when the community used the *herem* as punishment (Rabenu Gershom *Taqanot* in Louis Finkelstein's *Jewish Self-Government in the Middle Ages* pp 120 f). Extraordinary steps have always been taken to assure a *minyan* for mourners and for those unable to attend synagogue services.

In the medieval period when synagogues were often located in a common courtyard, access could not be blocked in any way, nor could it be made difficult (Meir of Rothenburg *Responsa* #541, 542 *Shulhan Arukh* Orah Hayim 150).

Landmark status is important and serves us well in our effort to preserve historic synagogues and to maintain the Jewish artistic architectural tradition, however, the primary object of the synagogue is to serve all the members of our community. As the number of aged increases so will the number of individuals who are handicapped. It is an obligation for us to serve all segments of the community and to provide access to our synagogues for those who are handicapped.

December 1988

44. POSITION OF THE READING DESK

QUESTION: The reading desk in our synagogue as in most synagogues is elevated. I have heard that the reading desk should actually be at a level lower than the rest of the congregation. What is appropriate? (Florence Lowenstein, Seattle WA)

ANSWER: A good deal has been written about the placement of the ark and the *bimah* in the synagogue. In a traditional synagogue the ark is to be placed in the Eastern wall and the *bimah* in the center so that all worshippers could hear the service (*Yad* Hil Tefilah 11.3; *Tur*; *Shulhan Arukh* Orah Hayim 150.5). If, however, the synagogue is small, the *bimah* may be placed by the Eastern wall (*Kesef Mishnah* to *Yad* Hil Hagigah 50.4, 3.4). The description of the great ancient synagogue in Alexandria demonstrated that even a centrally placed *bimah* could not always assure adequate sound quality for all.

Some authorities felt that the central *bimah* was akin to the placement of the altar in the ancient tabernacle or the temple (Moses Sofer *Responsa* Orah Hayim #19). In modern times, the placement of the *bimah* by the Eastern wall has been considered by some Orthodox authorities to be an imitation of non-Jewish practice and so must be avoided (*Imrei Esh* #7; *Sedei Hemed* Bet Hakneset #13). This matter remained controversial and there are Orthodox authorities who permitted the building of a synagogue with a *bimah* at the Eastern wall (Ezekiel Landau *Noda Biyehuda* II Orah Hayim 18; Solomon Schick *Responsa* Even Haezer #118).

The reading desk is called *almemar*, a word derived from the Arabic term for the reading desk in a mosque; the pulpit is known as *amud*. In the controversy whether the reading desk should be in the middle or at the end of the synagogue; the main consideration was practical so that the worshippers could hear the individual conducting the service (Isserles to *Shulhah Arukh* Orah Hayim 150.5). A statement in the *Zohar* stipulated that no more than six steps lead up to the *bimah* (Vayaqel), however, I can find nothing which indicated that the *sheliah tzibur* should stand in a position lower than the congregation. In these controversies a lower position for the reader was not mentioned.

The *minhag* which you cite may stem from the Psalm *min hametzar* "Out of the depth I cry unto you" (Psalm 118.5), but this verse has not been carried into practice. I have found references in the *halakhic* literature to a step which went down at the synagogue entrance so that the congregation would symbolically "call from the depth." Nothing, however, has been noted about a lowered *bimah*. There is no need to incorporate this thought into the rebuilding of a synagogue *bimah*.

April 1989

45. THE PORTABLE ARK

QUESTION: The architect engaged in designing a new synagogue wishes to introduce a portable ark for the *Torah*. This will be functionally useful as we plan many out of door services and he felt that it would bring the synagogue closer to the ancient desert Tabernacle. Is it permissible to imitate the Tabernacle in this fashion? (Fred A. Rosenberg, Los Angeles CA)

ANSWER: The Biblical ark to which you refer was very different both in function and in its theological implications from the ark of the later synagogue. The ark first appeared in the Book of Exodus (25.16; 26.33; 37.1-9) and again in Deuteronomy (10.3 ff). It was lovingly described with its precise dimensions and the material of its fabrication. The tablets of the Law were deposited within. The ark was subsequently mentioned a number of times in the Books of Samuel (I Samuel 4.7; 7.1; II Samuel 6.14 ff) and later in connection with the building and dedication of the Temple (I Kings 3.15; 6.19 ff. 8.1 ff; II Kings 23.12; II Chronicles 35.3 ff). In the ancient Temple the ark was central and was placed in the

Holy of Holies; after its disappearance the Holy of Holies remained empty (Josephus *Wars* V 5; *M* Yoma 5.2 ff). During the Biblical period a number of terms were used for the ark, the most common were *aron haqodesh, aron berit, aron adonai, aron elohim* or *aron haedut.* In the later synagogue the *Torah* ark was called *tevah* or frequently in *Sephardic* synagogues *hekhal.*

The synagogue ark also, of course, played a central role in worship as it served as the container for the *Torah.* In the early period the ark was mobile and was removed along with the *Torah* at the end of the service (Sotah 39b; *M* Meg 4.21); The remains of ancient synagogues at Bet Alpha Hamath-by-Gadara, Eshtemoa, Ostia, Sardis, as well as Dura Europa indicated a niche for the ark of the *Torah* (Franz Landsberger "The Sacred Direction of the Synagogue", *Hebrew Union College Annual,* Vol 28 pp 185 ff.; and Joseph Gutmann "Programmatic Painting in the Dura Synagogue," *The Synagogue: Studies in Art, Archaeology and Architecture* pp 217 ff; Lee I. Levine (ed) *Ancient Synagogues Revealed*).

The Temple and synagogue are related although very different in purpose, structure, and function. Psalms used in the Temple were carried over into the synagogue liturgy as were melodies (E. Werner *The Sacred Bridge*). The *menorah* of the Temple was not to be copied precisely (Men 28b; R H 24a; A Z 43a - notably only Babylonian references), but nothing was said about other architectural forms. There was no prohibition connected with the ark as it had disappeared long ago and certainly three dimensional cherubim were prohibited. It would be improper to copy the Temple ark in a contemporary synagogue not because of the fear of imitation, but as the function is totally unrelated.

We do not know when the ark became a permanent part of the synagogue building. An early reference was provided by R. Isaac (*Or Zerua* Vol 2 pp 386 f). Its sanctity was more than that of a synagogue and less than a *Torah* (*M* Meg 25; *Tur* and *Shulhan Arukh* 153.2 Orah Hayim). An ark which is permanently in the wall did not have any sanctity beyond that of the synagogue (*Shulhan Arukh* 154.3 Orah Hayim) and some scholars indicated that the ark could be used to store sacred books alongside the *Torah* (*Sefer Hassidim* #60; *Shulhan Arukh* Orah Hayim 154.8). Some authorities felt that the ark has become secondary as modern *Torahs* are covered with a special cloak and the ark no longer serves as the primary protection for the *Torah*. It has lost its former status (*Qorban Natanel* to *Rosh* 4.1).

The synagogue ark has developed in a very different direction from the lost ancient ark of the Temple. There would be nothing wrong with designing a portable ark akin to the earlier synagogue ark and reminiscent of it. We should, however, not imitate the Temple ark.

December 1990

46. JEWISH COLORS

QUESTION: My synagogue is redesigning the *bimah* and ark. When considering color combinations, some individuals have stated that the true Jewish colors are blue and white as in the flag of Israel, and that our design should be limited to those colors with perhaps some gold reminiscent of the ancient desert tabernacle. Are there specific Jewish colors? (Michael Horn, Miami FL)

ANSWER: I do not know how the Israeli flag came to be blue and white, and have not been able to find any answer for this in the literature. This may have followed the colors of the *tallit* which generally were blue or black and white (*Shulhan Aruk* Yoreh

Deah 8). However, in the Bible many different colors were used, as seen in the Book of Exodus (25.3 ff) which utilized gold, silver, copper, blue, purple, crimson, as well as the colors of various stones for the breast plate of the high priest. The desert tabernacle was not a drab affair. This may be seen in the reconstructed models (Moshe Levine *The Tabernacle*). This was equally true of the temple build by Solomon (I Kings 6 ff; II Chronicles).

If we look at the remnants of early synagogues which have survived, we can see a colorful floor mosaics as well as wall decorations (Lee I. Levine (ed) *Ancient Synagogues Revealed* etc). This may be seen clearly in the grand synagogue of Dura Europa which revealed magnificent multicolored wall paintings (C. Kraeling *The Synagogue of Dura Europa*; Erwin R. Goodenough *Jewish Symbols in the Greco-Roman Period*). These ancient synagogues were more colorful than anything to which we may be accustomed.

That tradition has continued in ritual objects, so we find it in synagogue textiles as well as home objects (Barbara Kirshenblatt-Gimbett and C. Grossman, *Fabrics of Jewish Life - Textiles from the Jewish Museum Collection*; Ruth Eis *Ornamented Bags for Tallit and Tefillin of the Judah L. Magnes Museum*). Illuminated manuscripts also demonstrate the wide variety of colors used in our tradition (Joseph Gutmann *Hebrew Manuscript Painting*). There are many other books which show this for the synagogue and home. We should note the colorful Isaac Mayer Wise Temple in Cincinnati built in the Moorish style of the 1870's, and decorated in a joyful multi-colored manner. Any color within the boundary of good taste may be used for the *bimah*, *Torah* curtains, or the remainder of the synagogue. There are no restrictions and there are no specific Jewish colors.

January 1991

ORAH HAYIM

47. ETERNAL LIGHT IN AN OUTDOOR SYNAGOGUE

QUESTION: During the summer months our synagogue utilizes a camp at which services are held each day in an amphitheater also used for other purposes. Should the eternal light be kept burning even when the ark and other synagogue appurtenances have been removed? (Tod Nathan, Los Angeles CA)

ANSWER: The eternal light is reminiscent of the fire which burned on the altar in the Tent of Meeting and the later Temple and the candelabrum eternally lit there (Lev 6.5; Hag 26b). The lamps of the candelabrum were carefully cleaned each day, but the western most light was always kept burning and from it the others were lit after they had been cleaned (Tamid 30b). Our synagogue eternal light may have been derived from this source, however, there is no reference to it until the seventeenth century writer Isaac Lamperonti (*Pahad Yitzhaq*; I. Elbogen *Gottesdienst* p 476). Undoubtedly various lights were kept burning in the synagogues through the ages, but they like the other lights in the Temple were lit each day (*Midrash Rabbah* 4.20; *Midrash Shir Hashirim Rabbah* 2.5; *Tosefta* Meg 3.3; Arakhin 6b). None of these citations or discussion of the synagogue mention the *ner tamid* as a light which was perpetually burning. We may conclude from Isaac Lamperonti that this light was lit only during hours of worship.

Although it has become our custom to have a light perpetually burning in the synagogue, it is not necessary as long as the light burns during the time of services. In the setting which you have described the eternal light should be removed with the ark and the other synagogue appurtenances.

July 1988

48. LILIES IN THE SYNAGOGUE

QUESTION: A woman who is fond of the lily has decorated the pulpit with lilies at her son's *Bar Mitzvah*. Some members of the congregation objected and stated that this flower has specific Christian connotation. Is the lily an appropriate decoration for the synagogue? (Shirley Swarz, Chicago IL)

ANSWER: A lot may be learned about the status of various plants used symbolically in art. As we review medieval and renaissance Christian paintings, we will see that many different plants have been utilized to symbolize aspects of Christianity. So, for example, the lily as a symbol of purity became the flower of the Virgin Mary. It has also been connected with various saints who are considered to be especially pure as St Francis or St Anthony. Other plants have different symbolic associations in medieval and renaissance paintings. The three leafed clover has become a symbol of St Patrick. The columbine, often compared to a white dove, is the symbol of the Holy Spirit; the cyclamen with its red spot is reminiscent of the Virgin Mary; the simple daisy is symbolic of the Christ child; the iris, like the lily, is a symbol of the Virgin Mary; the lily-of-the-valley is symbolic of the resurrection; the poppy is asociated with the passion, and the rose, especially the red rose, has served as a reminder of martyrs. The violet, which usually is bent over, is a symbol of humility and connected with St Bernard. This very partial list demonstrates Christian association with a large number of popular flowers. We would need to limit synagogue decorations to introduced rare species if we were to exclude the more common flowers from our pulpit decations. We should, perhaps, not use certain plants at precisely the same season as our Christian neighbors. It is better to avoid the lily at Easter for reasons of *marit ayin,* but there is no problem about using any flowers in synagogue decorations. Our congregants will rarely have the associations raised in the minds of Christians. We should, therefore, place no restrictions on floral decorations within the synagogue.

October 1989

49. A BRONZE HEBREW TABLET

QUESTION: A Biblical verse with the *tetragramaton* was inscribed on a bronze tablet which had a prominent position in our former synagogue. The congregation has moved to a new building, tastes have changed and the tablet does not fit into the current building. Some other tablets with names of individuals long forgotten have been abandoned. What rules govern this tablet which contains the *tetragramaton*? (Allen Goldstein, Boston MA)

ANSWER: We are, of course, aware of the special care given to the *tetragramaton* whenever it appears in printed or any other form. Tradition was concerned with reverence for the written name of God, the *tetragramaton.* This was one understanding of the third commandment (Ex 20.7; Deut 5.11), and also of the commentaries to an injunction in Deuteronomy (12.3 ff). In the considerable discussion which followed in subsequent literature, we find an emphasis on the sacredness of the name of God whether written in the *Torah,* another book, on a metal vessel, or even as a tattoo on the skin (*Yad* Hil. Yesodei Torah 6.1; *Sefer Hahinukh* #437). Ultimately, it was decided that the name was sacred only if there was a clear intent for it to be so (*Shulhan Arukh* Yoreh Deah 274 and commentaries).

Special care has always been given to the *tetragramaton*. We should therefore not dispose of this tablet lightly. It need not be given a prominent place in the new synagogue. One may very well wish to display it as a historic memento of another age It is also be appropriate to store it in a safe spot. This would be akin to placing a book which contains the *tetragramaton* into a *genizah*. Either way the tablet should be treated with reverence and should always be handled with appropriate care.

February 1989

50. PORTRAIT IN A SYNAGOGUE

QUESTION: Is it permissible to hang a large picture of the Four Chaplains in the vestibule of a synagogue? The oil painting depicts the chaplains who bravely sank with the Dorchester, in the Atlantic in World War II. (Wilham R. Guaroscio, Monongahela PA)

ANSWER: The prohibition against works of art in the synagogue is based upon the Decalogue statement "You shall not make unto yourself a graven image" (Ex 20.4; Deut 5.8). When the Talmud discussed these prohibitions it principally dealt with human figures, as well as those described by Ezekiel's vision along with the sun, moon and stars (A Z 43b; R H 24b). In the later codes the prohibition was further restricted to encompass only those objects which were three dimensional in nature; this excluded embroidery as well as wall paintings (*Tur* and *Shulhan Arukh* Yoreh Deah 141). Yet a statement in the *Talmud* described a bust of a monarch in a synagogue (Meg 29a; A Z 43b; Sherira Gaon *Sheeltot* (ed) Lewin p 72). Although Rav and Samuel attended this synagogue they did not object to the bust. Eventually the codes indicated that there

80

would be an objection only to a complete figure but not to a bust (*Tur* and *Shulhan Arukh* Yoreh Deah 141). Interestingly enough the further development of the prohibition against pictures and images was not connected with idolatry or the danger of idolatry, which was the concern of the second commandment, but simply with the possibility of distracting the worshipper from appropriate devotion in the synagogue or concentrating on the text of a decorated book (*Tos* to Yoma 54a; *Sefer Hassidim* #1625; *Shulhan Arukh* Yoreh Deah 141; Meir Katzenellenbogen *Avqat Rahel* #65).

These discussions stand in contrast to the decorations found in synagogues both ancient and modern. The synagogue at Dura Europa in Syria as well as various others in Israel have demonstrated that two dimensional figures were frequently used. Furthermore, the many volumes by E. Goodenough (*Jewish Symbols in the Greco-Roman Period*) show us a large number of pictorial images of plants, animals, as well as human figures on sarcophagi, ritual objects, coins and in synagogues. Josephus, Philo and other Hellenistic authors expressed themselves on the subject as well (Joseph Gutmann "The Second Commandment and the Image in Judaism" *Beauty and Holiness* pp 1 ff).

Abstract designs, in place of portraits or figures, were used in synagogues in Islamic lands as Muslims permitted no figures in their decorations. Other cultures influenced us in different directions so the *ketubot* of the Renaissance often showed human figures (Abraham Hiya De Boton *Lehem Rav* #15). De Boton felt that although we should not encourage decorations; it was not necessary to destroy the *ketubah* (Franz Landsberger "Illuminated Marriage Contracts" *Beauty and Holiness*, (ed) J. Gutmann pp 383 f). Although marriage contracts did not find a permanent place in the synagogue, the ceremony at which they were read took place in the courtyard of the synagogue or in the synagogue itself.

QUESTIONS AND REFORM JEWISH ANSWERS

In modern times Orthodox synagogues frequently restrict their window or other decorations to abstract designs. However, they continue to use lions and other figures on the *Torah* ark *parokhet* and *Torah* covers in two and three dimensional forms (Dov Baer Menkes *Anaf Etz Avot* #4; J. Greenwald *Zikhron Yehudah* Orah Hayim #63). Conservative and Reform synagogues use figures in their windows as the Tree of Life (Pittsburgh) where a window portrays Isaac Mayer Wise, the founder of Reform Judaism, in this Conservative synagogue, and Rodef Shalom with many figures.

There is no religious problem about hanging a picture of the Four Chaplains in the foyer of the synagogue. Questions about the artistic merit of the picture as well as other local considerations should be taken into account.

December 1987

51. A UNITARIAN CHURCH BUILDING USED AS A SYNAGOGUE *

QUESTION: May a congregation permanently share facilities with a Unitarian Church? The structure contains no Christian symbols and, in fact, is called "Hall of Worship" by the Unitarians. (Rabbi Joel S. Goor, New York NY)

ANSWER: Various aspects of this question have been treated in the responsum "Ark and *Torah* Permanently in a Christian Church" (W. Jacob *Contemporary American Reform Responsa* #148). That responsum indicates that Christians are considered as monotheist and cited a number of instances from the past in which the use of Christian or Muslim facilities has taken place under emergency conditions. The responsum also mentioned various instances in which facilities were used in common, as for example

82

the Greenwich Village Synagogue in New York City and most military chapels in the United States Armed Forces. Despite that, the responsum came to the conclusion that a *Torah* and ark should not be placed permanently in a church setting and that the congregation should be encouraged to build its own quarters.

There would be even stronger reasons for advising that the congregation move in this direction in this instance. The Unitarian Church stands at the very edge of Christianity and many Orthodox and fundamental Christians do not consider it a Christian body at all. That seems to also have been the perception of some Jewish families who have sought religion akin to Christianity, but without the creedal demands of Christian churches. As a result, most Unitarian churches have some members who were formerly Jewish. Although this poses no real threat to us, we also do not want to encourage confusion along those lines. In addition, we are engaged in a broad effort to limit the number of mixed marriages; therefore, anything which leads to syncretism or unusually close religious ties with Christians should be discouraged.

We are grateful for the good relationships between Christians and Jews which exist and intend to continue to foster them, both on the rabbinic and lay level. We primarily wish to maintain our identity and to strengthen Judaism. The common sharing of a building and all of the casual relationships which develop is not a practice that we would encourage on a permanent basis. We would, therefore, urge the congregation to consider permanent quarters of its own or to rent a space which has no Christian religious overtones.

September 1990

52. A CABARET GROUP IN THE SYNAGOGUE

QUESTION: In our Temple building we have a sanctuary and adjacent social hall. As the sanctuary's acoustics are better than those of the hall, a cabaret singing group has requested the use of the sanctuary for a show whose proceeds would go to the Temple. Is it appropriate to have a cabaret musical, or drama without Jewish content on the *bimah*? (Rabbi Steven A. Moss, Oakdale NY)

ANSWER: A synagogue possesses a special degree of sacredness, which begins when money has been pledged for the purchase or construction of such a building. This represents a transfer of the status of sacrifices dedicated to the ancient temple to articles or funds now dedicated to the synagogue. So, for example, in ancient times when individuals pledged inanimate objects to the temple, they became sacred although no transfer had occurred (*M* Kid 1.7). Funds collected for a synagogue, may on a temporary basis, be utilized for other sacred purposes, but ultimately must be utilized for the synagogue (B B 3b; *Yad* Hil Matnat Aniyim 8.10 f; *Shulhan Arukh* Orah Hayim 153.13). While the process of collecting money was underway students, could be supported by such funds. When building material has been assembled then funds could only be used for the synagogue during the process of erection, the structure possessed an element of the sacred, so funds may not be diverted for other purposes (*Shulhan Arukh* Orah Hayim 115.10).

Now we must ask of what did this sanctity consist? According to the traditional point of view, with which we agree, a synagogue is considered a small sanctuary. In other words it possesses some of the sanctity of the ancient temple in Jerusalem (Meg 29a based upon Ez 11.16).

The sacredness of the synagogue is akin to that of the Temple and rabbinic literature only disagreed whether this was an ordinance of the *Torah* or the rabbis (*Semag* Asin 164.1; *Tur* and *Shulhan Arukh* Orah Hayim 151; etc.).

Aside from regular services, the funeral of a congregational leader may be held there (Meg 28b; *Yad* Hil Tefilah 11.7; *Tur* and *Shulhan Arukh* Orah Hayim 150.5), as also circumcisions (*Tos* to Pes 10a; *Shulhan Arukh* Orah Hayim 131.4; Yoreh Deah 265.11).

The uses of a synagogue aside from prayer were defined. It may be used for study (Meg 28b; *Yad* Hil Meg 3.3; *Yad* Hil Talmud Torah 3.12; *Tur*; *Shulhan Arukh* Yoreh Deah 346.22); it may be utilized for congregational business (Ket 5a; 63b; *Yad* Hil Shabat 24.5; Hil Tefilah 11.7; Hil Ishut 14.9; *Tur* and *Shulhan Arukh* Even Haezer 77.2). Ten individuals might remain there all day in order to be present for a *minyan* or for any congregational business which might need attention (Maimonides *Responsa* #13 (ed) Freiman). Actual business matters could only be discussed if they were charitable or dealt with the redemption of captives (Meg 28a; *Yad* Hil Tefilah 11.6; *Shulhan Arukh* Orah Hayim 151.4). There are also some ancillary uses to which the synagogue could be put. Teachers and students are permitted to eat there as could others if it involved congregational business (Meg 28b; *Yad* Hil Tefilah 11.6; *Shulhan Arukh* Orah Hayim 151.1). Occasionally individuals slept in the synagogue or in adjacent rooms; the latter was preferable (*Tos* to Pes 101a; *Shulhan Arukh* Orah Hayim 151). Matters were different in villages where the inhabitants simply did not have room to house strangers and so they were permitted to sleep in the synagogue (Meg 28a; *Nimuqei Yosef*; *Shulhan Arukh* Orah Hayim 151.11).

During the early period of Nazi oppression in Germany, Yehiel Weinberg was asked whether it would be permissible to use a synagogue for concerts. He reluctantly agreed. However, he suggested that a few psalms or prayers be recited in conjunction with the concert to give it a slightly different context. One might say, therefore, in times of emergency, cultural events, of a non-religious nature, would also be permitted in a synagogue.

The main concern is that nothing untoward or irreverent should occur in the synagogue (Meg 28a; *Yad* Hil Tefilah 11.6; *Tur* and *Shulhan Arukh* Orah Hayim 151.1). The occasion which you described, however, does not fall into any of the permitted categories. The contents of the presentation may be offensive or border on what is inappropriate, and so it would be improper to use the synagogue facilities for a cabaret.

November 1987

53. A CONCERT MASS IN THE SYNAGOGUE

QUESTION: A community junior college, which is a friendly next door neighbor of our Temple, is planning a spring concert featuring the "Requiem" by Faure. The college auditorium is undergoing renovation and will not be available for this concert. May the Temple itself be used for the performance of this "Requiem" rooted in Christian theology or may it be presented in the Temple auditorium? (Rabbi Samuel M. Stahl, San Antonio TX)

ANSWER: We should divide this question into two segments. We will first deal with the use the synagogue itself for a musical performance and then for the performance of a specifically Christian piece.

Some traditional authorities have felt that all music, both vocal and instrumental, is out of place in Jewish life (San 101a; Git

7a). This was the opinion of Mar Ukba who based it upon the verse, "Do not rejoice O Israel among the peoples" (Hos 9.1). This was introduced as a form of mourning for the destruction of the Temple. This prohibition was also found in the later codes and some responsa (Maimonides *Responsa* (ed) Freimann #370; *Yad* Hil Taanit 5.14; *Tur* Orah Hayim 560). These strict statements were, however, modified by custom so that rejoicing and music at weddings became permitted. It was considered permissible to ask a non-Jew to play an instrument at this happy time (*Yad* Hil Taanit 514; *Tur* Orah Hayim 338; *Shulhan Arukh* Orah Hayim 560.3). Others permitted music and based it on the comment of Mar Ukba, at the beginning of the tractate *Berakhot*, stating that only love songs were prohibited, but music which praised God was permitted. Leon De Modena (1571 - 1648) provided a thorough discussion of the sources and indicated that there was no logic in prohibiting beautiful music which praises God without also asking cantors to sing off-key to obey such an injunction. According to him both instrumental and vocal music were permitted in the synagogue (*Zikhnei Yehudah* #6). Music which accompanied a *mitzvah* is permitted. A trend toward leniency may be seen in the *Shulhan Arukh* (Orah Hayim 561.3).

    In modern times the question has arisen again in a different fashion through the controversy over the organ in the synagogue. The numerous responsa on this issue dealt with instrumental music during the service (*Die Orgelfrage; Eleh Divrei Haberit*; David Hoffmann, *Melamed Lehoil* Vol 1 #16). Our question arose also during the Nazi period when synagogues suddenly became the center for all Jewish life, both religious and cultural. The Orthodox authority Yehiel Weinberg prohibited secular concerts in his synagogue in Berlin; he felt that even religious concerts should be preceded by psalms to provide a spiritual setting (*Seridei Esh*, Vol

2 #12). Liberal Jews, faced with the same problem in Nazi Germany, agreed to the use of synagogues for secular concerts. They felt that serious music did not violate the spiritual character of the synagogue. We would agree to the use of a synagogue for concerts in keeping with the mood and purpose of the synagogue.

Now let us deal with the use of the synagogue for a specific Christian performance as the Mass. Our attitude is determined by our feelings about Christianity. A historic review of Judaism's changing attitude toward Christianity demonstrates that we had moved from considering it as idolatry by the Middle Ages. We considered both Christians and Islam as monotheistic religions. Therefore, the ancient restrictions against pagans do not apply to Christians (W. Jacob *Contemporary American Reform Responsa* #167). We continue to emphasize that the Christian concept of God and its fundamental attitudes differs sharply from ours (Isserles to *Shulhan Arukh* Orah Hayim 156). In secular matters, Christians are *benei noah*, but in religious matters distinctions must remain.

We have gone considerably further than previous generations and have been willing to share facilities with Christian churches as the military chapels of the United States Armed Forces. In addition, many synagogues like my own have lent facilities within the building to various Christian groups over longer periods of time during emergencies. This meant that entirely Christian services were conducted within the synagogue setting.

The answer to your question, therefore, rests as much on the contemporary mood as on *halakhic* precedents. We stress openness and friendship, but with limits; it is permissible for Faure's "Requiem" to be performed within the synagogue building, but preferably not in the synagogue itself.

February 1989

88

54. A *MENORAH* ON THE EXTERIOR OF A SYNAGOGUE

QUESTION: During the restoration of the Rodef Shalom Temple in Pittsburgh, a seven branch *menorah* of terracotta in the facade above the main entrance of the Temple has been repaired. The *menorah* with its electric lights has been restored to its original condition. Is the *menorah* appropriate; may it be lit? (Stanley Rosenbaum, Pittsburgh PA)

ANSWER: When the Rodef Shalom Temple was built in 1905, Hornbostel and Palmer sought to create an imposing modern synagogue appropriate for the status of the congregation. It is located on a main thoroughfare in the cultural center of Pittsburgh. They borrowed the historic symbol of Judaism, the *menorah* from the ancient Temple. As this is a Reform Congregation, they felt no hesitation about copying directly from the Temple of Solomon and adding other elements which are reminiscent of that Temple, such as the terracotta decorations which surround the building at roof level which remind us of the ancient pomegranates. More traditional synagogues have avoided any replication of objects of the ancient Temple, so a *menorah* in a traditional synagogue would have six, eight or nine branches, but never seven. In our Reform synagogue those restrictions do not need to be observed.

The combination above the main entrance of the *menorah* along with the verse "My house shall be a house of worship for all people" (Is 56.7) visually emphasized Jewish traditions while also extending a welcome to the general community. The *menorah* is a appropriate; it may be lit on a regular basis.

February 1991

55. SYNAGOGUE PLANTING OF TREES

QUESTION: Should certain species of trees be prohibited on synagogue grounds as the Bible prohibits worshipping under trees? (Nathan Trachtenberg, Dallas TX)

ANSWER: The Biblical statement in Deuteronomy (16.21) demanded: "You shall not plant for yourself an Asherah of any kind of tree aside the altar of the Lord your God which you shall make for yourself." This law has been fully developed in later Jewish tradition by Maimonides (*Yad* Hil Akum 6.9), who stated that no shade or fruit tree could be planted in the temple sanctuary near the altar and in the courtyards of the sanctuary, although there was some debate about the latter. However, this applied only to the Temple in Jerusalem, and later tradition did not connect this with any prohibition against plantings outside the synagogue. We know, for example, that the ancient synagogues at Arsinoe and Palermo had gardens (I. Kraus *Synagogale Altertümer* p 315). In fact, we find no objection until Moses Schick who, in 1870, prohibited such plantings by reasoning that the synagogue is analogous to the temple (*Responsa* Orah Hayim #78, #79). Although this objection was widely discussed, it was not accepted by most authorities who cited Yomtov Lippman Heller's comment to the *Mishnah* (Midot 2.6) as well as other scholars who felt that his reasoning was faulty. Nothing would have prohibited planting trees even in the court of Israel in the Temple of Jerusalem. Some historic *Haggadah* illustrations which depicted the temple show it surrounded by plantings of shrubbery.

The great modern authority, Shalom Mordecai Schwadron (*Responsa* Vol I #127; Vol VI #17), specifically stated that the objection to trees in the Temple of Jerusalem did not apply to synagogues, and only cautioned individuals who decorated their synagogues in this way to make sure that the planting would be somewhat different from that of neighboring churches. He quoted Joseph ben Moses Trani, a sixteenth century scholar (*Responsa Yoreh Deah* #4), who reported that gardens and plantings around synagogues were widespread during his lifetime.

There is no analogy between worship of an Asherah, a form of ancient idolatry of which we know virtually nothing, and our worship. We need not be concerned with this Biblical prohibition. There is, therefore, no reason to be careful about the planting of trees or any other kind of greenery around the synagogue. We should be guided by the concern of Exodus for the beauty of the sanctuary. That thought was continued in the Temple of Solomon (I Kings 6 ff). We should follow the ideal of *hidur mitzvah* in all ceremonial objects as well as the synagogue building itself.

Circumstances have often forced us to use humble buildings as synagogues, but when it was possible to build more grandly we did so. From the nineteenth century onward when our synagogues were recognized and protected by the secular authorities; we no longer hid them behind a neutral facade, but provided them with a decorative exterior which often included plantings (Harold Hammer-Schenk *Synagogen in Deutschland;* Rachel Wischnitzer *The Architecture of the European Synagogue*). There would be no reason to exclude trees or shrubs from the grounds of the synagogue.

January 1990

56. WHY KINDLE TWO LIGHTS ON FRIDAY EVENING?

QUESTION: Why do we kindle two lights on Friday evening? (Aaron Cohen, Louisville KY)

ANSWER: The origin of the *shabbat* lamp goes back to the *Mishnah* (*M* Shabbat 2.1). There and in the appropriate sections of the Talmud we see that only one *shabbat* light was mentioned. The discussions dealt with the nature of the fuel for the single light; whether it could be tallow, or various kinds of oil. Further discussions dealt with moving the lamp as well as extinguishing the light (Shab 20b ff). In none of these places as well as the later *Talmudic* discussion was a second light for *erev shabbat* mentioned.

The first source of our custom seems to be Jacob ben Asher who wrote that it was customary to kindle a beautifully prepared light and that among some, two lights were kindled reminiscent of the two versions of the *shabbat* commandment in the Decalogue with the words *shamor* and *zakhor*. This custom was limited to the wealthy as the next sentences dealt with individuals who could not afford both *shabbat* and Hanukkah lights, or who did not have sufficient money for both the light and the wine for *qiddush* (*Agur* #358; *Tur* Orah Hayim 263; *Shulhan Arukh* Orah Hayim 263).

Another *minhag* which arose during more prosperous times called for kindling lights or candles for every member of the family or for each child in the family (*Shulhan Arukh* Orah Hayim 263.1 ff). For this reason we find some older *shabbat* lamps with a large number of arms, five, seven or eight are fairly common (A Kanof *Jewish Ritual Art* pp 102 ff, S. S. Kayser (ed) *Jewish Ceremonial Art* pp 74 ff; I Schachar *Jewish Tradition in Art* pp 206 ff; H. J. Spiller *The Cofeld Judaic Museum* pp 20 ff; *Journal of Jewish Art* Vols 1-15).

We can see that it has become a general custom to have two lights in order to usher in the *shabbat*. However, one would certainly be acceptable and any larger number presents the continuation of a fine *minhag*.

August 1991

57. WHITE BREAD FOR *HALOT*

QUESTION: Need the *halot* used on Friday evening and festivals be white bread? (Alan C. Marcus, Fort Worth TX)

ANSWER: The two *halot* used at the *shabbat* meal on Friday evening remind us of the double portion of *mannah* which was provided for the Israelites in the desert on Friday for *shabbat* (Ex 16.22). On *Pesah* two of the three *matzot* refer to this double portion of *mannah* (Ex 16.22; Shab 117b), while the third is broken early in the *Seder* ceremony. If we only had two, then one would remain whole at the time of the meal (*Sidur Rav Amram* p 113).

There are some regulations about covering the *halot* (*Shulhan Arukh* Orah Hayim 271.9) as well as how one should conduct oneself during the *motzi* (*Shulhan Arukh* Orah Hayim 274.1). In addition, the *halot* may be baked in unusual shapes for special occasions. On *Rosh Hashanah* they could be shaped like a ladder to remind those assembled that during the next year they may be elevated or humbled. Occasionally *halot* have been shaped like a bird, a reminder of Isaiah's statement that God will protect Jerusalem (Isaiah 31.5; *Shulhan Arukh* Orah Hayim 583.1).

These statements said little about the nature of the *halah* with the exception of *Rosh Hashanah*. On this festival the bread, which was normally salted as a reminder of the sacrifice in the ancient Temple (W. Jacob (ed) *American Reform Responsa* #42), remained sweet as we seek a sweet year. Both bread and apple may be dipped in honey (Ker 6a; *Shulhan Arukh* Orah Hayim 583.1).

White flour may have been used whenever possible in an effort to make the *halot* akin to the show breads of the ancient desert tabernacle and Temple. These were to be made of fine flour (Lev 24.7). Of course, those twelve loaves served a very different purpose and we do not know whether "fine" meant white. White flour may also have been part of our effort to distinguish the *shabbat*. This occurred in other ways as well, so poverty stricken households sought to serve some meat or fish on Friday evening.

In some traditions, raisins were added to the *halah* on festivals and it was baked in a round rather than rectangular form. Twisted *halot* were a medieval German Jewish custom.

In our prosperous American society the special nature of pure white flour has been forgotten. Even in my childhood in Germany white bread was special and more expensive. Undoubtedly its cost was beyond the means of some families, but in the past this may have been a way of stressing the festive nature of *shabbat*. It is preferable to have a white *halah* in keeping with the tradition, but any kind of bread is acceptable. There is no requirement that the *halot* be of white flour or to take any special form.

May 1990

58. JEWISH STUDIES ON *SHABBAT* AFTERNOON

QUESTION: A university would like to offer a college course for credit on *shabbat* afternoon in the Temple. A course given at this time will enable the largest number of students to fit a program of Jewish studies into their curriculum. In order to satisfy the college requirements, such a course would have to meet regularly and have scheduled exams. Is it appropriate to provide such a course in the synagogue? (Sylvia Nelson, Los Angeles CA)

ANSWER: The study of the *Torah* has always been considered more important than anything else (*M* Peah 1.1). Much of the *Mishnaic* tractate *Pirqei Avot* dealt with the significance of study and the need to engage in it constantly. Study has, of course, been a traditional part of *shabbat*. In order to assure at least some study by all individuals, the *Torah* reading on *shabbat* morning and afternoon along with the *Haftorah* and sermon are designed to provide for universal study. *Shabbat* provides study opportunities during the morning and afternoon services as well as the third meal (*Seudah Shelishit*; Shab 117b; *Tur* and *Shulhan Arukh* Orah Hayim 291). This meal is frequently accompanied by scholarly dissertations. In some traditions the *Mishnah* is studied on *shabbat* afternoon and groups (*hevrot*) are organized for this purpose. Regular study in a communal form is very much part of *shabbat*.

We must, however, ask about the format of a university course with the trappings of the weekday routine. The course will have quizzes, examinations, and the other requirements of the university. These are alien to the spirit of *shabbat* which inculcates a reverence for learning, but also the pleasure of learning.

This course will be appropriate if conducted in the right spirit. The instructor must provide the *shabbat* course with joy and the proper mood. Under those conditions such a course would be desirable. Examinations must be scheduled for another day as they certainly are not in the spirit of *shabbat*. A course planned to accommodate these considerations would be acceptable.

February 1990

59. RENTING A PORTION OF A SYNAGOGUE TO A UNIVERSITY

QUESTION: May a synagogue rent a portion of its building for university classes? The classes will be held both during the week and on *shabbat*. Is that rental appropriate as it involves a secular use of the building on *shabbat*? Does it make a difference that there are separate entrances for congregants coming to worship and for students coming to study? (Rabbi Robert T. Gan, Los Angeles CA)

ANSWER: Synagogues through the ages have been located in many different sites sometimes, especially since the Emancipation, in a completely secular environment. So, for example, the Orthodox synagogue in Springfield, Missouri was in an office building which also housed a movie theater, and the normal secular activities continued around the synagogue on *shabbat* as well as the holidays. Elsewhere, rooms rented by a congregation for religious school or adult activities during certain days were rented by others for secular purposes at different times.

In your instance, of course, we are dealing with a synagogue which owns the property and may rent to others. The fact that the rental is to a university for the purposes of study would make no difference to the traditional authorities such as Ezekiel Landau or Moses Sofer and many of their disciples who long opposed secular studies (A. Altman *Moses Mendelssohn* p 397; Ezekiel Landau *Derushei Hazelah* 53a pp; Moses Sofer *Responsa* #197). We, of course, do not share these feelings about the university and secular learning, and are joined by other Orthodox authorities such as David Hoffmann (*Melamed Lehoil*) and Samson Raphael Hirsch.

We must ask whether any particular feelings of holiness are attached to the synagogue building outside of the synagogue itself such as the social hall and other rooms. Such areas of the synagogue do not possess a special sanctified status. We would not hesitate to use the facilities of the synagogue for entirely secular purposes such as a social dance (S. B. Freehof *Recent Reform Responsa* #45; W. Jacob (ed) *American Reform Responsa* #166 ff). There are few restrictions on the use of a synagogue building.

All of the instances discussed have dealt with congregational or communal uses and were subject to restrictions on *shabbat* and holidays. No normal activities would continue during these sacred days especially during the hours of services.

We can only claim that university classes are inappropriate on *shabbat* under the rubric *marit ayin*. The appearance to the congregation and the general community of such a rental would be wrong. It would seem to violate the *shabbat* and secularize the synagogue building. Although technically such a rental arrangement would be alright, we should not neglect *marit ayin* and such sentiments unless the economic circumstances are extreme and this is the only way in which the synagogue can continue. The facilities should not be rented to a university if it is going to use them on *shabbat* and the holidays.

December 1990

60. FUND RAISING ON *SHABBAT*

QUESTION: Is it appropriate for a congregation to discuss matters of fund raising on *shabbat*? The officers of the congregation would like to meet before or after a *shabbat* service which they normally attend. (Charles Levine, Chicago IL)

ANSWER: The Biblical statement clearly prohibits work on *shabbat* as recorded in the Decalogue (Exodus 20.8 ff) and reemphasized by the prophets (Isaiah 58.13). The *Talmud* subsequently provided details and specifics which included the discussion of business matters on *shabbat* although no immediate commercial transactions may have been involved (Shab 150a). There were further discussions later about the permissibility of dealing with communal matters, and a general agreement that matters of charity as well as synagogue affairs might be discussed on the Shabbat (*Yad* Hil Shabbat 24.5; *Tur* and *Shulhan Arukh* Orah Hayim 306 and commentaries). The welfare of the congregation may certainly be discussed on *shabbat*, but how specific may the meeting become?

In answering these questions we must look at the circumstances which led to the permissive attitude. The only day of rest in most previous generations was *shabbat*. In many periods, therefore, this was the only day on which it was possible for individuals to gather together to discuss communal affairs. That is not our case, as virtually the entire society rests on both Saturday and Sunday and the vast majority in our society people restrict themselves to forty working hours per week. This means that there is ample time during the week for business discussions of all kinds. The necessity of holding such a meeting on *shabbat* either before or after service has been eliminated. It would be permissible to conduct such meetings during emergencies, but this should not become a regular habit of the congregational officers.

We have sought in every way to enhance *shabbat* and the spirit of rest. It will be difficult for individuals who are normally engaged in business to refrain on *shabbat* while at the same time engaging in the business affairs of the congregation. The line of demarcation may become gray. We should not do so.

January 1990

61. SYNAGOGUE TOURS ON *SHABBAT*

QUESTION: Our synagogue is a national landmark, and is visited by a large number of individuals throughout the year. Tour companies seek to schedule visits on *shabbat* afternoon. There is no problem about openning the building through a non-Jewish caretaker, however, our Jewish guides who normally take the groups through the building have objected to being scheduled on *shabbat*. Is it more important to show the synagogue or to rest on *shabbat*? (Alice Grafner, Pittsburgh PA)

ANSWER: During the last decades we have done a great deal to enhance the observance of *shabbat* and to minimize any activity akin to work or which would infringe on the spirit of rest, worship or study of this day. We may, of course, interpret showing the synagogue on *shabbat* as study, broadly understood.

A major segment of *shabbat* has traditionally been set aside for study. Such study should be pleasurable and not considered a task. As the guides do not view it in this fashion and see it as work, we cannot justify the tours on these grounds.

We should, of course, also consider the considerable effort we have made to teach the non-Jewish world about Judaism. There are national groups as well as special institutions like the Jewish Chautauqua Society of the National Brotherhoods which deal exclusively with Jewish/Christian relations, and make an effort to bring about understanding in the broader Christian community.

We have a clash of values. The members of the congregation want to inform the world around us about Judaism, but are also sensitive about *shabbat*; that should be honored. It is a good sign and indicates that our efforts to enhance *shabbat* are bearing fruit.

We could accommodate the Christian visitors through the use of modern technology, and provide them with an appropriate audio tape on *shabbat* which will explain the symbols of the synagogue and answer questions commonly asked. It should also indicate that no Jewish tour guide is on duty as *shabbat* is our day of rest. I am sure the Christian visitors will appreciate the effort on their behalf, as well as the desire of the guides to observe *shabbat* in the appropriate fashion.

February 1990

62. THE SABBATH COMMANDMENT AGAINST LIGHTING A FIRE

QUESTION: The tradition concerning *shabbat* lists thirty-nine prohibited types of work. Most of them are derived deductively, however, the commandment against lighting a fire on the Sabbath is specific. Why is that so? (Stanley H. Levin, Pittsburgh PA)

ANSWER: The commandment, which prohibits the lighting of a fire on the Sabbath (Ex 35.3), along with that against collecting *mannah* and the prohibition against planting, serving and harvesting represented the only specific injunctions which define work prohibited on *shabbat* in the *Torah*. The main statement which demanded rest was part of the Decalogue (Ex 20.10) and did not define work nor was a definition provided in Deuteronomy (5.14). The death penalty was specified for those who violate these ordinances (Ex 31.15; 35.2; Nu 15.32 ff).

The Bible provided only a few instances of work specifically prohibited on the Sabbath. Jeremiah mentioned transporting items or "doing work" on *shabbat* (Jer 17.21, 22) while Amos listed trading on the Sabbath as prohibited (Amos 8.5). Nehemiah included trading conducted by non-Jews (Neh 10.32). He closed the city gates as he found people loading their asses, carrying fruit and other items as well as working in their wine presses (Neh 13.15-21). The prohibition against the collection of *mannah* included its baking and preparation (Ex 16.22 ff). We can see from these statements that the Bible proceeded in the direction of specific prohibitions, but did not present us with a complete system as later found in the rabbinic literature. There, we find thirty-nine categories of work prohibited (*M* Shab 7.2; 11-24). All were associated with the construction of the desert tabernacle (Ex 35) principally because the specific Sabbath prohibition was associated with the construction of the Tabernacle (Ex 35.2, 3). Subsequently in the *Talmud* these categories designated as *avot* were further divided into *toledot* and so sub-categories became defined.

The prohibition against lighting a fire, collecting and preparing *mannah* and plowing, sowing and harvesting represent the *Torah's* steps toward defining work on the *shabbat*. It is not clear from the text why the prohibition against lighting a fire was singled out as a specific prohibited act. The commentators provide different interpretations on this. Some like Ibn Ezra indicated that it was intended to show how the Sabbath differs from other festivals like Passover. On them it is permitted to prepare foods and therefore to light a fire, but on the Sabbath this is prohibited. This had to be made clear from the outset. Others like Ramban indicated that acts, which might make the day more beautiful or comfortable like lighting a fire, were nevertheless prohibited. Both Ramban and Rashbam provided a number of other reasons from Midrashic sources. Benno Jacob in his classic commentary on Exodus cited this prohibition as one connected with the divine act of creation. As fire was part of the gift of light and so was among God's initial acts of creation, it therefore represents the ultimate and primaeval type of work. For this reason it is prohibited on the Sabbath.

The last of these reasons sounds more convincing than some of the others. However, ultimately we really do not know why this prohibition was specified nor do we have a reason for the others found in the *Torah* or the remainder of the Bible. We may, perhaps, best say that the Bible moved slowly toward a system of specific prohibitions. As the Bible is generally not systematic, it was left to the *Mishnah* and *Talmud* to carry this to its logical conclusion.

November 1987

63. THE TOWER AS A *HAVDALAH* SPICE BOX

QUESTION: What is the origin of the spice box in the form of a tower? Is this connected with the tower of David in Jerusalem? (Mitchell Davids, Albany, NY)

ANSWER: In the earliest discussions of *havdalah* the spice was held simply in the hand rather than in a container; for example a bunch of myrtle (Shab 33b; Jacob Moelln *Sefer Maharil* 19d). When a variety of spices rather than a single spice was used for *havdalah*, then a container became necessary (Isaac of Vienna *Or Zarua* II #92). Early illustrations show a round container (*Sefer Minhagim* Venice 1590). In some German illustrations from 1553, it appeared like a tower and the accompanying text indicated that this followed a traditional form (Franz Landsberger "Ritual Implements for the Sabbath" in Joseph Guttmann *Beauty in Holiness* p 186). Two suggestions about this form have been made: Kayser felt that the tower was reminiscent of the medieval fortified towers in which spices and other valuables were kept. Landsberger rejected this as the towers were too open for fortifications. He accepted the suggestion of Rachel Wischnitzer-Bernstein which related the tower to the Biblical verse: "His cheeks are as a bed of spices as *towers* of perfumes" (Song of Songs 5.13) and added that such towers were often among the gifts presented to the infant Jesus by the Three Kings along with myrrh and other spices.

Towers became a favorite form of the *besamim* box and were fabricated by Jews and non-Jews as the markings indicate. There is no connection with ancient Jerusalem.

September 1987

64. SHAPE OF THE *HAVDALAH* SPICE BOX

QUESTION: An artisan has asked whether a spice box need to take a special form. He remembers spice boxes in a shape of a tower as well as animals. What limits are there for this object? (John Rosen, Syracuse NY)

ANSWER: The spice box in the form of a tower has been discussed in the previous responsum. However, the form was not limited to towers. There are also spice boxes in the shape of a hand (Landsberger *Op cit* p 189), or a round container with an Islamic crescent at the top (A. Kanof *Ceremonial Art in Judaic Tradition* p 109), as a tree with birds, or a ship with some sailors (*Ibid* 64). In addition, spice containers in the form of flowers, fruit, buildings, a model synagogue, a Faberge egg, statues of Adam and Eve leaving Paradise, a windmill (A. Kanof *Jewish Ceremonial Art*; *Journal of Jewish Art*; Judith C. E. Belinfante *Joods Historisch Museum*; Isaiah Shachar *Jewish Tradition in Art*; Beverly R. Cohen *The Cofeld Judaic Museum*; and auction catalogs). I have also seen *besamin* boxes in the form of a miniature railway engine and a small airplane. In other words, it is possible to be playful and there are no restrictions. The artist in question may design a *besamim* box in any shape as long as it is not related to the object of another religion.

May 1990

65. ORDINARY OR HIGH HOLIDAY MELODIES

QUESTION: My cantor insists on using the traditional modes for the *Yamim Naroim* while the Ritual Committee and I have insisted that a large number of melodies ordinarily sung during the year be continued so that the congregation may participate in the service. There are, of course, also many holiday melodies which will be sung by the cantor or choir alone to set the mood for the *Yamim Naroim*. Is it permisable to use ordinary melodies on these holidays? (Fabian Levy, Los Angeles CA)

ANSWER: Synagogue melodies fall under the rubric of *minhag* and vary greatly between *Ashkenazim* and *Sephardim* as well as within each community. There are traditional modes not only for the *Yamim Naroim,* but also for other festivals as well as special *shabbat* services during the year (E. Werner *A Voice Still Heard*; A. Z. Idelsohn *Jewish Music* pp 110 ff). In all of these matters the local *minhag* is considered binding (Eruvin 20b; *Shulhan Arukh* Yoreh Deah 376.4). In an Orthodox congregation if the cantor, wishes to introduce a change in the melodies and the members object, then the melodies remain unchanged.

We might also add a very practical consideration. The services for the holy days should be participatory. That is always difficult as a large number of individuals attend synagogue only on those days and on few other occasions during the year. Through those rather sporadic visits to the synagogue they will have achieved a passing familiarity with some melodies. If they now attend a service which presents totally different music they will simply be spectators, and the service will lose much of its meaning.

Although it would be good to utilize the appropriate modes for a given holiday or *shabbat*, the introduction of those modes must be slowly and carefully undertaken so that participation in the service, which is vastly more important, will not be diminished.

January 1991

66. TWO DAYS OF YOM KIPPUR

QUESTION: Logic would demand that Orthodox Jews should observe two days of Yom Kippur. Why has this not been done? (Louise Marcovsky, Pittsburgh PA)

ANSWER: As you correctly surmised, traditional Judaism outside the Land of Israel observed two days of all the festivals due to the uncertainty of the calendar; let me review the reasoning. Each new month was established through the actual observation of the moon. The person who saw the new moon appeared at the Temple along with witnesses and the priest declared that a new month had begun (M R H 1.6 ff; 20a ff). When the precise date of each festival was established by observation in Jerusalem, the message could not arrive on time in Babylonia, and so two days were celebrated in order to assure the celebration of each festival on the proper day (Ber 4b ff; M R H 2.1 ff). It was for the same reason that two days of *Rosh Hashanah* were observed even within the city of Jerusalem, for the witnesses to the new moon might arrive too late to begin the full observance of the day (R H 30b).

Although these calendar reasons ceased to exist when the calendar was fixed by calculation rather than through the observation of the new moon in Jerusalem, the practice of observing two days outside the land of Israel continued. In modern times we Reform Jews abolished the second day of the festivals as no longer necessary and returned to the Biblical observance; subsequently most Conservative congregations have followed the same practice and given as their reason the wish to observe as the State of Israel. Of course, within Israel only one day of the festivals, except *Rosh Hashanah* has traditionally been observed.

Yom Kippur has been observed for only one day as two days of fasting would have presented an undue hardship (R H 30b). There were, however, pietists particularly in Germany who observed *Yom Kippur* for two days. This custom, as many pietistic customs arose in central Europe; the *Ashkenazi* mentality led to strictness. The custom was observed by some people, but it never became standard and was strongly opposed by such individuals as Ranenu Asher (*Tur* Orah Hayim 624; *Agur* Hil Yom Hakipurim #957).

August 1987

67. *YOM KIPPUR* "BREAK-THE-FAST"

QUESTION: It has been the custom of my congregation to conclude the Yom Kippur at 6:00 p.m., actually it is not completely dark with three stars until about 7:30 p.m. I wait until the traditional conclusion of the day to break my fast, however, now some of my congregants would like to hold a break-the-fast reception immediately after the *neilah* service at 6:00 p.m. How seriously does Reform Judaism take the fasting period "from eventide to eventide"? (Rabbi Gerald Raiskin, Burlingame CA)

ANSWER: *Yom Kippur*, like all festivals and the *shabbat*, extends from evening to evening and all Jews have always tried to honor this tradition and to fast on this day (Lev 16:27; 23.27; M Yoma 8.1 8l b, R H 9a, Shab 35b; *Shulhan Arukh* Orah Hayim 261.2, 293.2;610). We have not been particularly strict in some matters, for example in kindling the *shabbat* lights or making

106

qiddush on Friday evening. We do not insist that this be done at sunset but rather that it occur at the time of the family meal which actually begins *shabbat* for the family. As there is no prohibition against kindling lights on *shabbat* for us, the symbolism of the candles is better served when the candles are lit at the dinner table and then later at a public service.

Yom Kippur is observed by all our congregants and an effort is made to observe it from "eventide to eventide". Most of our people fast and take both the outward observance and the inner meaning of this holiday very seriously. Although individual families may not be fully observant, certainly congregations should not set that kind of an example. A congregational reception or dinner it should occur after the day is actually over.

There is, of course, some conflict between this kind of a reception and the general serious mood of the day and for that reason as well, it should not intrude into the day. The light mood of an evening reception may clash with the general tenor of the day. Some congregations, like my own, have satisfied the congregational desire for sociability at this time when almost all members are present by having a reception after the *Rosh Hashanah* morning services; others have chosen *Sukkot* as the appropriate time during this season for sociability. As the mood of that day is slightly different from *Yom Kippur* and as there are no questions of propriety, this has worked out very well for us.

Yom Kippur is concluded when three stars are visible, whether this be early or late; many of us are not absolutely strict about this, but there is no reason for breaking the fast before sunset and it is dark merely because the services have ended.

December 1988

68. NATURE OF THE *LULAV*

QUESTION: What is the nature of the *lulav* used on *Sukkot*? For how many days of the festival should it be used? (Stephen Paul, Indianapolis IN)

ANSWER: The *lulav* is the shoot of a palm tree which has remained in its folded state. In other words, before the palm leaf actually spreads out (Lev 23.40). It should measure at least three handbreadths in length. Two twigs of a willow and three of a myrtle are associated with it (Suk 29b, 32b, 34a). These three kinds of branches are tied together and used for *Sukkot* services with the *etrog*. Their use can be documented to the period of the Temple and its service throughout the seven days of the festival of *Sukkot*. The *lulav* was only used on the first day in the Temple. After the destruction of the Temple in 69 CE its use for the entire festival was mandated (Suk 41a, 43b).

The *lulav* is carried during the recital of the Hallel Psalms (Psalms 113-118). All of this, of course, is based upon the Biblical description of the festival (Lev 23.40).

No specific kind of palm has been mandated so the unfolded leaf on any palm branch is acceptable. Probably the most likely palm is the date palm (*Phoenix dactylifera*) as seems indicated by the sources (Suk 32b; Nid 26a; *Yad* Hil Sukkah 7.8). The palm leaf must be three handbreath in length. The following other palms have also been used: *Hyphaenae thebaica, corypha umbraculifera,* as well as the thorn palm (Suk 32b), but we need not limit ourselves to them.

October 1989

ORAH HAYIM

69. TYPE OF WILLOW FOR THE SUKKOT

QUESTION: There are a number of species of willows in our area and we are not certain which one should be used for the lulav? (Terry Osman, Philadelphia PA)

ANSWER: The Bible along with other ancient texts is not very specific about the nature of plants. For that matter, up to the time of Linneus plant identification was quite uncertain and popular names in various countries as well as various sections of countries often were used to identify entirely different plants.

All indications point to the willow species (*Salix Alba*) as the willow of the Biblical period. However, it might also have been *Salis Acmophylla*. The difference between the two trees is that one grows in a cooler climate and the other in the hot climate of the Jordan River Valley as well some of the oases. We shall also note that the tree mentioned in Psalm 137.2 which is sometimes translated as willow probably refers instead to the Euphrates poplar (*Populus Ephratica* which is a totally different species also mentioned in the Book of Ezekiel (17.5).

As the Jews moved into various other lands, we simply used the local species of willow tree and this varied from country to country and was never questioned. Probably once reason for this is that fact that in contrast to the palm branch and the *etrog* it would not be possible to transport a willow branch any distance and keep it looking green.

Any willow, therefore, is acceptable for use as the *lulav*. One need not be particular about obtaining the Israeli species.

October 1991

70. REFORM *HAGGADAH*

QUESTION: What is the rationale behind the Reform *Haggadah* which seems so different from the traditional text? (Norman Kline, Phoenix AZ)

ANSWER: We must understand that the *Haggadah*, which represents the ritual of the *Seder* Eve, began as a very simple ceremony in which only the recital of the verse "My father was a wandering Aramean..." (Deut 26.5) was required. Through the ages a vast amount of additional material accumulated. Some of it in the *Mishnaic* and *Talmudic* period. Portions are Aramaic while others are in Hebrew. There are reflections of *Midrashic* literature, synagogue poetry, popular poetry, some of doubtful value, undercurrents of anti-Christian polemic, some mystical leanings and much more. The study of the text of the *Haggadah* provides a fascinating insight into Jewish history as well as a broad effort to encourage learning for children and adults over many different generations. A number of good studies of the *Haggadah* exist and a great deal more remains to be written on this wonderful book (D. Goldschmidt *Haggadah shel Pesah;* S. Wiener *Bibliographie der Oster - Haggadah;* C. Roth, *The Haggadah;* J. D. Eisenstein *Otzar Perushim al Haggadah*).

The American Reform movement was the first to create a *Haggadah* for itself at the beginning of this century. This reflected a number of different issues both ideological and practical. The traditional text had grown too long and so people abbreviated it in their own fashion. Rather than permitting this and omitting significant segments, the movement felt it should present a version which would appeal to its new American constituency. English was widely used so that the text would be readily understandable.

At the turn of the century, the strong traditional emphasis on Zion and Israel was considered wrong and more stress was placed on America. This was part of a broader movement to Americanize the new immigrant and to bring them closer to the ideals of this country. Therefore, we find songs like "America the Beautiful" as well as the elimination of the rebuilding of Jerusalem and *leshanah habah berushalayim*. The early versions of the *Haggadah* also eliminated elements considered hostile to Gentiles or simply too bloody, so for example the ten plagues and their *Midrashic* enlargement. These along with both playful and serious sections were removed. The text was reduced to a reasonable size and aesthetically printed in 1905.

The second version of the *Haggadah* (1923) made other changes for aesthetic and textual reasons. They, however, were relatively minor. A larger historic introduction was added as were contemporary photographs which illustrated some of the thoughts stressed in the volume. The art deco engravings added a touch of fancy which is otherwise missing in the earlier *Haggadah*.

The latest *Haggadah* (1974) has taken us in a somewhat different direction. It added much traditional material and rather than only eliminating text, it has freely added contemporary pieces and practices some choice to those conducting the *Seder*. They may select from relevant material of the Holocaust, twentieth century thinkers, modern Israelis and a good deal more. The result is a *Haggadah* which is longer than the traditional *Haggadah* if it were read in its entirety. A properly prepared leader can bring a contemporary touch to the text. References to Zion and Israel have been restored as have the ten plagues, but not their *Midrashic* exuberance. Some traditional poetry is back. We should realize that this *Haggadah* represents the most popular liturgical work of the creative decades from the 1960's through the 1980's during which

111

a large number of modern *Haggadahs* were published.

The Reform *Haggadah* therefore represents an attempt to eliminate what does not seem to appeal to our generation while adding elements which are new and contemporary. Some of these changes will be permanent and be reflected in the general Jewish liturgies of all movements eventually; others will be temporary and have simply demonstrated the mood of our age.

July 1991

71. *MATZAH* AND BAKED GOODS

QUESTION: At various meals held during *Pesah* items, akin to bread have been placed on the table along with *matzah*. The caterer is kosher so it is clear that this is not bread, but these goods have been baked from ground *matzah* as the taste also quickly reveals. Is it appropriate to use these items during *Pesah* or does this violate the spirit of the holiday? (Frances Stein, Baltimore MD)

ANSWER: *Matzah* meal has been used for baking items during *Pesah* for some time and in this way certain kinds of cakes and cookies have been prepared. There is also an older use described by Simon Ben Zemah of Duran who advised Marranos, often especially watched during the *Pesah* season, to bake *matzot*, reduce them to meal, and bake bread from that meal. In this way they could observe *Pesah* without endangering their lives. Undoubtedly something akin to this has occurred elsewhere as well.

Our circumstance is, of course, entirely different as we are free to use *matzah* and to celebrate the festival appropriately. We should not use an item akin to bread or rolls baked from *matzah* meal. Although technically it is not forbidden, we would discourage it because of *marit ayin*. The presence of this kind of "bread" raises the suspicion that the festival is not being observed properly and it is not in the spirit of *Pesah* to use items which appear like bread.

March 1986

72. AN OLIVE WOOD *HAGGADAH*

QUESTION: The synagogue has been given a *Haggadah* with a cover made of olive wood. Several individuals have asked whether this is an attempt to connect the story of Noah with the tale of Passover, two acts of divine salvation. (Ernest Wolf, New York NY)

ANSWER: The olive branch has been associated with the story of Noah, as a dove flew to him in the evening with an olive branch in its mouth; then Noah realized that the flood waters were receding from the earth (Gen 8.11). Through this symbolism it became a sign of peace between God and humanity. The olive branch in the mouth of a dove has been used frequently in Christian art where it possesses a completely different meaning. We should also remember the special status accorded to the olive tree in the poetic verses of Judges (9.8f).

The use of olive wood to create covers for the *Haggadah* has other origins. In the early decades of this century the new Jewish settlements of Israel produced little which they could export. It was not yet possible to ship citrus fruit or other agricultural products as the necessary refrigeration did not yet exist. In an effort to find products which were specifically related to the land of Israel and which were plentiful and easily worked, objects of olive wood were created. Almost all of these were small and were designed to

113

appeal to individuals in Europe or North America. Olive wood was used for *besamim* boxes, *havdalah* sets, candelabra, Bible and prayerbook covers, as well as the *Haggadah* cover which your synagogue possesses. The fabrication of such objects continues to the present time, but on a diminished scale as Israel now exports many other goods as well.

February 1990

73. SCHOOL CEREMONIES ON A JEWISH HOLIDAY

QUESTION: A private school, which has a fairly large number of Jews enrolled, has planned its graduation on *Shavuot*. They have mandated the attendance of all students. How should we deal with this situation? (Ned Deutsch, Boston MA)

ANSWER: Let us begin by reviewing the past records of conflicts between Jewish children and education authorities. Our children began to attend government schools in the nineteenth century. In Eastern Europe the hostile government school legislation met vigorous opposition. Western European legislation was not hostile and most families complied especially as the schools openned new economic possibilities. There were times in the last century when it was unavoidable for Jewish children in public schools to avoid classes on *shabbat*, as the school week extended for six days. David Hoffmann, the Orthodox rabbi of Berlin, permitted students to attend school on *shabbat*, carry books to their class, etc., as this was the only way in which students could graduate from these schools and qualify themselves for a decent livelihood (*Melamed Lehoil* Vol I #58). They were to modify their conduct on *shabbat* and observe *shabbat* in every way which remained possible;

114

special *shabbat* afternoon services were instituted for them. There were occasions when this was absolutely unavoidable.

Our situation in contemporary America is different. Both private and public schools have regularly made special provisions for Jewish students. If a private school like the one in question seeks to enroll Jewish students then it must also be sensitive to the Jewish calendar. Jewish agencies provide both private and public schools with Jewish calendars so that such conflict may be avoided.

In this instance the Jewish students should indicate that they will not attend graduation if the graduation ceremonies cannot be moved and they expect future graduations to be held on a day other than a Jewish holiday. I am sure that the authorities sensitive to religious issues and to bad publicity which may result from a mass protest by Jewish students will excuse the Jewish students or move the graduation. Perhaps, a special graduation ceremony for the Jewish students can be arranged if the graduation cannot be moved. In any case, a firm stand should be taken.

April 1987

74. PALM TREES ON *SHAVUOT*

QUESTION: Some members of my congregation remember that palm trees were displayed on *Shavuot* in the synagogues of their childhood in Central Europe. They would like to introduce this custom to our synagogue. Would this be appropriate? Is there such a *minhag*? (Peter Rostow, Boston MA)

ANSWER: The festival of *Shavuot* has been augmented by a variety of traditions through the ages. Each of them sought to add to its significance or stressed a special element of this day. So, for example, the association with Sinai and the giving of the law (*zeman matan toratenu*) has been stressed through the custom of studying throughout the night of *Shavuot*. This was initially mentioned by the *Kabalists* of Safed and is found in the *Zohar* (Emor 98a). For this purpose a special reader was created (*Tiqun Leil Shavuot*). This volume contains brief excerpts from each of the Books of the Bible, the entire Book of Ruth and selections of each book of the *Mishnah*. These readings were selected from the beginning and end of the book, or in the case of the *Torah* from the very opening or closing verses of each *parashah*. In some traditions the six hundred and thirteen commandments, according to the Maimonidian sequence, were added along with portions from mystical texts as the *Zohar* or *Sefer Yetzirah*. These readings were accompanied by a festive mood and continued either until midnight or more commonly throughout the night. This custom was found in many Eastern European lands and continues in some circles today.

A less intellectual reminder of the giving of the law has been created through eating dairy foods because the *Torah* is akin to milk and honey (Song of Songs 4.11). As Reform Jews, of course, we have added the custom of Confirmation to *Shavuot*. This ceremony originated with Israel Jacobson in 1810, in the German town of Seesen. Through involving both boys and girls it declared the equality of the sexes and the need to educate young women Jewishly. Confirmation celebrated additional educational achievement as it lay beyond the age of *Bar/Bat Mitzvah*.

The other element of *Shavuot* is the harvest so the synagogue has often been decorated with greens as are the homes of each family. In some synagogues it became customary to decorate the synagogue itself with branches of trees or with trees planted in tubs. This is also a reminder that *Shavuot* occurs at the season when fruit trees are to be judged (*M* Rosh Hashanah 1.2).

116

In other words, on this day whether the fruit tree harvest will be abundant or slim is determined.

I have been unable to discover how widespread the custom of putting potted trees into the synagogue became. It was customary in many synagogues throughout Central and Eastern Europe. It would, therefore, be good to incorporate this custom in your *Shavuot* celebration.

January 1990

75. *HANUKKAH* AND CHRISTMAS DECORATIONS IN AN APARTMENT COMPLEX

QUESTION: A large apartment building has both Jewish and Christian residents. Traditionally the foyer has been decorated with Christmas trees and wreaths. Recently the board has had requests for *Hanukkah* decorations as well as the *menorah*. Is this appropriate? (Teresa Dorfan, Kansas City MO)

ANSWER: We have traditionally opposed both *Hanukkah* and Christmas decorations in public offices and schools. Although an apartment complex is somewhat different, it would probably also be best to follow this pattern in apartment buildings and leave religious celebrations to individuals. However the removal of Christmas decorations in this setting will only arouse animosity, so it may be better to add *Hanukkah* decorations to create a sense of fairness. There is nothing wrong with displaying a *menorah* in such a setting (see *Responsa* #76). Other decorations such as *dreidels* or colorful illustrations of the Maccabee story could also be used.

We should remember that *Hanukkah* remains a minor holiday for us and, is not the equivalent of Christmas. The display of a *menorah* for *Hanukkah* would be appropriate in an apartment setting. It will add to the festivity of this holiday season.

January 1989

76. AN APARTMENT HOUSE *MENORAH*

QUESTION: A condominium council is debating the placement of a *menorah* in the lobby of the apartment house during *Hanukkah*. Is this a sacred object? If a *menorah* is placed there, may it be an electric *menorah*? Should an additional light be kindled each night? (David Weiss, Houston TX)

ANSWER: Most of us have taken a public stand against the display of religious objects in government buildings or schools. We along with groups such as the American Jewish Committee have sought to minimize both Christmas and *Hanukkah* displays as well as religious displays at other seasons. Here we have a private dwelling and the owners of the condominium are interested in displaying a *menorah*. Let me turn to each segment of this question.

It is appropriate to display a *menorah* publicly, in fact the traditional statements about the *menorah* prescribe that the lights be visible from the outside (Shab 24a; *Shulhan Arukh* Orah Hayim 1.5). In the warmer lands of North Africa and the Near East, almost every *menorah* was designed to be placed on the outer wall of the home and lit there in the Jewish quarter. Publicizing the miracle is the intent and so there is no problem about displaying the *menorah* in a public setting of an apartment house lobby.

118

The *menorah* itself is not a sacred item and there is no degree of sanctity connected with it. Of course, the ancient *menorah* in the Temple itself was a holy object, but it was lost after Titus transported it to Rome for his triumphal march through the city. Subsequently we hear no more about it. Every later *menorah* is purposely sufficiently different so that it does not imitate the original *menorah*. Most have eight arms rather than the seven of the ancient Temple. The *Hannukah menorah* has nine with the *shames*.

The traditional rabbinic authorities opposed an electric *menorah* (Y. E. Henkin *Edut Leyisrael* p 122; Unterman *Mishpatei Uziel* 1.25). We would certainly agree with that decision for a home, but for public display an electric *menorah* will be safer and more aesthetically pleasing. We can assume that every Jewish family in the condominium will kindle their own *menorah* each evening, so we need not be concerned about an electric *menorah*. They are also used frequently on public buildings in Israel.

It would be possible to either kindle all the lights during the entire eight days of the festival, or more appropriately to kindle an additional light each evening. This need not be accompanied by the traditional prayers in the same fashion, as *Hanukkah* lights are often lit in the synagogue before the morning service without prayers, as a reminder of the number of candles to be lit on the subsequent evening (Ziv *Haminhagim* p 263; J. D. Eisenstein, *Otzar Dinim Uminhagim* p 141).

In a condominium in which a large number of Jews live, it is appropriate to display an electric *Hanukkah menorah*. This would add to the festive nature of the holiday.

December 1988

77. DRUMS AT A *PURIM SERVICE*

QUESTION: May drums and other musical instruments be used at a *Purim* service with a specific instrumental setting, in order to create the noise necessary to drown out the name Haman; this would add a festive touch to the service? (Walter Finegold, Bloomington IN)

ANSWER: Let us begin by looking at the Orthodox rejection of instrumental in the synagogue. Generally this objection has been connected with mourning for the destruction of the Temple, and so instrumental music is permitted only at weddings (*Shulhan Arukh* Orah Hayim 560.3). In addition, there is the prohibition against the use of music on *shabbat* or festival days partly because of the work involved, and partly because this would imitate non-Jewish customs (*Shulhan Arukh* Orah Hayim 338.1 ff; *Eleh Divrei Haberit*; David Hoffmann *Melamed Lehoil* 1.16). The latter opinions are part of a controversy about the use of the organ as an instrument in the synagogue. This represented one of the major disputes between the Reform and Orthodox community in the last century. *Nogah Hatzedeq* along with other lengthy essays in German, represent the Reform point of view (Samuel Krauss *Zur Orgelfrage*).

This controversy is behind us; we do not observe the restriction against instrumental synagogue music or continue to mourn for the destruction of the Temple, so we must ask what kind of instrumental music is appropriate in the synagogue. The music should not imitate gentile music around us (Joel Sirkes *Responsa* #127). Of course, we should remember that music and musicians played a major role in the ancient Temple in Jerusalem (I Chron 15.16; II Chron 5.13; 2.76; Neh 12.35, etc). In addition, we have many musical notations in the Book of Psalms, although a large number of them are no longer understood. Some psalms dealt specifically with the musical instruments, as Psalms 149 and 150.

The *Purim* Service has always been among the most relaxed of the entire year. The festival has had a carnival like atmosphere attached to it. Costumes were permitted (Judah Mintz *Responsa* #16; *Shulhan Arukh* Orah Hayim 696.8). In addition, noise accompanied the reading of the *Megillah* and objections were only raised when it became excessive and made it difficult to listen to the text. *Greggars* have been made available to children for several centuries. Some are beautifully ornamented and others very simple (*Siehe der Stein Schreit aus der Mauer - Geschichte und Kultur der Juden in Bayern* p 127 ff; Isaac Shachar *Jewish Tradition in Art* p 158 ff). None of these examples antedated the nineteenth century but they certainly existed earlier. Our collection here in Pittsburgh displays a fine brass *greggar*.

The inclusion of musical instruments in the service for the reading of the *Megillah* when Haman is mentioned is appropriate. As the instruments will play a special flourish rather than just making noise this will add to the festivities.

February 1988

78. FOODS AND OUR HOLIDAYS

QUESTION: What is the origin of foods such as *latkes* for *Hanukkah, hamantaschen* for Purim, etc? (Daniel Lehman, Pittsburgh PA)

ANSWER: Little research into traditional food has been done. Most of the dietary customs which we consider part of our holiday traditions are associated with Jews from a particular locale. *Ashkenzai* Jews of central Europe have different traditions than those of Eastern Europe which are not akin to those of the *Sephardic* communities of North Africa or the Near East. Many traditions can be traced only for a century as the older literary references are vague and do not specify dishes. So, for example, dairy dishes have been associated with *Hanukkah* (*Shulhan Arukh Orah Hayim* 670.2) because of a tale in the Book of Judith. The heroine gave the Greek general, Holophernes, milk as a soporific and then killed him, which liberated the Jewish community.

However, there is no simple connection between milk dishes and *latkes*. Certainly the custom of potato pancakes must be recent as potatoes were not introduced to Poland before the late seventeenth or early eighteenth century (C. B. Heiser *The Fascinating World of the Nightshades*).

The *hamantaschen* which are a three cornered pastry may reflect some old medieval illustrations of Haman which showed him wearing a three cornered hat common in the Middle Ages. I do not know the reason why they were originally filled with poppy seed. Such questions deserve more attention.

April 1990

79. GRACE AFTER MEALS

QUESTION: The traditional grace after meals is quite lengthy. While the Reform version has been considerably abbreviated, what is the justification or the rationale for this abbreviation? (Irene Jacob, Pittsburgh PA)

ANSWER: As we look at the traditional grace after meals, we will see that it was composed over a very long period and stems from many different times in our past. Actually, it is to a large extent a collection of Biblical and *Talmudic* verses. The earliest statement about the grace after meals was found in the *Mishnah* (Ber 6.5 ff). The concern there was not with the text, but over when it is necessary to recite the prayers and how they are to be said with various groupings of individuals. We have some discussion of some possible texts in the next chapter (7.3). In the *Talmud*, the whole matter is taken somewhat further and we have not only a detailed discussion about the questions raised by the *Mishnah*, but also of texts and subjects to be included (Ber 48b). The earliest complete text is that of the *Sidur Rav Amram* and that is somewhat different from ours; it is considerably shorter. Maimonides later presented us with a long and short text.

As we review the text we will see that additions were made to each paragraph in the *Gaonic* as well as the medieval period. It is not possible to find any rationale for these additions except that they reflected favorite Biblical verses of various anonymous individuals. The longer section *"harahaman"* may reflect the suffering of the Middle Ages, the renewed hope for Elijah and the Messianic Age, as well as a desire to be more specific about blessings for the family. A variety of melodies for the grace after meals exists both in the *Ashkenazic* and *Sephardic* traditions.

An abbreviated version of the grace after meals has always been available for those individuals who did not have the time to recite the longer grace. This included servants and women who were busy with other duties. It was also used during emergencies.

The Reform abbreviated version of the grace is, to the best of my knowledge, first found in the earliest edition of the Union

Haggadah (1905) and subsequently in pamphlets and other longer liturgical works. Its main emphasis has been to eliminate redundancies, to abbreviate the number of quotations, as a large number no longer appealed or were meaningful, and generally to shorten this prayer into a form into which it was more likely to be widely used. That effort has been successful. Some continue to read the longer version and that number has increased with a broader understanding of Hebrew among our people. The longer version of the grace is appealing, as the Biblical character of the Hebrew text is easy to understand. Except for a few passages, as those which deal with the Messiah, there are no ideological problems with the grace after meals.

September 1990

80. BERAKHAH LEVATALAH

QUESTION: In a new service for the minor festival of *Tu Beshvat*, a number of blessings for trees, fruit and wine are repeated. Would such a repetition, intended both for children and adults, be considered *berakhah levatalah*, a blessing in vain? What is encompassed by that concept and what role does it play in tradition? (Rabbi Adam D. Fisher, Stony Brook New York)

ANSWER: The concept of not reciting a blessing in vain is intended to guard against the misuse of the divine name; this is one possible interpretation of the third commandment (Exodus 20.7; Ber 33a; *Tur* and *Shulhan Arukh* Orah Hayim 215.4), the third commandment encompasses other prohibitions as well, and tradition provided a large number of possible interpretations (W.

Jacob, "The Expression 'To Take God's Name in Vain': A History of its Interpretation" Unpublished Prize Essay Hebrew Union College, 1953). Anyone who heard a blessing said in vain should not respond with "amen" (*Tur* and *Shulhan Arukh* Orah Hayim 215.4).

The definition of what is involved in a "vain blessing" is a little more difficult. It may consist of one of the following: The recital without the action connected with it, as not consuming the food or drink for which the prayer has been said (*Tur* Orah Hayim 213-215 and commentaries); the recital of blessings after they had already been spoken by someone else, the recital of erroneous blessings, the recital of proper blessings at an inappropriate time and the recital by inappropriate persons such as the priestly benediction by non-*kohanim* in a traditional setting.

There are, of course, numerous instances in which blessings are repeated intentionally as by the reader at a service. These were considered customary repetitions and were appropriate. The repetition of the *qiddush* in the *Pesah Seder* is considered appropriate before the meal. The blessing over bread is sufficient for any other food or drink which might be served during a meal. The only exception is wine which merits a special blessing at the beginning of the meal; that is sufficient for any number of cups of wine (*Shulhan Arukh* Orah Hayim 174.1; 177.1). When a blessing had been recited, the act for which it had been made should be executed whether it consists of eating, or anything else (*Shulhan Arukh* Orah Hayim 167.6; etc). When a number of different foods were consumed, then the most important food determined the blessing to be recited (*Shulhan Arukh* Orah Hayim 204.12).

When an individual recited a blessing or a set of blessings as a leader for others, as for example the *qiddush* or the *birkhat hamazon,* and someone present did not consider that individual fit to act in this leadership capacity, he could refuse to say "amen" or could repeat the blessing. In this way blessings have been used as a way of determining status.

The training of children was exempt from the prohibition against reciting blessings in vain. The normal designation for God could be used in those blessings - when they are taught although, some prefer to omit it (*Tur* and *Shulhan Arukh* Orah Hayim 215.3).

The complete terminology of blessing had to be erroneously used in order to consider it a "blessing in vain". In other words if a blessing called for the statement "Lord, our God" and only "Lord" was used, it was not considered "a blessing spoken in vain" (*Tur* and *Shulhan Arukh* 206.6).

Some authorities felt that it is meritorious to add blessings and prayers to those normally recited. This was deemed necessary to fulfill the obligation of reciting one-hundred benedictions a day (Men 43a). This need was felt particularly on *shabbat* when the *tefilah* contains fewer benedictions and so the required number is not fulfilled. The blessing recited in connection with the "third meal" has been discussed in this context (Rosh *Responsa* Rosh 22.4; *Tur* and *Shulhan Arukh* Orah Hayim 291.3 and commentaries). Repetition is also an appropriate mechanism to involve individuals throughout the day (Ber 21a and *Tos*; *Or Zarua* II pp 91).

Now let us turn to your specific situation which not only celebrates a holiday, albeit a minor one, but also seeks to educate the entire family. It is appropriate to repeat benedictions for various trees and the blessing over wine before the meal. The ritual planned is akin to the *Pesah Seder* and will teach blessings now not frequently used. In general we need to be much more careful about the misuse of the divine name in other settings than in that of "benedictions spoken in vain."

June 1988

81. A BLESSING FOR PETS

QUESTION: The local animal pound had a community celebration in which the Rabbi was asked to participate along with other clergy. Is there a Jewish approach to blessing animals? (Rabbi Robert A. Raab, Wantagh NY)

ANSWER: The general Jewish attitude toward pets has been discussed in responsum "Kaddish for a Pet" (W. Jacob *Contemporary American Reform Responsa* #124). One can see from the literature that the exaggerated American feeling for pets is a contemporary phenomena and has no basis in our Jewish past. Rabbinic literature does mention cats and dogs but mostly for very specific tasks rather than as pets. There is, of course, respect for animals, in general, as living beings created by God and so one of the Noahide commandments which are incumbent upon all human beings, not just Jews, prohibits cruelty to animals (*Midrash* Rabbah Noah 34.8). In addition the Sabbath commandment of the Decalogue insisted that animals rest on the Sabbath along with their masters (20.9; Deut 5.14). Kindness toward animals appears with some frequency in the literature, in connection with the Noah story and in general discussions (Git 62a; *Midrash Rabbah* Shemot 2.2; *Mekhilta* Yitro 1 *Tanhuma* Noah 17a ff etc).

In some instances the care for animals was raised to a level akin to that for human beings. So the Bible stated that ox should not be muzzled while treading out corn (Deut 25.4). This line of thought is then continued in the later rabbinic literature (B K 54a; B M 87b, 88b, 90b, 9a; *Yad* Hil Zekhirut 12; *Shulhan Arukh* Hoshen Mishpat 338; 339). Even when man could exercise his dominance over animals, something which Jewish tradition felt had been ordained from the very beginning of creation, he must refrain from cruelty. So, cows or sheep are not to be slaughtered with their young on the same day (Lev 22.28) or a mother bird along with its young (Deut 22.6). This thought is also developed further in the subsequent rabbinic literature (Ber 33b; Hul 78a ff, 81b, 82a, 85a, 138b, 139b, 140a, 141a; Yad Hil Shehitah 12, 13; Maimonides *Guide to the Perplexed* 3.48, etc). The medieval work *Sefer Hahinukh* felt that the prohibition against yoking an ox and a donkey together to pull a plow (Deut 22.10) intended to spare the animals from difficulties (*Sefer Hahinukh* Mitzvah #249). Sick or injured animals were to be healed if that was possible (Shab 144a; Ker 22a; *Tos* M K 2.11). In each of these instances the literature has dealt with animals which are useful not pets.

Our tradition has also dealt with the wonder of seeing an unusually beautiful or exotic animal, the like of which had not been before. A special benediction is to be recited "*Barukh atah adonai elohenu melekh haolam shekakhah lo beolamo*" - Blessed are You O Lord, our God, Sovreign of the Universe who has such things in the world". Such a prayer, along with a preamble, which deals with the place of animals in the Jewish tradition would probably be appropriate on an occasion akin to the one you have mentioned.

June 1987

Yoreh Deah

82. A FISH IN THE SHAPE OF A SHRIMP

QUESTION: A wedding at which I recently attended was strictly kosher. Much to my surprise the fish course was served in the shape of a shrimp. Would this be permissible according to our tradition? (Vigdor Kavaler, Pittsburgh PA)

ANSWER: The whole pattern of tradition has sought to keep clearly non-kosher items away from our people. Items which are kosher should not be made to look like non-kosher foods because of *marit ayin* (Betza 9a). In addition rabbinic Judaism built "fences" around the law in order to be quite certain that no violations of the laws of *kashrut* would occur. So, for example, the prohibitions against legumes among *Ashkenazim* for Passover (*Shulhan Arkuh* Orah Hayim 453.1). It would, therefore, be wrong as well as in poor taste to present any item in the form of shrimp or let us say a pig at a kosher dinner. Strictly speaking it would, of course, not be wrong to consume such an item, but it is in bad taste and contrary to the spirit of tradition.

The Reform attitude toward *kashrut* has changed during the last two centuries; it continues to evolve and no clear pattern for North American Reform Jewish life has been established (W. Jacob (ed) *American Reform Responsa* # 49).

Although Reform Jews do not observe the laws of *kashrut* strictly, those who do should observe the spirit as well as the letter of the law.

April 1989

83. ARE DINOSAURS KOSHER

A Light Hearted *Purim* Responsum

QUESTION: Are dinosaurs kosher? (Vigdor Kavaler, Pittsburgh PA)

ANSWER: There are several elements involved in this question. All of them eventually lead to the same negative conclusion, however, let us look at the possibilities?
We must begin by dividing dinosaurs between carnivorous and vegetarian animals as all kosher cattle whether tame (*behemot*) or wild (*hayat*) consume plants (Lev 11:2). The rabbinic tradition makes that distinction specific in the case of birds as the Bible does not provide ways of identifying kosher birds (Hul 63b). Carnivorous dinosaurs would definitely not be kosher, furthermore we must make a division between warm-blooded and cold-blooded dinosaurs as the latter would be considered as reptiles and be forbidden. As there is currently some difference of opinion among scientists about this fact we must reserve judgement on this issue.
Finally, we must ask whether dinosaurs have cloven hoofs and are ruminants which chew the cud. Some dinosaurs may actually fall into that category and so theoretically it should be possible to eat their meat. However, this is not possible on two grounds: (a) The animals were not known to the ancient Jews and only those animals clearly identifiable from the Biblical sources are considered kosher (Lev 11:21; Deut 14.4); Maimonides considered this list as complete and final (*Yad* Hil Maakhalot Asurot 1.8)

though Rashi at least in the case of birds felt that a folk tradition of *kashrut* was sufficient to declare a specific bird kosher even if some questioned it (Rashi to Hil 62b). We, however, possess no such folk tradition or *bobo meise*. (b) It would not be possible to slaughter them in the traditional pattern of *kashrut* as the *shohet* would have to stand on a very tall ladder and the animal would need to stand quite still. It is not permissible to stun an animal before slaughtering it.

Even if that requirement were met, (dinosaurs had unusually small brains) the *shohet* would place himself in grave personal danger as the collapsing dinosaur would propel him from his ladder. So because of *pikuah nefesh* the *shohet* would not be able to slaughter the dinosaur even if it were kosher.

We may approach the entire problem in a different fashion. Dinosaurs existed only before days of Noah and the Flood. In that early period of human history, according to the *Torah*, animals were not consumed as food and people simply lived from fruit and vegetables. The killing of animals was not permitted until after the Flood (Gen 9.3). If we follow this line of reasoning the question would not have been asked in the appropriate time. Furthermore if none of these reasons sound convincing we would have to follow the *Talmud* dictum, "this is a question which can only be settled by Elijah in the days of the Messiah" (Men 45b; *Midrash Rabbah*, Numbers 3).

Should you, therefore, find a dinosaur steak listed on your menu you should refuse it on the grounds of *kashrut* and due to the age of the meat.

April 1989

84. RED WINE OR WHITE WINE

QUESTION: At a recent wedding the groom insisted that red wine be used, while the bride afraid that some of it might spill demanded white wine. Does our tradition have a preference? (Daniel Jacob, Pittsburgh PA)

ANSWER: Discussions of red wine or white wine goes back to the days of the Talmud and the use of wine in the service at the Temple. The debate also dealt with the question whether various kinds of white wine *boreq* or *hivrin* were appropriate. *Boreq* was generally rejected except *bediavad.* while *hivrin* was considered acceptable as it was akin to red wine which was considered to be stronger and better (B B 97a ff and commentaries). The *Tosfos* who lived in the wine producing provinces of France considered *hivrin* as white and therefore not acceptable. There was, therefore, a general preference for red wine (*Tur* Orah Hayim 472 and Commentaries). Yet, even Jacob ben Asher felt that if the white wine was superior to the red wine it should be used. Earlier Simon ben Zemah of Duran indicated that both red and white wines were acceptable on the altar at the ancient Temple as well as for *qiddush* (Tashbetz *Responsa* #85). Joseph Caro in the *Shulhan Arukh* provided us with a decision which went in both directions. When discussing the ordinary *qiddush,* he indicated that white wine was acceptable (Orah Hayim 272.4). On the other hand when he discussed wine for the *Seder* his preference was for red wine (Orah Hayim 472.11). The commentaries on this passage provide a caution and warn that red wine be avoided in those places where the accusation of blood libel had occurred.

As one can see from these traditional discussions as well as from responsa not cited, either type of wine is appropriate; tradition would simply state that the best wine should be used.

November 1989

85. A NON-DENOMINATIONAL SERVICE WITH A PEACE PIPE

QUESTION: A service which stresses peace and disarmament for both the Soviet Union and the United States has included the American Indian ritual of the peace pipe as well as rituals of the Hindu and Shinto religions. Should we participate in such a service? (Karen Fine, Philadelphia PA)

ANSWER: Our relationship with other religions has been divided into two categories. Those which we consider monotheistic and those which are idolatrous. Christianity and Islam have been considered monotheistic for more than a thousand years (W. Jacob *Contemporary American Reform Responsa* #167). Despite these friendly views, all of the traditional authorities made it quite clear that major distinctions continue to exist between them and Judaism. Maimonides felt that we should restrict our relationships with Christians (*Yad* Hil Akum 10.2) and also prohibited Jews from dealing in Christian wine (*Yad* Hil Maakhalot Asurot 17). He and all the other medieval authorities thought that both Christianity and Islam had strange concepts (*shituf*) which impinged on the absolute unity of God (Isserles to *Shulhan Arukh* Orah Hayim 156; Maimonides *Peer Hador* 50, etc). In secular relationships Christians could be treated as *benei noah*, but in religious matters, distinctions were to remain.

The factors outlined above have provided a Jewish basis for good Jewish-Christian relationships in the last centuries. They have enabled us to participate in many joint social and charitable programs. American Reform Jewish practice has permitted participation in interfaith services which remain neutral and are non-Christological. We have also participated in Christian services when our participation is limited to our presence, Biblical readings, or a sermon to promote good relationships. Reform rabbis have participated by their presence and some appropriate words in the installation of bishops or ministers, the dedication of new churches and other services as a gesture of friendship.

Such relationships with Christianity have led to common Thanksgiving Services, Memorial Day tributes, and patriotic services on the Fourth of July. In each of these services the prayers dealt with the specific occasion and were not tied to the theology or ritual of either Judaism or Christianity.

As the number of followers of other religions in America increases and as we have more and more contact with Hindus, Buddhists, Shintos, etc., we must work out a relationship with them as well. This will depend on the specific form of each religion which has been transferred to North America. Each contains both polytheistic and monotheistic tendencies. There is no problem about a common celebration of national holidays with representatives of these religions. We should stipulate that no specific rites or prayers which we would consider inappropriate be included, for example Hindu prayers to various deities or prayers to Buddha or any of the Bodhisattvas. We are not willing to participate in services which are polytheistic.

This would hold equally true for the ritual of the peace pipe which according to my reading represents not only the common smoking of a pipe among the participants in an effort to create friendship among them, but is also an invocation of American Indian deities. This is inappropriate; we should not participate in such a service.

November 1990

86. HINDUS AND JEWS

QUESTION: Several members of the Brotherhood have established good relations with a number of Hindu businessmen. They have invited them to various Brotherhood functions at the synagogue which have taken the form of lectures, meals or simply attending a Jewish service. The Hindu businessmen have responded and have asked members of the Brotherhood to attend various Hindu rituals. Now, some members have been asked to participate in those rituals. What are the limits of such participation? (David Deutsch, Trenton NJ)

ANSWER: The ancient Hindu religion contains some fine philosophical writings as well as many fascinating insights into the human condition. However, its popular worship with a large pantheon of deities is polytheistic. Some Hindu thinkers view these manifestations as related to a single dominant life giving force, however, it is not at all clear whether this is the interpretation accepted by most adherents.

It would certainly be wrong for us to participate in a polytheistic ceremony of any kind. There is no barrier to watching the ceremony, hearing about it from those who are conducting it and maintaining a general atmosphere of friendship with adherents of the Hindu religion. We can not go beyond this and must refrain from any kind of participation. My own discussions with Hindus has indicated that such restraint on our part will be accepted and viewed as the normal reaction of our religion. We should also not ask Hindus to participate in a specifically Jewish service, but should be content to establish good relationships and a mutual understanding of each others ways. In all of these discussions we should remember that it took a very long time before Judaism was willing to acknowledge Christianity as a monotheistic religion as we were not sure of the status of the Trinity (W. Jacob *Contemporary American Reform Responsa* pp 250ff). We may wish to review our stance toward the Hindu religion at another time when the nature of the Hindu religion practiced in North America has become clearer. At the present time we should *not* participate in such a service in any way.

February 1989

87. JEWISH SOLDIERS IN A FUNDAMENTALIST ISLAMIC LAND

QUESTION: A young Jewish Marine has been assigned to an embassy in an Islamic land. His dog tag indicates that he is Jewish and he realizes in case of medical problems that his Jewish identity may cause him problems. Should he remove that identifying letter? (Daniel Roth, Washington DC)

ANSWER: Desperate persecution has sometimes forced us to assume other religious identity although most of the traditional authorities sought to prohibit this and no Jew is to abandon his religion and take on another even outwardly (*Sefer Hamitzvot Taaseh* #9; *Shulhan Arukh* Yoreh Deah 157.1 ff.; E. Oshry *Memamakim* #13). However, a Jew could be ambiguous in his answer to the authorities (Isserles to *Shulhan Arukh* Yoreh Deah 157.2) or might also dress himself in Christian garments.

The problems raised by disguising one's Jewish identity were divided by Oshry into matters which indicated a permanent separation from Judaism which he prohibited and temporary measures which were permissable. One could obtain a Christian passport (See also R. Kirschner *Anthology of Holocaust Responsa* pp 97 ff; and H. J. Zimmels *The Echo of the Nazi Holocaust in Rabbinic LIterature* pp 77 ff).

Every effort was made to escape danger to life, but also to avoid apostasy. Tradition always insisted that death was preferable to the sin of idolatry, incest or murder. For these three prohibitions a person must surrender one's life (San 60b ff; A Z 43b, 54a; Ket 33b; Shab 149a; *Shulhan Arukh* Yoreh Deah 157.1).

In this instance eliminating the designation for a Jew on the dog tag would represent a temporary disguise, but we must ask whether it is really necessary. After all, any individual connected with an American embassy possesses special status protected by international law and the likelihood of an accident or some other mishap which would place him into a foreign hospital is slim. We would, therefore, strongly discourage the marine from taking this step and encourage him to serve there as a proud American Jew. His stand would be another clear indication that the United States intends to protect all its citizens irrespective of their religion.

May 1987

88. A CHILD AND TWO RELIGIOUS TRADITIONS

QUESTION: During a bitter divorce settlement a non Jewish father took his four year old and had her baptized as an Episcopalian. This was without the mother's consent. Now he wishes to have the child raised one Sunday in a Jewish Religious School, and one Sunday in an Episcopalian Religious School and he used the child's baptism as part of the rationale. What is the Jewish attitude toward this? (Rabbi Joseph Levine W. Palm Beach FL)

ANSWER: As you know, according to tradition, the child of a Jewish mother remains Jewish irrespective of baptism. An individual who was baptized was considered an apostate, a sinner who remained a Jew (San 44a), and the act of baptism itself has been considered irrelevant by the Tradition. We as Reform Jews have, however, recognized the right of an individual to choose a religious identity and would honor the baptism of an adult who willingly and knowing joined a Christian denomination. We would consider such an adult a Christian with the concomitant conclusion that should the individual wish to rejoin us more than a simple statement would be required (W. Jacob *Contemporary American Reform Responsa* #64, 65; Solomon B. Freehof *Modern Reform Responsa* #30).

Your case is, however, somewhat different as we are dealing with a child, whose baptism occurred without the mother's consent, and as this was part of a bitter divorce proceeding we would, therefore, not recognize the baptism and follow our earlier tradition in this matter. If it is not too late, the religious identity of the child should be firmly established in the divorce document. The suggestions that the child attend a Jewish Religious School on one

138

Sunday and an Episcopalian Religious School on the other is not acceptable or practical. Such a child will possess no religious identity and will get very little out of either of these Religious School experiences.

What is perhaps more important than the Religious School training is the actual religious life of the child. If the child lives with the mother and therefore spends most of her time in a Jewish environment, then there is at least a good opportunity to raise this youngster as a Jew. If, of course, the bitterness of the divorce has led the father to emphasize Christianity during his time with his daughter then the mother's efforts will be partially compromised.

It is important for these parents to settle the religious identity of their daughter outside their own bitter struggle. It cannot be postponed by attempting to raise the child in two religious traditions - that simply will not work. Naturally the child should be raised in such a way that she has respect for the religious tradition of the parents whose religion that she has not followed, but this is very different from attempting to be part of two traditions.

We would encourage the mother to raise her daughter as a Jew. We reject any attempt to follow two religious traditions.

December 1990

89. CHRISTIAN CHILDREN IN THE RELIGIOUS SCHOOL

QUESTION: The family of a mixed marriage with a Jewish mother and a Catholic father have two male children. They have agreed to raise the children as Catholics and the children are currently enrolled in Catechism classes on a regular basis. The parents would like the children to attend the synagogue Religious

School in order to provide the youngsters with some understanding of their Jewish heritage. I have agreed to meet with the family privately but do not feel that they belong in the Religious School. What should our attitude be toward this kind of situation? (Rabbi T. P. Liebschutz, Winston-Salem NC)

ANSWER: There is little in the tradition which has any bearing on this question. We have long ago, as a Conference, decided that enrolling children in our Religious School is tantamount to the beginning process of conversion (Report of the Committee on Mixed Marriage, *Central Conference of American Rabbis Yearbook* 1947). This involves children whose parents have decided on a Jewish direction for their future even though the non-Jewish parent has not converted to Judaism. We have also decided in a number of responsa that children cannot be raised in two traditions, but the parents must make up their mind about the religious future of their offsprings (W. Jacob *Contemporary Reform Responsa* #61; etc). Each of these responsa indicate that it is the task of parents to decide on the religious education of their child, and that it must be Jewish *or* Christian, but cannot be both.

In this case the parents have decided to raise the children as Catholics. Although we may not like this decision, we must accept it. As you indicated we should not place these children into the regular Religious School classes as this may lead to confusion for them rest of the class. Furthermore, we do not want to indicate to our children or our congregation that we consider this kind of family as normative.

Your suggestion of meeting with the family or the children privately is certainly a good one and would provide an introduction to their Jewish heritage and minimally a feeling of closeness to Judaism. In larger communities it may be useful to organize this on a broader basis.

January 1989

90. ASBESTOS VERSUS REFUGEES

QUESTION: The congregation has found some asbestos in its Religious School and discovered that it can be contained at a modest cost, but some parents have demanded its removal which would cost several hundred thousand dollars. At the same time other members of the congregation have petitioned vigorously to use these funds for the rescue and resettlement of Soviet Jews. What would tradition see as more important - the health of our children or the rescue of the Russian Jewish immigrants? (Nora A. Ellenson, Philadelphia PA)

ANSWER: Let us begin by looking at the *mitzvah* of *pidyon shivuyin* (the redemption of captives). Tradition has considered this a major *mitzvah* (B B 8a) and Maimonides for example cited a long series of Biblical verses to prove how significant the *mitzvah* was (*Yad* Hil Matnot Aniyin 8.10; *Shulhan Arukh* Yoreh Deah 352). In the *Talmudic* citation the rabbi permitted funds to be removed from a designated charity to this purpose as it was so important. Even if the funds had been specified only for the rebuilding of the Temple they could be diverted for the sake of redeeming captives. The literature then sadly enough felt it necessary to deal with the order of priority among the captives. Obviously there often were

141

insufficient funds to rescue everyone. The primary importance of this task has been very clearly established by tradition.

Now let us look at the matter of health. It is a duty for all Jews to look after their health and for that matter the health of their fellow human beings (Deut 4.9, 15; 22.8; B K 91b; *Yad* Hil Rotzeah 11.4 ff; *Shulhan Arukh* Hoshen Mishpat 427; Yoreh Deah 116.5 and Isserles). This means that no product which can cause harm should be used in any way. These citations would certainly apply to the danger of asbestos and, of course, we need to protect both children and adults from problems which may be caused by it. In this instance, however, two solutions are available. Both will assure the safety of the children; one is much more expensive than the other. It would, therefore, be preferable to encapsulate the asbestos and have it checked from time to time rather than spend a very large sum of money on its total removal especially as those funds can be used to rescue Jews from the Soviet Union. This must be done first and the smaller sum of money utilized for the safety of the children.

March 1990

91. FINANCIAL RESPONSIBILITY TOWARD JEWISH HOMES FOR THE AGED

QUESTION: Many Jewish institutions for the elderly require that all assets be placed into the custody of the institution before placement can take place. This has resulted in a large number of elderly individuals either refusing to use the institutions or giving their assets to their children before placement. The latter method is often used as a way of evading financial responsibility. The individuals then either become wards of the state or place an undue burden upon the Jewish community which supports the institution. What is the Jewish attitude toward this kind of subterfuge? (Howard Fagin, Temple Sinai Atlanta GA)

ANSWER: The law as presently constituted intends to view the state as the care provider of last resort. Although this was the intention of the Congress, the rising cost of care for the elderly and the inability of private institutions to provide adequate care has led to the subterfuge mentioned above. It is, of course, wrong to cheat the government especially a friendly government or helpful institutions to avoid fiscal responsibility (B K 113 a, b; *Or Zarua* 110; Solomon ben Aderet *Responsa* III 165; IV 35, 111). This should be considered as *genevat daat* or possibly outright theft (Hulin 94a; *Yad* Hil Genevah 18.3; *Tur* and *Shulhan Arukh* Hoshen Mishpat 228.6). We must see this matter in the light of various aspects of tradition as well as other factors which may ameliorate this initial judgement.

Let us begin by reviewing some economic considerations presented by our tradition. We should recall that the *Talmud* set a poverty level for those eligible to receive the second tithe. The net worth had to be below 200 *zuz* or 50 *zuz* if the funds were invested as capital (*M* Peah 8.8f; *Yad* Hil Matnat Aniyim 9.14; *Tur* and *Shulhan Arukh* Yoreh Deah 253.1 ff). The party may retain his home, essential household goods and clothing. However, if the household goods are made of gold or silver, they are to be sold and replaced with ordinary ones. The assets must be accessible so a person with property in another place (as for example frozen bank accounts in another land) may qualify for assistance as he/she has no assets in his current domicile (See *Bet Yosef* to above quoting Isaac of Vienna).

This approach of the *Talmud* and codes is appropriate when

143

sufficient public assistance is available; it demands the depletion of assets and guarantees a safety net. We should note that the tradition indicated that we are not obliged to provide luxuriously for the poor (*M* Ket 6.8; 67b; *Yad* Hil Matnat Aniyim 7.3), yet if the individual was once wealthy we should provide some luxuries as this will make poverty more bearable (*Yad* Hil Matnat Aniyim 7.3; *Shulhan Arukh* and *Tur* Yoreh Deah 250.1). We must remember that this legislation dealt with poverty in general and not with our specific problem of the aged who have not been poor, but who may be thrust into poverty because of the inadequacy of the pension/welfare system or due to the high costs of providing elderly and nursing care.

We must also be concerned about the psychological implications. The expectations of exhausting ones resources entirely provide a devastating psychological blow to aged individual. The aged individual independent and middle class to this point will now become destitute and helpless. This person sees himself\herself as a ward of the state or completely dependent upon children even for the most minor luxuries. This may well lead to depression and an early death. Furthermore the children see the institution which will care for their parents robbing them of the hard earned savings of their parents in short period of time. They feel that a disproportionate burden has been placed on their shoulders in the semi-socialist society in which we live.

The subterfuge is wrong; as the law is not functioning as intended, it needs to be changed. This is especially necessary in this case as the old system has broken down and has led to a general disrespect for the law. However, until that change occurs we must deal with the morality of the present situation and reality as we find it.

YOREH DEAH

We should discourage aged parents from committing *genevat daat*. If they nevertheless leave all assets to their children before placement, an increased financial responsibility falls upon the children especially if major assets were involved. Although no secular law may demand sizable contributions toward the care of their parents Jewish law does make such demands.

Rabbi Meir of Rothenburg indicated that charity must begin with close relatives; parents are first, then brothers and sisters; other relatives follow, and the total stranger comes last (*Responsa* Vol II p 118 f; *Yad* Hil Matnat Aniyim 7.13; *Seder Elijahu* Chap 27 p 135; *Tur* and *Shulhan Arukh* Yoreh Deah 251). It was normal in medieval Europe to support family members from the tithe allocated to the poor (Meir of Rothenburg *Responsa* (ed) Bloch #75 p 10b; Isaac of Vienna *Or Zarua* Tzedaqah Sec 26). The community could go to considerable length to force a son in this direction. Solomon ben Aderet, for example, suggested that the synagogue be closed to such a son and he be publicly shamed until he supported his father, yet he should not be placed under a ban (*Responsa* Vol 4 #56). In this case there was some doubt about the economic deprivation of the father. Somewhat similarly, David ben Zimri felt that children could be compelled to support their parents in a manner appropriate to the financial status of the children (*Responsa* Vol 2 p 664). A decision akin to this was rendered much later by Moses Sofer (*Hatam Sofer* Yoreh Deah #229). It further indicated that anything which the son possessed must be placed at the disposal of the parents. These situations dealt with a society in which no social services existed and individuals might be left completely helpless. Our situation is somewhat different yet our communities may make reasonable demands of the children. We do not expect them to support their aged parents alone, but we can also not permit financial abandonment.

The community may exert both moral and social pressure in order to bring about appropriate support according to the means of the children. This will bring enhanced support for the homes for the aged within our Jewish community and be in the spirit of our tradition.

March 1989

92. REFORM SUPPORT FOR ORTHODOX INSTITUTIONS

QUESTION: Should the members of a Reform Congregation support an Orthodox congregation in the city or Orthodox institutions elsewhere, which do not recognize Reform and are unwilling to accept the pluralism of American Jewish life. It is the policy of these institutions not to involve themselves in any activities associated with Reform congregations or the Reform movement. What should our attitude be toward providing funds for such organizations and what should our attitude be toward members of such organizations? (Rabbi Morley T. Feinstein, South Bend IN)

ANSWER: Through our long history our people have continually sought unity, although it has often been difficult to attain. Bitter struggle among various segments of the Jewish community have occurred in virtually every century. The battles against Hassidism in the eighteenth century led to the opposing forces demanding intervention by the hostile Polish and Russian governments (S. Dubnow *History of the Jews in Russia and Poland*; *Geschichte Des Chassidismus*) Eventually, however, the Hassidic movement was recognized as part of Judaism and generally a *modus vivendi* exists although violence occasionally occurs between groups in Brooklyn or Jerusalem. The nineteenth century saw the *herem* invoked against the Reform movement in Germany and Hungary (David Philippson *The Reform Movement in Judaism*; Alexander Guttmann *Struggle over Reform Judaism*; Michael Meyer *Jews of Modernity*). Eventually the Reform movement became dominant in Germany and very strong in Hungary and so it was accepted. We should also remember the hostility against the Zionist movement which was long and bitter. A remnant of that is the *Neturei Karta* which refuse to recognize the Jewish state although its members live in a section of Jerusalem (A. Bein *The History of Zionism*; B. Halpern *Zionism and Anti-Zionism in Orthodox Judaism*). We should, therefore, understand the new Orthodox hostility in the light of history. We should not encourage that position. For forty years since the creation of the State of Israel, we Reform Jews have taken abuse along with the Conservative movement in Israel in order to avoid rupturing Jewish unity. That worldwide unity, which has existed since the Second World War, has prevailed for a longer period than ever before.

Militant Orthodoxy in Israel, which seeks to change the Law of Return with the support of Orthodox institutions in the United States, threatens this unity in the United States. We must now deal with this new state of affairs and support unity and pluralism. We and our members should *not* support institutions which are unwilling to recognize pluralism or to work for unity within our community. We should note that Mosheh Feinstein long ago prohibited Orthodox Jews from supporting Reform institutions (*Igrot Mosheh* Yoreh Deah #149) through the United Jewish Federations which have emphasized unity and pluralism. Their resolution on this subject stressed unity and pluralism:

"We reject any effort to divide our people by Israeli state legislation which seeks to amend, directly or indirectly, the Law of Return, which defines Who is a Jew.

We associate ourselves with the overwhelming majorities of the Jews of Israel and the Diaspora who oppose any such legislation.

While only a few people would be personally affected by this political action, millions would suffer a deep symbolic wound from this insult to our religious traditions and sense of peoplehood.

Any such initiative threatens our community at a time when unity is essential to support Israel, still besieged by external foes, facing new internal uprising and fresh world-wide propaganda assaults."

We and they intend to reconstitute pluralism and unity in the worldwide Jewish community. We should not support institutions or congregations who are unwilling to recognize us or our movement. We should discourage any individual from offering such support and we should insist that Federations and other joint fund raising agencies refuse such support. We must distinguish between friendly and unfriendly Orthodox institutions. We will continue to labor for the unity of the Jewish community and will do everything possible to bring it about. Orthodox institutions which disrupt such efforts should not be rewarded. We and our members should *not* support them.

December 1988

93. A CIRCUMCISION WITHOUT PARENTAL CONSENT

QUESTION: A baby boy born to Jewish parents required a one week hospitalization due to a serious illness. The parents indicated that they wished to have the child circumcised but did not want a *berit*. The grandmother inquired about a *berit*. The physician who is a trained *mohel* subsequently circumcised the child. As he performed the medical procedure on the eighth day, he decided to recite the blessing for a *berit milah*, reasoning that a *berit* is a *mitzvah* central to Judaism and that in this case the recital of the blessing was known only to the individual and to God. Was this an appropriate act? (Stanley Berkowitz, Los Angeles CA)

ANSWER: As you have appropriately indicated in your letter the *berit milah* does not affect the Jewishness of this child who is the offspring of two Jewish parents and is Jewish by birth. The obligation of *berit milah* rests upon the father. It is the duty of the father, or in some instances of the mother, to circumcise the child or to delegate the responsibility to their agent (*shaliah*). Under some special circumstances a *bet din* may perform this task for the father. (For full references see W. Jacob (ed) *American Reform Responsa* #54).

We might argue that the *berit milah* performed by the physician/*mohel* benefits the child and one may benefit a person even without his consent. That is true only when the individual or those responsible for that person would consent if the situation became known. That is not the case here. We might also follow another line of reasoning which would state that *berit milah* is a *mitzvah* which is incumbent upon every Jew and which if not accomplished by the father may be enforced by a *bet din* (Kid 29a; *Shulhan Aruhk* Yoreh Deah 261.1) or by the entire Jewish

149

community in the absence of a *bet din* (*Arukh Hashulhan* Yoreh Deah 261.2 and *Shulhan Arukh* 265.1 and commentaries). In other words, one could look upon this *mohel* as a delegate of the entire Jewish community upon whom the obligation of *berit milah* rests even without parental consent. This line of reasoning is the one used by the *haredi* group in Israel for all *mitzvot*. As they are obligatory upon all Jews they consider it their obligation to enforce the *mitzvot* with or without the consent of those for whom it is being done. We reject this line of reasoning and have always felt strongly that no form of religious coercion can be permitted.

The Jews have fought many battles against religious coercion. In the Middle Ages and in modern times we have struggled against baptisms carried out without the consent of parents by well intentioned Christian maids. In our own century we have fought against Sunday legislation, obligatory prayer in the schools, mandatory attendance at baccalaureate service, etc., so we can certainly not condone religious coercion in this instance either.

We would like to persuade the parents in this instance as well as many others to follow the *mitzvot* and encourage them to provide this minimal beginning of a religious life for their child.

The *mohel*/physician may feel strongly that *berit milah* is an absolute obligation. Therefore he has good grounds for refusing to do this circumcision unless it is to be done as a *berit milah* and it may be wise for him to take this road so that his own integrity is not violated.

Discussion with the family may change their attitude toward *berit milah* especially if they had only vague objections to the ritual. The ritual is fundamental to Jewish life and that should be explained fully. If they have strong objections we should honor them, although we believe the parents to be wrong. The physician should *not* have performed this *berit milah*.

July 1988

94. A *BERIT* FOR A CHILD OF AN UNMARRIED MOTHER

QUESTION: A Jewish man and a non-Jewish woman, who have no intention of being married, have had a child. They have asked the rabbi to preside at the *berit*. Is it appropriate for him to do so? (Rabbi Theodore S. Levy, Syracuse NY)

ANSWER: Let us view this question through the eyes of tradition and then seek a modern approach to it. Tradition would not recognize the sexual relations of a Jewish man with a non-Jewish woman. Even if the couple were married civilly or by common law the marriage would not be considered *qidushin* (*Yad* Hil Ishut 115; *Shulhan Arukh* Even Haezer 154.23).

Jewish recognition of marriage to non-Jews in a limited non-religious way was provided by the Napoleonic Sanhedrin of 1807 (N. D. Tama (ed) Kirwan (tr) *Transactions of the Parisian Sanhedrin* Kirwan p 155). We should remember that such marriages were not recognized by the various Christian churches in earlier periods either.

The child of such a union is, of course, traditionally not considered Jewish (Kid 68b; Yeb 23a; *Shulhan Arukh* Even Haezer 4.5 ff). Such a non-Jewish child may then be converted by a *bet din* and would be accepted as any other infant who was converted to Judaism (Ket 11a; *Shulhan Arukh* Yoreh Deah 268.7; Shelomo

Kluger *Tuv Taam Vedaat* II 111). We should note that the famous last century controversy (1864) between Rabbi Bernard Illowy and Rabbi Azriel Hildesheimer against Rabbi Tzvi Hirsch Kalischer centered around this matter. Rabbi Illowy of New Orleans felt that a child in that isolated, small Jewish community would probably not be raised as a Jew and might be mistaken as a Jew because of his circumcision.

Subsequent discussions inquired whether the conversion actually benefitted the child; some traditional authorities felt that this would only be true if the child were raised in a traditionally observant household. This consideration, however, represented only a recent modern restriction. The general consensus moved in the direction of permitting such a circumcision. That also was the decision of Moses Sofer (*Hatam Sofer* Yoreh Deah #253).

We should note Maimonides' decision about Jewish soldiers who cohabited with non-Jewish women during wartime. If these women converted they would, of course, be considered Jews; they could then be married by the soldiers and their offsprings would be Jewish. If, however, a woman decided not to marry her Jewish soldier and continued to live with the soldier for as long as a year, then any child from such a union could be converted by a *bet din* (*Yad* Hil Melakhim 8.1-8).

These traditional answers indicated that under a variety of circumstances it would be perfectly possible to have a *berit* for an infant child whose father was Jewish and whose mother is not Jewish. The *berit* would be for the sake of conversion and so it should be with us as our resolution on patrilineal descent deals with mixed *marriage*. It assumes marriage, a stable family and a Jewish education for the child.

In this instance we seem to have some assurance that the child will be raised as a Jew. We should, of course, encourage the mother and father to marry, however, our primary concern here is with the child and not with the status of the parents.

May 1988

95. CESAREAN AND *BERIT*

QUESTION: May a child born of Cesarean section be circumcised on *shabbat*, or should the circumcision be postponed? This question is asked because there seems to be a difference of opinion between the traditional sources and the response given by Solomon B. Freehof in *Today's Reform Responsa*. (Rabbi B. H. Mehlman, Boston MA)

ANSWER: As you have indicated, the traditional sources which deal with this question state that a child whose sexual status is doubtful, who has two foreskins or who is born through Cesarean, should not be circumcised on *shabbat* (*Yad* Hil Milah 1.11; *Shulhan Arukh* Yoreh Deah 266.10; *Yad* Hil Milah 1.11). These statements were very clear and the commentaries on them did not present any arguments in another direction. They were based on the decision of the *Mishnah* (Shab 19.3) which prohibited the circumcision of an androgynous child on *shabbat*. It is correct that a child born of Cesarean section was not mentioned in the *Mishnah* nor in the subsequent discussion of the *Talmud* (Shab 134a). Although there were numerous discussions of children whose sexual status is doubtful (hermaphrodites or androgynous) in the classical literature both in connection with this matter and

153

others, there were none to the best of my knowledge which dealt with the question of circumcision of a Cesarean birth on *shabbat*. The tradition of not circumcising on *shabbat* developed and was accepted.

We must now ask why Solomon B. Freehof in his last volume of responsa answered in a different vein. I have looked through his *halakhic* correspondence as well as various papers in order to discover some reason for his conclusion. In the responsum itself, he only indicated that he felt the decision of Maimonides and Caro "overextends the statement of the *Mishnah*." That is perfectly correct and we may add that no reason for this extension of the *Mishnahic* prohibition has been provided. We might guess that it took place for one of two reasons: a) An extension of the statement that *pidyan haben* was not required for those born through a Cesarean (*Yad* Hil Bikurim 11.16; *Tur* and *Shulhan Arukh* Yoreh Deah 305.24); b) there was a hesitancy about violating *shabbat* for a child whose birth was surrounded by any doubt, not only an androgynous or hermaphrodite child, but also one who was born at twilight as it may have been born on Friday or *shabbat*. Such a "doubtful status" might have been extended to the Cesarean as well. In any case we do not know the reason for the traditional statement which may also have simply followed *minhag*.

Solomon B. Freehof's conclusion in this matter was surprising as he advocated change only when there was a specific reason. It is, of course, possible to argue that the *Mishnah* has limited itself to the child of doubtful sexual status, and as it did not include a child born of Cesarean section we should not either. He mentioned that Rabbi Judah disputed the conclusion of this *Mishnah*, however, the decision went against him.

I believe that in this instance we must respectfully disagree with the decision of Solomon B. Freehof. As there is neither a Reform ideological reason for a change nor any other reason we would state with the tradition that a child born of a Cesarean should not be circumcised on *shabbat*, but on the next day.

August 1990

96. TERMINATED PREGNANCY AND *BERIT*

QUESTION: For various reasons (i.e. post term pregnancy, medical complications, convenience of the doctor or patient) it was decided that a woman who was pregnant should have her pregnancy ended before labor commenced. Labor was then artificially induced either through the use of Pitocin or by having the doctor rupture the amniotic membrane. In either case it could be argued that because labor had been started artificially the actual delivery date has also been altered by artificial medical intervention. If the child was born on the *shabbat* after such an artificially induced labor, should the *berit* ceremony then be postponed to Sunday (ninth day). (Mark Lebovitz, Cherry Hill NJ)

ANSWER: Tradition has mandated that the *berit milah* shall be conducted on the eighth day as a mark of the covenant (Gen 17.9 ff; Lev 12.1 ff; *Yad* Hil Milah; *Tur* and *Shulhan Arukh* 264). The circumcision was to take place on the eighth day as indicated by the Biblical citations and also in later literature even if it was *shabbat* (*Tur* and *Shulhan Arukh* Yoreh Deah 262.1, 266.2). There were some circumstances in which the child was not circumcised on

155

shabbat although it may have been the eighth day. It was not done if there was some uncertainly about the time of birth. For example if the child was born at twilight (*Shulhan Arukh* 264.4, 266.8). In addition a circumcision was postponed if the child was ill or there is some other medical reason for doing so and then the postponed circumcision would not be permitted on *shabbat* or a festival (Yeb 64b, *Shulhan Arukh* Yoreh Deah 262.2, 263.4, 266.10). A child born through Cesarean section is also not circumcised on *shabbat* (see responsum # 95).

As far as drugs or any other methods which hasten the delivery of a child are concerned, they would make no difference with the *berit*. That would be determined by the time of birth irrespective of the method of birth.

We should remember that a child born by Cesarean does not need to be redeemed (Nu 18.15 f). This is so because the child did not "open the womb" as would occur with a normal delivery (*M* Bek 8.2; *Shulhan Arukh* Yoreh Deah 305.24). The other male babies who do not need to be redeemed were the firstborn of a priest or a Levite (*Shulhan Arukh* Yoreh Deah 305.18), and the son of a woman who had a miscarriage after the first forty days of conception (*M* Nidah 3.7; *Shulhan Arukh* 305.23). This ritual, of course takes place on the thirty-first day after birth and is never held on *shabbat* or a festival but postponed until the next day.

Circumcision therefore under all circumstances except a Cesarean section and those listed above takes place on the eighth day when it falls on *shabbat* irrespective of what has induced the labor which led to the birth of the boy.

June 1989

97. A *MINYAN* AND *BERIT MILAH*

QUESTION: Is a *minyan* required for a *berit*? (Morris F. Rosenberg, El Paso TX)

ANSWER: Reform practice follows the Orthodox tradition in regard to the *minyan*. It is preferable to have the *berit* in the presence of ten adults (of course, for us, men or women), but this has not been considered essential (*Tur* and *Shulhan Arukh* Yoreh Deah 265.1, see also *Itur* and *Maharil*).

It is considered of primary importance to have the *berit* on the appropriate eighth day unless the illness of a child prevents that. This takes precedence over the ability to gather a *minyan*, and so even if the *berit* is held only in the presence of the mother and father without any of the other attendants, this is considered perfectly acceptable.

Without doubt the custom of having a *berit* in the synagogue, and even setting aside a special chair for Elijah for this purpose is a way of assuring the attendants of a *minyan* at the service. So the *berit* is frequently held in conjunction with the *shaharit* or *minhah* service and all those in attendance formed a *minyan* for both the service and for the *berit*.

For us in the United States it should usually be easy to get a *minyan* except in the more isolated small communities. If it is possible we should do so. If not, the *berit* should be conducted in as festive a manner as the circumstances permit.

December 1990

98. A *BERIT MILAH* IN THE SYNAGOGUE

QUESTION: Some couples have recently asked that a *berit milah* be conducted in the synagogue rather than at home. They feel that the setting is more appropriate for a religious service, and furthermore it makes it easier for a large group of friends to attend there rather than in a small cramped apartment. (Loren Rabinowitz, Cleveland OH)

ANSWER: It is unclear when the custom of a *berit milah* in the synagogue began. The earliest traces are ninth century Persian, and may reflect Islamic influence as Muslims also require circumcision. The custom subsequently spread both among Karaite and rabbinic Jews (L. Löw *Die Lebensalter in der Jüdischen Literatur*). Later this custom became rather common and many synagogues throughout the world set aside a special "chair for Elijah." This served the practical purpose of providing a setting for the *berit milah* and also stressed the desirability of having a *berit* in the synagogue.

Undoubtedly having the *berit* in the synagogue also made it much easier to assemble a *minyan* for this occasion. As it was to be festive, this enabled the entire community, who assembled for services either at *shaharit* or *minhah*, to participate in the joy of parenthood.

In the liberal congregations of Western Europe and North America a *berit* was been rarely held in the synagogue. Partly this may have been due to the size of the synagogues which made a small gathering seem inappropriate. More than likely it was due to the prosperity of the families who now had sufficient space at home to conduct the *berit* even with a fairly large number of guests present.

A *berit milah* in the synagogue is appropriate for both religious and practical reasons. We have for many years stressed the necessity of having the *berit milah* as a religious ceremony properly conducted on the eighth day irrespective of the medical reasons for circumcision. An assembly in the synagogue stresses the religious aspect of the occasion, and emphasizes the importance of children and the need to begin their religious involvement to the community. The synagogue should welcome this opportunity to bring young couples into it's midst and perhaps provide a special "chair for Elijah" as have so many other synagogues in the past.

December 1990

99. *BERIT MILAH* IN THE EVENING

QUESTION: May a *berit milah* be conducted at twilight or at night? (Mark Lebovitz, Cherry Hill NJ)

ANSWER: The stipulation that circumcision must take place during the day, on the eighth day, rests on a Biblical foundation (Gen 17.12; Lev 12.3). The *Talmudic* discussion was first concerned with how early it might be possible to circumcise. The *Mishnah* stated that the sun should have risen but if the circumcision or other matters there discussed were performed after dawn it would be acceptable (*M* Meg 2.4; 20a ff). It was always considered preferable to have the *berit* early in the day in order to display eagerness to perform the commandment just as Abraham had been eager to obey God (Gen 17.12; Kid 29a). There was general agreement that circumcision may not take place at night and that circumcision must occur on the eighth day unless postponed for health reasons. There was some *Talmudic* discussion about evening circumcision when the *berit* had been postponed. Despite a lengthy debate which hinged upon the interpretation of a Biblical verse (Lev 12.3), the final decision was for daytime circumcisions (Yeb 72b; Kid 29a; Meg 20a ff; Shab 132b ff). We should note that during the *Talmudic* period, when some of these matters were still in flux, one authority, R. Papa, felt that no circumcision should occur on a cloudy day or during bad weather. This injunction may have been made to guard the infant's health. The *Talmud* indicated that it was not to be followed (Yeb 72a).

All of the later authorities agreed that circumcision may occur only during the daytime. Solomon ben Aderet wrote a responsum on this specific question and came to the same conclusion (*Responsa* I #877). This subsequently was also the decision of Maimonides (*Yad* Hil Milah 1.8) and Joseph Caro (*Shulhan Arukh* Yoreh Deah 262.1). Later authorities agreed with it (*Sheelat Yaabetz* I #35).

The *Mishnah* and the *Talmud* discussed the whole issue of twilight in connection with the specific time for various commandments (Meg 20b ff; Yeb 72b; Shab 137a ff; etc). For circumcision this discussion was principally connected with *shabbat*. In other words should a child born during twilight, eight days earlier or whose head emerged at that time, be circumcised on *shabbat*? The definition of twilight was not clearly provided; for some it was the period after the sun had set but daylight remained. For others it was a period of fifteen or twenty minutes before three stars were visible (*Yad* Hil Milah 1.12 and commentaries, *Shulhan Arukh* Yoreh Deah 262.4 ff and commentaries; B. Auerbach *Berit Abraham* page 126 ff).

If the circumcision occurred at night, and twilight was generally considered as night, then it was obligatory to take at least a drop of blood during the next day according to some (Solomon ben Aderet *Ibid; Shulhan Arukh* Yoreh Deah 262.2). There were, however, early authorities who indicated that no drop of blood needed to be taken (Rabenu Asher as quoted by *Bayit Hadash* to *Tur* Yoreh Deah 262), while the custom of taking a drop of blood seems to have originated in the *Hagahot Maimuni*.

We conclude that a *berit milah* should not take place at twilight under normal circumstances. If it nevertheless occurred; we would consider the *berit* valid as did our forefathers and would not require a *tipat dam*.

The specific time frame for each of the *mitzvot* including *berit milah* has been specified in the *Talmudic* tradition and has usually been derived from a specific Biblical verse without any other reason. We do not, for example, know specific logical reasons for the long list of religious rituals to be performed during the daylight or at night, given at the end of the second chapter of *Mishnah* Megilah (see also Meg 20b). We should follow the tradition in these matters as there is no compelling reason to change it.

April 1988

100. THE PRESSURED *MOHEL*

QUESTION: A Reform *mohel*, who has been properly trained, is the only individual active within this community. The mother of a child wishes to have this particular *mohel* do the *berit milah* of her child because of his Reform philosophy or his surgical skill. In this instance it has not been possible for the *mohel* to accommodate her and she inquired whether it would be possible for him to perform the *berit milah* on the following day.

Should the *mohel* accommodate the mother or should he insist that someone else, with perhaps a different philosophy, be chosen in order to conduct the *berit* on the eighth day? (Mark Lebovitz, Cherry Hill NJ)

ANSWER: The pressure of time on a *mohel* will be as great as other practical pressures for the postponement of *berit milah*. We should resist all these pressures and the temptations to move the *berit milah* from the eighth day for any reason except the health of the child.

Berit milah maintains specific traditions and have been connected specifically with the eighth day. All other matters should become secondary. Here we follow our tradition and which assigns such significance to *berit milah*, it overrides the *shabbat* and *Yom Kippur*. This unique status precludes moving the ceremony to another day for personal reasons or as a convenience (W. Jacob (ed) *American Reform Responsa* #55 and #56). Great emphasis has been placed on circumcising a child on the eighth day. The *Septuagint* translated Genesis 17.14, "He who was not circumcised in the foreskin of his flesh on the eighth day that soul shall be cut off from its people". In other words the Greek text added the phrase "on the eighth day" which did not occur in our Hebrew Bible. Philo was puzzled by this and stated that the punishment fell on the parents or upon the child when it became an adult. But that caused him other difficulties because the child became an adult at thirteen while the punishment of *karet* was not considered possible before the age of twenty. Later, Christian commentators indicated that this had to refer to punishment of the parents which is also in keeping with a *midrash* found in the *Mishnah*. It stated that Moses was almost punished by death because he did not quickly carry out

162

the command of circumcising his second son who was born when they were traveling from Midian to Egypt (Ned 32a; *Midrash Rabbah* Exodus 5.8).

The matter discussed in the legal literature in connection with the punishment of *karet* which could not be carried out before the age of twenty (Sab 89b, *J* Bik I 64c; *Yad* Hil Milah 1.3; etc). All of this indicates the importance tradition has placed on the eighth day for a *berit milah*.

Every effort should make The Reform *mohel* to accommodate the family even if the *berit milah* must be very early in the morning of the eighth day. If that is not possible then another *mohel* or, perhaps a Jewish physician not yet certified as a *mohel*, should perform a *berit milah*.

As a larger number of Reform *mohalim* are trained this question will arise less frequently.

April 1988

101. ANESTHESIA FOR A *BERIT MILAH*

QUESTION: At a recent *berit milah* the Jewish physician who performed the surgery asked me why it should not be possible to apply a local anesthetic superficially to the penis of the infant before the operation. This is routinely done before a cystoscopy or similar examination. (Rabbi Karl Richter, Sarasota FL)

ANSWER: We must remember that the widespread use of anesthesia is rather recent. It is now utilized generally for minor surgery and even for routine dentistry. Although there was some early opposition to the use of anesthesia in circumcision as with all suggestions of change (N. Arik *Imrei Yosher* II #130). Later

163

authorities indicated that there was no objection (Gedalia Felder *Nahalat Tzevi* p 57). A number of individuals have written on the subject and indicated that it is the operation itself which is important and not the reaction to it. In other words, the child or adult who is circumcised may be asleep or awake. Either way the operation is valid. He may feel pain or no pain. That too makes no difference although a *midrash* declared that Abraham gained merit because of the pain of circumcision which he bore stoically (*Midrash Rabbah* Gen 47.9). Furthermore, the *mohel* usually places a drop or two of wine on the lips of the child which may have a slight pain alleviating effect although this is not mentioned by any of the traditional authorities.

We do not know whether an infant, eight days old, suffers more than slight discomfort due to the circumcision. I have seen a number of children virtually sleep through the whole operation. So it is not clear that anesthetic is necessary. If, however, the physician feels in a particular case that some kind of local anesthetic would be useful there would be no objection to using it.

August 1989

102. CIRCUMCISION AND AIDS

QUESTION: What precautions should a *mohel* take for his own protection and for the protection of other children in view of the AIDS epidemic? (Mark Cohen, New Orleans LA)

ANSWER: As AIDS is transmitted through blood and it is possible that the *mohel* may injure himself in the process of the circumcision, he should take every precaution possible. There would be no problem about wearing gloves. This would also be in keeping with the tradition (*Sefer Haberit* #179). The *mohel* should, of course, always be careful about the cleanliness and sterility of instruments used for the circumcision. It is presumed that our Reform *mohalim* would use the highest medical standards in their procedures and that there would be no reason to question them on these matters.

As we do not perform *metzitzah* either directly or indirectly and use other methods for seeing to it that the wound is clean and the danger of infection is minimized, we would have no other contact with the blood of the child. From *Talmudic* times we have sought and followed the best current medical opinion (Nidah 22b; *Yad* Hil Deah 4.1, 23ff; *Shulhan Arukh* Orah Hayim 571; Moses Sofer *Hatam Sofer* Yoreh Deah 175; Even Haezer Vol 2 #2; Moshe Feinstein *Igrot Mosheh* Yoreh Deah Vol 2 #69). In all of these matters we, therefore, rely on current medical advice and take the necessary precautions.

January 1991

103. DOUBTS ABOUT A SOVIET *BERIT*

QUESTION: A recent Soviet immigrant had his son circumcised at some risk in Russia. Some blessings, as best as they could be remembered, were recited at the ceremony, but without a *minyan*. The child is now eight years old; should there be a second *berit*? (Derryl Levi, Chicago ILL)

ANSWER: A *berit* is valid *bediavad* even if conducted in an irregular manner, without a *minyan*, or at the wrong time as the references in the earlier responsa demonstrate. We should congratulate this couple on taking the risk of a *berit* when this was very dangerous in the Soviet Union. The child need not go through any other ritual and should proceed with his normal Jewish education.

April 1989.

104. *SANDEQ* AND *MOHEL* AT PUBLIC SERVICES

QUESTION: Does a *sandeq* or a *mohel* have particular rights or obligations at the public service on the day on which the circumcision takes place? I have heard some rumors that this may be so. (Robert D. Feingold, St. Paul MIN)

ANSWER: The *mohel* in some traditional circles led the prayers on the day of the *berit milah*. This was done in keeping with a Biblical verse in the Book of Psalms (Psalm 149.6; *Shulhan Arukh* Yoreh Deah 165.11). It also sought to fulfill the thought that someone who is about to perform a *mitzvah* should pray that he be fit to accomplish it. Usually it was the *mohel* and the *sandeq* who divided the appropriate psalm and read it responsively.

In other traditions, some of the prayers before the *barkhu*, the formal call to worship, were recited by these two individuals.

It would, therefore, be appropriate to have both *mohel* and *sandeq* or the *sandeq* alone participate in the service in this fashion. This would provide additional public recognition of the *berit* and the individual honored as *sandeq*.

August 1989

105. A GENTILE AS A *KEVATER* AT A *BERIT MILAH*

QUESTION: May a Gentile sister of a convert serve as a *kevater* or *kevaterin*? The tradition requires the *kevater* or *kevaterin* to present the child in the place of circumcision. Is it appropriate for a Christian to participate in this ceremony? (Rabbi Leonard Winograd, McKeesport PA)

ANSWER: Generally three individuals are honored through a special participation in the circumcision ceremony. They are the *kevater*, and *kevaterin* and the *sandeq*. All of these may be appropriately designated as godparents of the young lad. The usual procedure is for the *kevaterin* to bring the child into the place of circumcision and hand him to the *kevater* who in turn gives the baby to the *mohel*. The *mohel* continues with a brief prayer and then presents the child to the *sandeq* who may hold the child upon his knees during the circumcision or on a table (*Midrash* to Ps 36:10; *Roqeah* 109). The same procedure was used whether the circumcision was held at home or in the synagogue. The custom of having the *berit milah* in the synagogue may have originated in Persia in the ninth century and may reflect Muslim influence as Islam required circumcision. This custom then spread among both Karaite and Rabbinic Jews (L. Löw *Die Lebensalter in der Jüdischen Literatur*). Subsequently it was also followed partially among

167

Northern European Jews. The *kevater* and *kevaterin* are not mentioned in the early sources at all. Later they play an extremely limited role in the ceremony. They also have no responsibility for any of the social aspects connected with the ceremony which frequently fell upon the *sandeq*. He provided a meal and other refreshments connected with the *berit*. In order to prevent this from becoming an unusual burden, some authorities like the *Tosafists*, and Peretz De Corbeil stated than an individual could serve in this capacity only once. Much later Ezekiel Landau (1713-1793) disagreed and felt that the same individual could be asked any number of times. Landau mentioned that it was the custom in Poland of his time to appoint the local rabbi as the permanent *sandeq*. He participated in every *berit* presumably without obligations for the festivities (*Nodah Biyehudah* I #86). This and later debates on these matters deal only with the *sandeq* mention no *kevater* or *kevaterin*.

Christians participated in the ceremony as *sandeq* in the Middle Ages. The literature also stated that it was inappropriate for a woman to be a *sandeq* (*Shulhan Arukh* Yoreh Deah 265.11) which confirmed that women filled this role. A Christian as a *sandeq* was reported in Castro Giovanni in Sicily in 1484 (L. Zunz *Zur Geschichte und Literatur* p.499). Several medieval church councils prohibited such Christian participation as for example the Council of Terracinana in 1330. Similar statements of prohibition were found in Protestant ordinances; Christians obviously acted in this capacity.

The *kevater* or *kevaterin* represented an Eastern European tradition as the words indicated and found no echo in the earlier literature. Both of these individuals are incidental to the circumcision itself. As Christians have been honored with the position of *sandeq* in the Middle Ages there would be no reason to prohibit a Christian from serving as *kevater* or *kevaterin*. In this instance it honors a members of a family. Furthermore, participation in the ceremony indicates recognition and acceptance of the fact that this child will be raised as a Jew.

July 1987

106. ELIJAH AND THE *BERIT*

QUESTION: Some young parents would like to provide a chair for Elijah for the synagogue to be used at any *berit* held in the synagogue. Are there any specifications for such a chair? What is the connection between Elijah and the *berit*? (Norman Goldberg, New York NY)

ANSWER: Elijah has been traditionally connected with the *berit* because of his concern with Israel forsaking its covenant with God (I Kings 19.10). This verse, when understood narrowly, could refer to the *berit*, so one of the early rabbinic books indicated that for this reason a chair of honor for Elijah has been provided at every *berit milah* (*Pirkei Rabbi Eliezer* 28). The connection may also reflect our Messianic hopes; there is the unspoken wish that the child about to enter into the covenant will live to see the Messianic Age and help to bring it about. In the traditional ritual and our own, Elijah is mentioned on several occasions. These passages seek a hopeful Messianic future.

The few chairs for Elijah which I have seen in museums or synagogues are nice pieces of furniture without any specific design. The oldest surviving chair is from the eighteenth century. If this young couple wishes to design a chair which may symbolize the

Messianic future then any theme of peace and prosperity mentioned by the prophets, or some aspect of the life of Elijah himself, would be appropriate in the decoration. There is nothing in the traditional literature nor in the examples from the past which may guide us.

December 1989

107. A *BERIT MILAH* PLATE

QUESTION: A family which has seen some *berit milah* plates in a museum would like to commission one for their grandson, soon to be born. Is there a specific design which tradition suggests? (Allen Levy, San Francisco CA)

ANSWER: There is nothing in the traditional *halakhic* literature which deals with this subject. It is interested in the problems of the *berit* itself and the various individuals involved.

As we turn to the literature on Jewish art objects, we will find a variety of silver plates designed for the *berit* (A. Kanof *Jewish Ceremonial Art*, Isaiah Shachar *Jewish Tradition in Art*, Beverly R. Cohen *The Cofeld Judaic Museum*, Cissy Grossman *A Temple Treasury*, etc). Some depicted the *berit* itself with a large group in attendance, while others dealt with the theme of Elijah and the Messianic Age. Some of the other plates appear to be more personal and referred to family events which were to be stressed for the next generation. Any of these themes or others which the family many suggest would be appropriate.

June 1990

108. *TIPAT DAM*

QUESTION: A perspective male convert has asked about the requirement of *tipat dam* for conversion. He is circumcised and wants to know the origin of this custom and whether it is required for Reform conversion. (Morton Cohen, Montreal Quebec)

ANSWER: Let us begin by looking at the traditional sources. This question represents a controversy between Hillel and Shamai. Shamai indicated that it was necessary while Hillel stated that it was not (*Tosefta* Shab 9.7; Shab 135a). This controversy then continued in the later literature and was further complicated by the question whether the individual may have been born without a foreskin. This *Mishnaic* discussion, of course, has a Biblical basis as circumcision was part of the ritual of joining our people from early times onward as shown by the story of Shechem and Hamor (Gen 34:13). In addition, anyone who participated in the *Pesah* meal was required to be circumcised (Ex 12.45). Of course, this might have meant that no uncircumcised Jew was supposed to eat the pascal sacrifice (Rashi to Ex 12.45). All of these statement referred to circumcision not *tipat dam*, and circumcision was mandated in the *Mishnah* with some debate, and the debate continued into the *Talmud* (Moed 5.2; Pes 8.8; Yeb 46a ff). Circumcision became a general requirement in later Judaism and has been so indicated by all the codes (*Yad* Hil Milah 17; *Shulhan Arukh* Yoreh Deah 268 1.1). Yet there were discussions in the responsa literature which indicate that it is not indispensable (Elijah Mizrahi *Mayim Amukim* #34; Leon deModena *Kol Sokhol* p 59; Mordecai Eidelberg *Hazon Lamoed* #7). We may, therefore, say that the rite of circumcision

171

for a proselyte although well established by the codes was vigorously debated in *Mishnaic* and *Talmudic* times and echoes of that debate continued in the later responsa literature.

Although there was virtually no discussion in the responsa literature of *hatafat dam* for proselytes the same considerations would be applied. There was some debate whether a court of three individuals must be present at all rites connected with the conversion. Tradition stipulated that it is only the final act of conversion which necessitates a *bet din*. The various steps along the way as circumcision or *tipat dam* and immersion in a *miqveh* would not require it (Yeb 45a ff; *Shulhan Arukh* Yoreh Deah 268.3). The *Shulhan Arukh* indicated that there is absolutely no doubt *bediavad*.

The whole question of proselytes and any ritual necessary for their acceptance was debated at the end of the last century by the Central Conference of American Rabbis (W. Jacob (ed) *American Reform Responsa* #68). The final decision mandated that no rites were necessary for acceptance and that was followed well into the last half of the twentieth century. During the last decades, however, the custom of immersion in a *miqveh* has become widespread and is practiced in a large number of Reform congregations. Mandatory circumcision or *tipat dam* is less wide spread. We may wish to encourage it, always with the stipulation that the ritual is subsidiary to the learning process and the spiritual element of conversion.

February 1990

109. *BERIT* AND BAPTISM

QUESTION: A *mohel* has been asked to officiate at a *berit milah* of the child of a mixed marriage. The mother is Jewish with a strong Jewish identity and background. The father is a believing Catholic. They have agreed that the child should have a *berit* and then be baptized. He is to be educated in both religious traditions so that he may make a choice at the age of maturity. Should the *mohel* conduct the *berit*? (Lewis M. Barth, Berit Milah Board of Reform Judaism, Los Angeles CA)

ANSWER: We might argue that it is our task to bring the child into the covenant of Abraham, and the later actions of the parents are not our primary concern; this finds some justification in the tradition. As the child is Jewish by matrilineal descent, irrespective of what is done, the child would be considered potentially Jewish by us and fully Jewish, but an apostate, by traditional Jews. This would be true whether he is circumcised or not. We should remember that duty of circumcision rests upon the father (Kid 29a; *Shulhan Arukh* Yoreh Deah 261.1); a secondary obligation rests with the *bet din* (*Ibid*). If the mother does not have her son circumcised, the duty falls upon him as an adult (*Shulhan Arukh* Yoreh Deah 261).

These reasons might move us in the direction of a *berit*, however, in this confused setting should we permit it? Had the parents indicated that they would have a *berit* but no baptism, and that they would determine the religious education of the child later, then we could, in clear conscience, proceed. The *berit* would represent an initial tentative step toward Judaism. In accordance

173

with our decision on patrilineal descent other steps must follow. Even without a *berit* we would later accept the child in our religious school.

A *berit* now, without baptism, would provide some time for discussion and persuasion about the needs of a Jewish religious education. However, in this instance they intend to have a baptism immediately after the *berit*, and continue this dual path through the child's life. He would be brought to Religious School and Hebrew School and as well catechism instruction. He would celebrate all the Jewish and all the Christian holidays and later prepare for *Bar Mitzvah* and First Communion simultaneously.

We cannot condone such religious syncretism and must avoid it from the beginning of the child's life. We must indicate to the family that this is the time to choose one religious path or the other for their child. If they are not prepared to make this choice, let them surgically circumcise the child so that a possible entry into the covenant can later be effected by the painless *tipat dam*.

A choice at this junction will avoid confusion for the child and problems with various Jewish authorities throughout his life. This has been our decision in an earlier question which dealt with a child raised in two religious traditions (W. Jacob, *Contemporary American Reform Responsa* #61). We would recommend the same path here at the beginning of life and we cannot proceed with the *berit*.

September, 1987

110. *BERIT* FOR "MESSIANIC JEWS"

QUESTION: A woman who just delivered asked for a *mohel* to do the *berit milah*. While he was talking to her she had a visitor who she introduced as her "minister". When the *mohel* asked the "minister" if he was a rabbi, an evasive answer was given. The *mohel* wanted to know what to do as it was clear these were "Messianic Jews". (Lewis M. Barth, Berit Milah Board of Reform Judaism, Los Angeles CA)

ANSWER: We consider "Messianic Jews" as apostates who have adopted another religion without coercion in contrast to those who were forced to take this step in the Middle Ages. The attitudes toward these individuals who have converted to Christianity has been expressed by several responsa (W. Jacob (ed) *American Reform Responsa* #150; W. Jacob *Contemporary American Reform Responsa* #66-68).

The small group of "Messianic Jews" or "Jewish Christians" pose little danger to the Jewish community, but they do cause considerable confusion. The real threat is minimal but nevertheless they have the capacity to lead some peripheral members of the Jewish community astray and misinform the general American public about the nature of Judaism. We, therefore, have been stricter in our relationship with these groups, and its members, than with other apostates. We will continue to make every effort to create a clear line of demarcation and indicate that they are, in every way, to be considered as Christians and not Jews. The *mohel* should not circumcise this child or bring him into the Covenant of Abraham as that, in fact, is not the intent of these parents.

September 1987

111. BAPTISM AND EDUCATING A CHILD AS A JEW

QUESTION: A couple in which the husband is Jewish and the wife is Catholic were civilly married. When their daughter was born the father was not particularly interested in Judaism and so the child was baptized. Now the father has rediscovered his Jewish identity, joined a congregation in which he is vaguely active and the mother is considering conversion, but in any case intends to raise the child as a Jew. They would like a Jewish naming ceremony for the child. Is this possible? Should we simply consider the child Jewish by patrilineal decent? Would our approach be different for a child already enrolled in a Catholic school program? What are the ramifications as a baptism occurred about a year ago? (Rabbi Jonathan Adland Lexington KY)

ANSWER: There have, of course, been tragic cases in our past when individuals entrusted with the care of a Jewish infant brought it to church to be baptized and later the church as well as the Christian official demanded that the child be surrendered to them. The last instance of this was the infamous Mortara case (1858 - Bologna) in which the child was subsequently kidnapped by church officials. Traditional Judaism does not recognize baptism and would simply look upon such a Jewish child as an apostate. This is in accordance with a decision made for Marrano children by Solomon ben Simon Duran (*Responsum #89*). In those instances baptism occurred against the will of the parents, which is not our situation.   We as Reform Jews look at this situation somewhat differently. First we should note that if there is either a Jewish mother or a Jewish father a presumption of Jewishness exists, but it must be acted upon (W. Jacob (ed) *American Reform Responsa* 547 ff). Here, however, we are dealing with precisely the opposite situation. The parents made a decision for Catholicism and now they have changed their minds. This family illustrates very well the current American situation in which religion is determined less by family background and more by conscience, choice, or whim, at least in families in which a mixed marriage has taken place.

We must ask ourselves whether the presumption once rejected can be activated through a vague kind of Jewish identification; our response needs to be negative. More must be required for otherwise couples like this would simply move back and forth according to the whim of the moment. I am not suggesting that this couple is not serious, but it is easy to imagine others who may not be.

Once a firm action like baptism or enrollment in a Christian religious institution has been taken, then a formal step toward Judaism must be required. This will also settle any doubts about the status of the individual in the future. This little girl should not, later in life, need to respond to an inquiry about her status that although she was baptized she attended a Jewish religious school and now thinks of herself as Jewish. Rather than leaving matters in this indefinite state it would be wise to formally name the child and do so in conjunction with a conversion ceremony appropriate for an infant. The certificate should indicate that a formal conversion took place. If the child is older then the conversion ceremony alone would be appropriate.

This way of approaching the problem will be useful for the child, the parent and the Jewish community. All will understand that this is a serious step taken after considerable deliberation. Furthermore no one will be able to question the status of the child in the future.

March 1990

QUESTIONS AND REFORM JEWISH ANSWERS

112. THE SELECTION OF A HEBREW NAME

QUESTION: Adults frequently come to me with an inquiry about their Hebrew name. Sometimes this has occurred before weddings, and at other instances when an inscription must be placed on a tombstone. How should the Hebrew name be selected on those occasions? (Thomas Pearlman, Phoenix AZ)

ANSWER: A good deal has been written on the choice of names. Among *Ashkenazim*, it is the general practice to name children after a deceased ancestor, while among the *Sephardim* both deceased and living forbearers' names are used. The history of the development of naming in Jewish tradition is long and complex (Jacob Z. Lauterbach *CCAR Annual* 1932 Vol 42 pp 316 ff; W. Jacob (ed) *American Reform Responsa*).

A name was chosen in a number of different ways, either at random or through opening a *Torah* scroll and utilizing the name of the first Biblical figure which appeared, excluding names prior to Abraham (Joseph Trani *Responsa* I #189).

An adult should make every effort to inquire from parents or other members of the older generation about his/her Hebrew name. Sometimes certificates or other records can be found. If no records of any kind can be located then the individual should be enouraged to honor a deceased member of the family by selecting that Hebrew name. In this way a name would be preserved within the family in keeping with tradition. Even more important, the memory of individuals and their accomplishments will be recalled whenever the Hebrew name is used. We should remember that it is possible to select more than one Hebrew name, and in a considerable number of instances two or three are used by a single person.

178

Matters are a little more difficult and complex with the names of parents. If their Hebrew name is not known then an equivalent of their English name should be chosen. This involves some educated guesswork, but it may be reasonably correct.

Hebrew names when selected should be placed in a permanent record within the congregational files so that they can be rediscovered if forgotten.

August 1988

113. MALE AND FEMALE NAMES

QUESTION: The parents of a recently born baby boy wish to name the child after a grandmother as names of other male ancestors have already been used for other children. Is it appropriate to name a male for a female ancestor or vice versa? (Ellen Levine, Omaha NE)

ANSWER: The entire question of Jewish names is complex and has a fascinating history. Jacob Z. Lauterbach and others have written long essays on names and the changes which have taken place with them over the ages (W. Jacob (ed) *American Reform Responsa* #59; L. Löw *Die Lebensalter in der Jüdischen Literatur* pp 94 ff; L. Zunz "Namen der Juden" *Gesammelte Schriften* Vol II). In the Talmudic period some names were used interchangeably for both men and women (Yeb 65e). This practice had also occurred already earlier. In later Jewish literature we find names like *Simhah* used for both boys and girls. Generally, however, an effort was made to modify the name in a manner appropriate for that sex, so for example a boy named after a grandmother Sarah was called Abraham, and vice versa. In other cases the name itself has been modified so that *Shelomoh* became *Shelomit* or *Daniel, Daniela.* Such efforts assured that the child was comfortable with the name so that it was not a source of irritation. The primary reason for naming a child after an ancestor is to recall some good qualities and the provide a personal link with tradition. This will not succeed if the name is disliked. It should also be at least sufficiently akin to the original name to serve this purpose.

Another way of approaching the matter is by providing the child with several Hebrew names. There is very good historical precedent for this. One of those might, therefore, represent the incorrect gender and it would not cause embarrassment.

A feminine name should not normally be used to name a male child or vice versa; it should be modified in an appropriate fashion.

September 1989

114. A YIDDISH NAME

QUESTION: A lad now about to become *Bar Mitzvah* was given a Yiddish rather than a Hebrew name after a deceased grandfather. May the lad be called to the *Torah* with a Yiddish rather than a Hebrew name or must he be given a Hebrew name? (Nathan Silver, New York NY)

ANSWER: The history of Jewish names is long and involved. A number of books and essays have been written on the subject. (J. Z. Lauterbach *Central Conference of American Rabbis Yearbook* 1932 Vol 42 pp 316 ff; L. Zunz *Die Namen der Juden*; L. Löw

Geschichte der Jüdischen Namen) Even a cursory glance at our past indicates that we have borrowed generously from the surrounding cultures. While a large number of Biblical names have Hebrew roots, the meaning and origin of the name *Mosheh* (Moses) is far from clear; it may be Egyptian (Ex 2.10; B. Jacob *Exodus Commentary*) Mordecai, the uncle of Esther, had a Babylonian name (Esther 2.5). Other *Biblical* names also reflected a foreign orientation as they included the prefix *Baal*. In the later Biblical books obviously foreign names were used as in the long list of Levites (Neh 7.45-59). In the Hellenistic period a number of famous Jews bore names as Alexander, Jason, Nicanor, Philo, Zeno, etc. The same occurred in the Roman and later Persian periods. In some eras of our past there was a tendency to return to Biblical names but at the same time names of local origins were also used. So, for example, in the medieval period we have Kalonymus, Maimon, Al-Harisi, Ibn Gabirol, etc. It would be easy to compose a list of hundreds of names commonly used during various periods of our past which have no Hebrew origins.

Our renewed emphasis on Hebrew through the establishment of Israel has led us to emphasize Biblical and Hebrew names. This effort may present a useful tie with contemporary Israel but we should remember that many modern Israelies have invented new names in an effort to Hebraize the linguistic heritage of their diaspora origin.

There is nothing wrong with giving a child a Yiddish name of a grandparent who came from Eastern Europe and thereby recalling that segment of our Jewish tradition. When the boy is called to the *Torah* he should insist that his correct name be used rather than permitting a Hebrew substitute.

July 1988

QUESTIONS AND REFORM JEWISH ANSWERS

115. THE NAME OF A CONVERT

QUESTION: A mother and daughter wish to convert to Judaism. They have studied for two years and are ready to become part of the Jewish community. The mother will be named *bat Avraham Avinu*; may the daughter be designated as the daughter of her mother rather than *bat Avraham Avinu* if she is converted somewhat later than the mother? (Rabbi M. I. Silverman, Albany NY)

ANSWER: The practice of naming a convert as "daughter/son of Abraham" is a custom rather than the law and so it is not mentioned in either the code of Maimonides (*Yad* Hil *Issurei Biah*) or by Joseph Karo (*Shulhan Arukh* Yoreh Deah). The custom is old and was mentioned in the *Tosefta* (Git 6.6) in connection with a *get* (divorce). The notation of "daughter/son of Abraham" may have been used to remind the community that this proselyte may marry a *mamzer* (*Shulhan Arukh* Even Haezer 4.22), and that a proselyte may not be appointed as the King over our people. As these and a few other matters are of little significance for us in modern times we need not be strict about using the term "daughter/son of Abraham". There is no obligation to use it at all. If, however, because of custom you wish to use it with the mother, that is appropriate. However, for the daughter it would be better to use the name of the mother and thereby to indicate both the family relationship and that the daughter has followed in her mother's footsteps in her religious choice.

January 1989

116. NAMING A DYING BABY

QUESTION: The perspective mother of a baby boy knows that the child will be born with serious defects which will make it viable for only a short period, perhaps a few days. Should this child who will die soon be given a name? (Richard Meyers, New York NY)

ANSWER: We should begin by inquiring about the status of an infant who dies at an early age. Jewish law is clear; an infant who dies before reaching the age of thirty days does not require a formal burial. A child who dies before thirty days have elapsed is considered a *nefel* and for such a child (considered stillborn if it does not survive thirty days), no burial or mourning rites are required (Ket 20b; Shab 135b; *Evel Rabati* I; *Shulhan Arukh* Yoreh Deah 266; Ettlinger *Binyan Zion* #133; Jacob Reischer *Shevut Yaaqov* Vol II #10). From *Gaonic* times onward it became customary to circumcise and name a male infant who died before reaching his thirtieth day. Such a circumcision was conducted without the normal prayers. If they forgot to circumcise, the grave was not opened for this purpose, but a name was given the the child (Ezekiel Landau *Nodah Biyehudah* Yoreh Deah #164; *Meir Netiv Responsa* #47).

Another statement also gives us some idea of the attitude to the death of infants in our tradition. The discussion dealt with a eulogy (*hesped*) for a young child; it concluded that for children of the poor there may be a *hesped* from age of five and onward, and for the children of the rich, six and onward (M K 24b; *Shulhan Arukh* 344.4). All of this indicated that relatively little was made of infant deaths or still born babies. Such sad events occurred quite frequently and the communities would have been in a constant state of mourning if rites had been required (*Shulhan Arukh* Yoreh Deah 263.5; 353.6; *Berit Olam* pp 68 ff).

We do not follow the practice of circumcision at the grave and regret the custom. However, we would encourage the parents to give a name to the infant.

In our age when infant mortality is low, the feeling of loss and grief is great. It may help the young parents to overcome their sorrow if the child is given a name, and therefore possesses a definite identity. This should be done in an informal way soon after the child is born. Through it we seek to help the mother and the rest of the family through this difficult period.

January 1991

117. NAME OF A TEENAGE CONVERT

QUESTION: The son of a Christian father and a mother who is about to convert to Judaism also wishes to convert to Judaism. When a Hebrew name is given to him what are the alternatives? Should he be treated simply as a convert or should the name of the parent, now Jewish, be included? (Rabbi Elyse M. Goldstein, Randolph MA)

ANSWER: Let me refer you for some of the references to a portion of this matter to, "A Hebrew Name for a Child with One Jewish Parent" (W. Jacob *Contemporary American Reform Responsa* #34). In that situation, however, we were dealing with a newborn child of a Jewish mother and a non-Jewish father; the status of that child was that of a potential Jew not a convert. In this instance, as the mother has converted to Judaism already and her son wishes to follow her, we should honor the relationship between mother and son by using the mother's Hebrew name. We cannot designate the natural father as he is not Jewish and so might mention no father at all. That is the path followed for example in a *mi sheberakh* recited for someone who is ill. Of course, this prayer is recited at a time of crisis. The other possibility would be to use the mother's name and then designate Abraham (*ben Avraham*) as the spiritual father as is customary with most converts. This would certainly be appropriate and should not be offensive by the father.

We should also consider the possibility of the father's later conversion in order to join the religious community of the rest of his family. If that is judged likely then it would be wise to simply use the mother's name and later add the father's name on occasions when the Hebrew name is used. In this way an even stronger family bond would be forged.

June 1988

118. JEWISHNESS OF AN ADOPTED CHILD

QUESTION: A young adult woman, who has been very active in the synagogue and on our board for many years, has recently discovered that her biological parents were not Jewish. At infancy she was adopted by a Jewish couple. Her adoptive parents openly told her about her adoption, though not about her non-Jewish parentage; they may not have known. Her adoptive parents raised her as a Jew. She has always seen herself as a Jew and has worked within the Jewish community. Now an element of self doubt has affected her. Would Reform Judaism recommend a formal conversion in this case? (Rabbi Alan Henkin, Arleta CA)

ANSWER: Our tradition has always considered it a *mitzvah* to raise an orphan or a child without a home, although formal adoption in the modern sense was not been discussed in the Biblical or *Talmudic* period (Meg 13a; San 19b; *Midrash Rabbah* Exodus 45 interpreting Isaiah 64.8). The subsequent discussion dealt not with the issue of Jewishness, but with the status of abandoned children and possible suspicions of *mamzerut* (*M* Kid 4.2; 73a; *Yad* Hil Issurei Biah 15.30f; *Shulhan Arukh* Even Haezer 4.30 f). However, generally all children were considered *kasher* unless there was definite proof to the contrary and that was virtually never possible.

Nowadays when a child comes from non-Jewish parents and is adopted into a Jewish family the child is converted as any other individual. For an adult, of course, such an assumption of a new religion is a conscience act. For a child this is done by the parents, and a *bet din* to benefit the child. The rituals for a boy consists of circumcision and immersion in a *miqveh*, and for a girl simply immersion in a *miqveh* along with a naming ceremony. When such children reach the age of maturity (*Bar/Bat Mitzvah*) they may without prejudice reject Judaism (*Shulhan Arukh* Yoreh Deah 268.7) and that remains theoretically possible today. This means that up to that time an infant convert, while considered totally Jewish retains the option of leaving. Among us as Reform Jews, if no formal conversion took place during infancy then the act of raising the child as a Jew is tantamount to such conversion and nothing else needs to be done. This is in keeping with our emphasis on education and a pattern of life rather than ritual. This has been our practice for most of the twentieth century as formalized in a resolution passed by the Central Conference of American Rabbis in 1947. We have followed this position for many generations so this young woman is to be considered as Jewish. She should consider herself as Jewish and nothing needs to be done. In fact a formal conversion now would be redundant and would needlessly call into question all that she had done earlier.

February 1989

119. NAME CHANGE OF AN ADOPTED CHILD AFTER THE *BERIT*

QUESTION: A baby boy has been circumcised in the traditional manner and was given a name on that occasion. Now this child is to enter a new family, through adoption, and they wish to give the child a different name. Is this possible? What needs to be done in order to effect such a change, if it is possible? (Deborah Rosenthal, Salt Lake City UT)

ANSWER: The general problems of changing a Hebrew name and presumably in this case the common name has been addressed in a previous responsum "Changing a Hebrew Name" (W. Jacob *Contemporary American Reform Responsa* #33). We should begin by remembering that on several occasions God, himself, changed the name of Biblical figures (Gen 17.5, 32.29, 35.10) while other Biblical persons had their names changed for various reasons. In the Middle Ages names were changed principally in periods of serious illness in order to confuse the Angel of Death (*Sefer Hassidim* #363; *Sefer Toldot Adam Vehavah* I 28; *Bet Yosef* to *Tur Orah Hayim* 129). Furthermore, when a foster parent raised an orphan, which unfortunately occurred frequently in earlier periods of our history, often the name of the father who raised the child was added to the child's name followed by the Hebrew word *hamgadlo* (*Midrash Rabbah* Shemot 46-end; Isserles to *Shulhan Arukh* Even Haezer 129.10). Here, we are not only concerned with identifying the new family, but also giving an identity to the child.

The child in this instance is a baby, has no memory of a former name and the process of adoption once formalized cuts all previous ties with his original natural parents. There would, therefore, be no reason to retain the original name nor would that be desirable. Furthermore, there would be no obstacle as in the case with adults whose names may appear on various legal documents (marriage, divorce, etc).

After the adoption is finalized and the given name has been changed in accordance with the laws of the state or province in which the family lives, then the child should be named in the synagogue and an appropriate certificate of naming should be issued. The previous name may then be ignored just as the previous common name. Such a ceremony would provide an opportunity for the parents to celebrate the adoption and to make the child formally part of their family.

August 1987

120. *PIDYON HABEN*

QUESTION: What is the status of *pidyon haben* (redemption of the first-born) within Reform Judaism? May it take place after the mother has had a miscarriage? (Rabbi Cyril Stanway, Hattiesburg MS)

ANSWER: Reform Jews have only seldom practiced this ritual. As we do not recognize any special status for priests and Levites (Philadelphia Conference Proceedings *Yearbook Central Conference of American Rabbis* Vol I 1890 p 178; W. Jacob *The Pittsburgh Platform in Retrospect* p 108) it is therefore not logical to demand the redemption of the first born. If it is done in Reform circles it is a symbol of a tradition and a tie to the past. Those who want to conduct the ritual should note the following matters:

The Biblical tradition informs us that the first-born sons were devoted to the service at the Temple and earlier at the tent of meeting. However, this special sanctity which they possessed could be redeemed (Ex 13.15; 34.19; Lev 27, 1-8; Nu 18, 14-16; Deut 15.19). It, of course, became necessary to follow such a system as soon as priests and Levites were designated for service at the sanctuary.

Naturally priests and Levites and their daughters who married Israelites do not need to redeem their first-born (Bek 2.1). As for the rest of Israelites, it is incumbent among traditional Jews to redeem all firstborn males. In matters of inheritance "first-born" means the first son of the father. With *pidyon haben* it means the first son of the mother. The child, however, is not considered first-born if the mother had a miscarriage and if that fetus was more than forty days old (*Shulhan Arukh* Yoreh Deah 305.23). Furthermore, if there is any question whether the child really is the first-born or not then no redemption is necessary (*Ibid* 305.22 ff). We should also note that the duty of redemption falls upon the father and if for some reason he fails to do so it is up to the son to redeem himself at maturity (Kid 29a; *Shulhan Arukh* Yoreh Deah 305.15). In time it became customary for some other male relative or perhaps a *bet din* to act in lieu of the father and to redeem the child.

Five *shekels* is the sum set by the Bible (Num 18.16) for the redemption and according to tradition it had to be presented in coinage (*Shulhan Arukh* Yoreh Deah 305.14). In some periods of Jewish history special coins were minted for this purpose. In most periods the money was either returned to the child's father or was distributed to the poor (Bek 51b; *Shulhan Arukh* Yoreh Deah 305.8). The act of redemption may also be used to give money to a poor individual of priestly descent.

The ceremony itself is held on the thirty-first day after birth for by that time tradition found that the child was viable. It may occur even if for health reasons circumcision has not yet taken place (*Shulhan Arukh* Yoreh Deah 305.11). The ceremony involves a simple Aramaic or Hebrew formula in which the father presents his son to the priest and the priest asks whether he wishes to redeem it and the father replies and the coins change hands; it concluded with a blessing over a cup of wine as well as the priestly benediction (*Shulhan Arukh* Yoreh Deah 305.10). In some periods special beautiful trays of silver have been fabricated for use during this ceremony.

Whether a male son is actually the first-born depends on the testimony of either the midwife, the mother or the father. This question, of course, arises principally during multiple births (*M* Kid 4.2; 65d; Yeb 47a Kid 74a; *Shulhan Arukh* Even Haezer). As stated at the beginning the ceremony is not necessary but optional.

December 1987

121. A *PIDYON HABEN* AND *KOHANIM*

QUESTION: An intermarried couple knows that their first child will be a boy. They are thinking about a *pidyon haben*. The mother is Jewish. Her mother's family are *kohanim*. Her father's are Israelites. What status does the child have if his father is not Jewish? (Rabbi Avi Magid, White Plains NY)

ANSWER: The question essentially here is whether the status of *kohen* is passed through the female line. It is clear that in the first generation it is passed through both the masculine and feminine line at least as far as *pidyan haben* is concerned although not in other matters. So neither the son's first born male child nor the daughter's first born male child need to be redeemed if their father was a *kohen* and if both are married to Israelites (Bek 47a). On growing up, however, the children of the male are considered *kohanim* while those of the female are Israelites (*Shulhan Arukh Yoreh Deah* 305.18).

In this instance we are one generation further down the line and the status of *kohen* does not continue; the woman is an Israelite who has married a non-Jew. If they are part of a more traditional family they would then have to consider a *pidyon haben*. Of course, in Reform Judaism this is somewhat incongruous as we do not provide a special status to *kohanim*. Nevertheless some families continue the practice simply as a tie to tradition. This may also be the initial act which begins the identification of the child.

June 1990

122. *BEN ZAKHOR*

QUESTION: What is the origin of *Ben Zakhor*, the ceremony which occurs on the birth of a male firstborn child. (Rabbi Harold B. Waintrup, Abington PA)

ANSWER: The ceremony about which you asked continues to be observed by some families. The tradition concerning it varies, some celebrate on the eve of the day of circumcision while others do so on the Friday evening following circumcision. Moses Isserles refers the celebration on the eve of the circumcision day when he calls it "The night of vigil" (Isserles to *Shulhan Arukh* Yoreh Deah 265.12)

The ceremony itself is simple and consists of a few psalms, some prayers for the child and for the recovery of the mother, the *shemah* and the blessing of Jacob from Genesis (48.16 ff) In some of the communities of the Near East other prayers and readings are added. Occasionally they refer to Elijah who is the patron of all the children who are circumcised *(Berit Olam; Berit Yitzhaq)*. Following the ceremony food is served according to local custom.

The origin of the ceremony is obscure. The words *shalom zakhor*, another term for the ceremony, are found in the *Talmud* in a phrase which indicates that peace enters the world upon the birth of a boy (Nid 31b; San 32b; B K 88a), but we hear nothing about a ceremony in these sources It was sufficiently popular for mention by the *Shulhan Arukh,* but I have not found it earlier.

July 1987

123. CONVERSION ACCORDING TO REFORM *HALAKHAH*

QUESTION: During some conversion ceremonies the phrase "according *halakhah*" has been used. What does this mean for us as Reform Jews? (Leonard N. Fineberg, New York NY)

ANSWER: Let us begin by looking at the tradition. The traditional texts which deal with *gerut* indicate that the prospective convert must be instructed in some of the major and minor *mitzvot*, and then accepts Judaism in accordance with the interpretation of the tradition. That "interpretation," of course, has changed through the ages; in a specific period it may vary both in major and minor matters as seen in contemporary Orthodox discussions. "According to *halakhah*" therefore has some flexibility within traditional circles. It broadly indicates an acceptance of the written and oral law as sacred and as given by God at Sinai; it would allow some flexibility in interpretation.

Our view of this a phrase is somewhat different. "According to *halakhah*" means according to our Reform Jewish tradition. Over the last two centuries we have developed a considerable body of *halakhah* of our own. Some of it in the form of books of guidance (S. B. Freehof *Reform Jewish Practice*; P. Knobel *Gates of Mitzvah* among others); through statements made at synods and conferences (W. G. Plaut *The Rise of Reform Judaism*; M. Meyer *Response to Modernity*), and through more than a thousand responsa written by Solomon B. Freehof and myself. There is therefore a Reform tradition which has been expressed in an expanding *halakhah*.

Our view of the *halakhah* is progressive; portions of the *Torah* came from Sinai and it continued to develop subsequently. We consider the principles enunciated by later prophets and sages also divinely inspired. Revelation continues as does our interpretation of the past. Interpretation has adapted Judaism to new ages and conditions; that is the "oral law" which we as modern Jews continue to adapt and alter. We view the tradition as a continuum and see ourselves not only as bearers of the tradition, but also as interpreters and innovators. Interpretation, along with new decisions become the basis for our *halakhah*. As time goes on these blend and create an authoritative *halakhah* (Elliot Stevens (ed) *Rabbinic Authority*; W. Jacob and M. Zemer *Dynamic Jewish Law*).

"According to *halakhah*" in our tradition therefore means according to the Reform *halakhah* as stated by the various Reform documents and *halakhic* sources.

December 1990

124. THE COURSE OF STUDY FOR *GERUT*

QUESTION: Several members of a congregation have questions about the conversion of a woman who has recently joined the congregation. She has moved to our city from another state and they claim that the study which led to her conversion was insufficient. Upon investigation it was discovered that the woman in question was converted to Judaism after only an afternoon of instruction. She followed the normal ritual of conversion with the appropriate witnesses. Since that time she has lived as a Jewess and since her arrival in this city she has attended the synagogue with some regularity and affiliated almost immediately. May her conversion be questioned? (Ernest Levi, Los Angeles CA)

YOREH DEAH

ANSWER: For many decades the North American Reform movement has provided a fairly uniform course of study for conversion. This has been followed in most communities throughout the country. The length of time spent studying may vary from six to eight months as may the intensity of the instruction provided. The intent, however, has been to give the convert a reasonable background of the major aspects of Judaism and a understanding of basic concept, holidays, practices, liturgy and theology. There have, of course, been deviations from this norm usually due to very specific circumstances, as for example a perspective convert who has long been active in the Jewish community or one who has privately studied Judaism for years; under such circumstances the normal course would be redundant.

In all instances the primary consideration remains the intent of the individual to convert. If intent is present and sincere then it will usually be accompanied by a desire to learn far more than the introductory course. A major aspect of our courses is the exposure of the convert to many aspects of Judaism which may test his/her sincerity in ways which could not be anticipated. The course of study, therefore, is important both for what is learned and the additional level of sincerity which it elicits.

In this instance we must say that there really was no course of study at all and this perspective convert was hurriedly moved through the ritual. *Bediavad* conversion is valid. This is in keeping with the traditional sources which simply stated that a few major and a few minor commandments were taught to the perspective convert. He/she was asked whether they accepted the commandments, and that was followed by the ritual of conversion (*M* Nedarim 3.11; B K 5.4; *Shulhan Arukh* Orah Hayim 199.4). We can see that in previous times the instruction was much less formal although, of course, the perspective convert had to be warned and discouraged, but if he/her persisted the authorities accepted the individual.

In this instance the life pattern of the woman in question has indicated that she is serious about conversion. She has made Judaism very much part of her existence, she participates in the synagogue and has been actively involved in the Jewish community. There is no reason to question her conversion. It is valid and must be accepted.

March 1990

125. CONVERSION OF A CHILD

QUESTION: A non-Jewish woman, previously married to a non-Jew, with an eight year old daughter, has married a Jewish man. They have had a child who has been named in the synagogue and is being reared as a Jew. The second husband has now adopted the older daughter. She wishes to become Jewish; should there be a formal conversion or may she be considered under "patrilineal descent?" (Rabbi Morley T. Feinstein, South Bend IN)

ANSWER: Whenever we discuss individuals and patrilineal descent, one of the physical parents must be Jewish. When there is one Jewish parent, either father or mother, a potential for Jewish life exists. The Central Conference has therefore declared "Depending on circumstances, *mitzvot* leading toward a positive and exclusive Jewish identity will include entry into the covenant, acquisition of a Hebrew name, *Torah* study, *Bar/Bat Mitzvah*, and *Kabbalat Torah* (Confirmation). For those beyond childhood claiming Jewish identity, other public acts or declarations may be

196

added or substituted after consultation with their rabbi" (W. Jacob (ed) *American Reform Responsa* p 550).

In this instance the child has no Jewish parents and is being adopted relatively late in her life. She should therefore be formally converted. This would, of course, be different from the conversion of an adult and would consist of her enrollment in religious school at the appropriate grade level, and a formal ritual in the synagogue, as well as immersion in a *miqveh,* if that is customary. These acts on her part would make the religious transition real and undoubtedly be important to her. They will strengthen her ties to her new family and should be considered an extension of the formal adoption which has taken place.

December 1988

126. A CONVERT AND HEBREW

QUESTION: A middle aged convert is hesitant about conversion. She has given up all identity with Christianity, studied Judaism diligently to the best of her ability, and has learned enough to qualify as a convert. She feels that she is ready and the rabbi also indicates that conversion is now possible. She has, however, hesitated to take this step on the grounds that she knows very little Hebrew, has no linguistic aptitude. and feels that she can not be a good Jewess without a firm grasp of Hebrew. Would we agree with her or would we state that Hebrew is not essential? (Tillie Lebowitz, Tulsa OK)

ANSWER: The Hebrew language has played an important role in Jewish life throughout our history. Throughout the ages we have done our best to encourage the study of Hebrew; our greatest literature has been written in Hebrew or Aramaic.

Within the Reform movement we have put less emphasis on Hebrew and more on the vernacular in our services, in order to enable the worshipper to understand the service fully. Yet we retain a considerable amount of Hebrew in the liturgy.

Problems with understanding the Hebrew language go back to the end of the Biblical period. A large proportion of our people were no longer familiar with Hebrew, even in the time of Ezra and Nehemiah (Neh 8:8), so the Scriptural reading had to be translated for them. By the time of the *Mishnah*, the common people no longer used Hebrew, therefore, the *shema, tefilah* and the *birkhat hamazon* were permitted in the vernacular (*M* Sotah 7.1). This, then, also was the later decision of the *Talmud* (Sotah 32b ff); it enabled individuals who recited petitions to pray sincerely and with full knowledge of what they were saying. A parallel stand was taken by later authorities, so the *Sefer Hassidim* of the eleventh century (#588 and #785) stated that those who did not understand Hebrew should pray in the vernacular. Maimonides provided a similar statement (*Yad* Hil Ber 1.6), while the *Tur* and *Shulhan Arukh* made a distinction between private and pubic prayers. Private prayers were preferably said in Hebrew, while those congregational prayers might be recited in the vernacular. They expressed a preference but did not exclude the vernacular in either instance (*Tur* Orah Hayim 101; *Shulhan Arukh* Orah Hayim 101.4). Aaron Chorin, Eliezer Lieberman and others, who defended the changes made by the Reform movement in the last century and its use of the vernacular, however, insisted that a number of prayers should continue to be recited in Hebrew (*Qinat Haemet*; *Or Nogah* Part I). Of course, they felt that nothing stood in the way of using the vernacular.

In most conversion courses the study of a minimal amount of Hebrew is encouraged, although with the limited amount of time available real familiarity with the language is impossible. In many instances the convert will be able to read simple prayerbook Hebrew and know the meaning of a text by association. The continuation of Hebrew studies has always been encouraged but not made a mandatory part of the conversion process. We would, therefore, say to this individual that a minimum knowledge of Hebrew will be helpful for familiarity with religious services and as an association with tradition. More advanced knowledge of the Hebrew is desirable, but may not be possible for everyone. The sincerity of this convert is enough to lead to her acceptance. She should be assured that a fuller knowledge of Hebrew is not required of her. We will welcome her with the hope that she will be a good addition to our people.

February ,1989

127. A CONVERT FROM ANOTHER LAND

QUESTION: A young woman has come to the United States from Australia. She was converted to Judaism there and possesses the proper documentation; the conversion in this instance seems to have been done rather hurriedly. Should we accept it? She wishes to marry an American Jewish boy. (Robert Gold, Baltimore MD)

ANSWER: Unless we have very good reason for rejecting the conversion from a foreign land, we should accept it. Those reasons would primarily deal with the behavior or knowledge of the convert. If the convert's attitude towards Judaism raises doubts, then we are entitled to question the conversion. Otherwise, someone who comes to us with appropriate documentation should be accepted.

We may, of course, suggest further study to the young woman on the grounds that her knowledge of Judaism seems limited. This would make it easier for her to establish a Jewish home and to raise her children within the Jewish community. Such suggestions made in a positive manner will have the desired effect; they will avoid the problems of questioning the efforts of colleagues elsewhere while at the same time maintaining our own standards for conversion.

May 1989

128. CONVERSION OF A CHILD WITH TWO NON-JEWISH PARENTS

QUESTION: A mixed married couple were members of a congregation. The woman had no desire to convert to Judaism but was committed to raising her son as a Jew. She became a regular Temple goer and has continued after his death. She had another child by a non-Jewish man with whom she had a brief relationship. She intends that the child be raised as a Jew just as his brother. Should a *mohel* perform a *berit milah* on this child? (Lewis Barth, Los Angeles CA)

ANSWER: The new born baby here is clearly non-Jewish. The fact that the mother was not married to the father plays no role in our discussion. It has always been possible for *bet din* converting a young child and thus stand in *loco parentis*. We have used this procedure since *Talmudic* times (Ket 11a) although in modern times we refrain from it as we do not want to convert any minors who may come to us because of specific family problems or some temporary youthful attraction. We have frequently counseled teenagers with an interest in Judaism to study it academically but not to convert (W. Jacob *Contemporary American Reform Responsa* #50). In this instance, of course, we face a different situation as this is a baby and is not the child of an outsider, but of an individual who has made a commitment to Judaism albeit without conversion. The *mohel* should circumcise this child as an act of conversion with the appropriate special blessing; *milah leshem gerut* is frequent among us. *Tevilah* should also be considered in accordance with local custom. Technically the child possesses the right to renounce his conversion when he reaches maturity (W. Jacob *Contemporary Reform Responsa* #49). The previous actions of the mother guarantee that the child will be raised as a Jew along with his older brother.

The rabbi should take whatever opportunities this and other occasions present to encourage the young woman to convert to Judaism and in this way to bring religious unity to her young family. Without this step and therefore without a Jewish parent in the home it will be difficult to raise these children as Jews. We should encourage her in every way possible.

September 1987

129. RUMORS ABOUT STATUS OF SOVIET JEWS

QUESTION: A family has emigrated to the United States from the Soviet Union. They received help from the Federation and were adopted by a synagogue. Now several Soviet Jews have protested and indicated that they do not feel that this family actually is Jewish. The protest is based on alleged mixed marriage which took place two generations ago. What is the status of this family? Need they do anything formal to adjust their status? (Steven Thomas, Detroit MI)

ANSWER: The nature of this question is rather sad as it revealed some tensions, and an antagonistic spirit among a few of our new Soviet immigrants.

Let me begin with the resolution of the Central Conference of American Rabbis passed in 1983 which stated: "The Central Conference of American Rabbis declares that the child of one Jewish parent is under the presumption of Jewish descent. This presumption of the Jewish status of the offspring of any mixed marriage is to be established through appropriate and timely public and formal acts of identification with the Jewish faith and people. The performance of these *mitzvot* serves to commit those who participate in them, both parent and child, to Jewish life.

Depending on circumstances, *mitzvot* leading toward a positive and exclusive Jewish identity will include entry into the covenant, acquisition of a Hebrew name, *Torah* study, *Bar/Bat Mitzvah*, and *Kabbalat Torah* (Confirmation). For those beyond childhood claiming Jewish identity, other public acts or declarations may be added or substitutes after consultation with their rabbi."

From this we can see that in the current generation we would definitely consider the family Jewish. As they suffered as Jews while in the Soviet Union. Upon arriving in the United States they have established close ties with a synagogue. Even if there was some vague Christian tradition in the past through mixed marriage this family has identified itself as Jewish.

What of questions about the past? Such an aspersion was raised against the descendents of the Exilarch Bustenai ("Maasei Bustenai" *Bruell Jahrbücher* 1876 pp 102 ff; G. Margoliouth "Some Fragments" *Jewish Quarterly Review* Vol 14 pp 303 ff). The facts in that case are clouded by political implications, but we do know that some of the descendants assumed the same high office and brushed aside the allegations.

We should also take into account the statement of Solomon ben Simon of Duran who claimed for Marranos that if the mother in each generation was Jewish the Jewish lineage would continue indefinitely (*Responsa #89*). In this case we do not know whether the allegations were made about the mother or the father. We must anyhow condemn the gossip which surrounds this family. There are strong statements against gossip (Hafetz Hayyim *Sefer Hafetz Hayyim* Rehilut).

As the family in question has thoroughly identified itself with the Jewish community we should accept them and vigorously defend their Jewishness against any and all who question it.

March 1990

130. A TAROT READER AS A CONVERT

QUESTION: A prospective convert has indicated that she reads Tarot cards approximately once a month. Although in the past she has done so for a fee she is now doing it only for her friends at no charge. She feels that the information which she receives is from God and that she is thus privileged to be the channel for God. She has indicated that this is a new small part of her life. In every other respect she seems to be a fine candidate for conversion; shall we accept her as a convert? (Rabbi Stephen J. Einstein, Fountain Valley CA)

ANSWER: Jewish opposition to all kinds of fortune telling has been very strong. It is based upon verses in Leviticus and Deuteronomy (Lev 19.26, 31; Deut 18.10,11; as well as Ex 22.17). The prohibition includes soothsayers and fortune tellers of all kinds. There are numerous discussions in the *Talmud* (Hul 7b; 95b Ber 33b; Shab 75a; San 65a ff; Pes 113b; Ned 32a; etc). The matter has also been treated in the various books of *mitzvot*, for example, *Sefer Hamitzvot* (Lo Taaseh 8,9,31,38), as well as by Maimonides' Code (*Yad* Hil Akum Vehuqotehem 11.14 ff) and the *Shulhan Arukh* (Yoreh Deah 179). Some modern discussions have been equally negative (*Responsa Daat Kohen*). We have sought to avoid superstitious influences and to keep our monotheism free from strange practices.

As this candidate for conversion feels that she has direct access to God through her Tarot cards, her concept of God is different from that of normative Judaism and the influences which she feels cannot be incorporated in a Jewish life.

This perspective convert should be encouraged to look at her ties to the Tarot card reading once more. As this has become a minor part of her life, it may be possible for her to give this up entirely. If she can do so, then we can accept her as a convert. If not, we should reject her at this time.

April 1988

131. ASSURING THE STATUS OF A CHILD

QUESTION: A child, a member of my congregation, has a Jewish father and a non-Jewish mother. I understand that in accordance with the decision of patrilineal descent this child is potentially Jewish if appropriate action is taken by the family, i.e. berit, a naming, a Jewish education. The couple, however, feels that there is a period of uncertainty therefore in the child's life, and they wish to remove that uncertainty about his status. How may this be done? (Fieda Rosenfeld, New York NY)

ANSWER: The resolution on patrilineal descent (W. Jacob (ed) *American Reform Response* Appendix p 547) was designed to provide complete equality between men and women as we have done in all other matters connected with Reform Judaism. Furthermore it was intended to meet the different conditions of our own time when descent and a cohesive community no longer guarantee Jewish identity. Therefore we have placed a vigorous emphasis upon commitment to Judaism on the part of the individual in accordance with his/her ability and age. This has meant that from an adult we expect participation in Jewish life, and from a child education towards such participation. A number of responsa have discussed both the rationale behind the resolution as well as problems associated with the resolution (W. Jacob *Contemporary American Reform Responsa* #38-42; 59-62; 96).

If parents wish to remove any doubt, and this may be desirable for a variety of reasons, they may do so through a formal *gerut* (conversion). By taking this step either at the time of the *berit milah* or later they will assure that no one can question the Jewish identity of their child. We would, of course, continue to stress the need for a Jewish education and for later involvement in the Jewish community for the infant *ger*.

September 1989

132. A BLACK JEW AND FALASHAS

QUESTION: A young black woman who has attended services regularly and studied Judaism in the customary introductory course has stated that she wishes to be considered as Jewish in accordance with the Reform decision on patrilineal descent. She claims that her forbearers were Falashas and states it unnecessary and inappropriate for her to go through a conversion ceremony. (Joanne Freeman, Pittsburgh PA)

ANSWER: Let us begin by taking a careful look at the resolution passed by the Central Conference of American Rabbis in 1983. "The Central Conference of American Rabbis declares that the child of one Jewish parent is under the presumption of Jewish descent. This presumption of the Jewish status of the offspring of

206

any mixed marriage is to be established through appropriate and timely public and formal acts of identification with the Jewish faith and people. The performance of these *mitzvot* serves to commit those who participate in them, both parents and child, to Jewish life.

"Depending on circumstances, *mitzvot* leading toward a positive and exclusive Jewish identity will include entry into the covenant, acquisition of a Hebrew name, *Torah* study, *Bar/Bat Mitzvah*, and *Kabbalat Torah* (Confirmation). For those beyond childhood claiming Jewish identity, other public acts or declarations may be added or substituted after consultation with their rabbi."

From what I have gathered from conversations after the initial question, the parents of this young woman consider themselves to be Christians and she, herself, was raised in a Baptist community. In her mother's family, there was a family tradition of descent from African nobility which the daughter has interpreted, because of some customs about which she is rather vague, as descent from the Falashas.

The closest parallel to this would be if we looked at the Spanish-Jewish family which did not preserve its Marrano traditions, and only had a vague memory of the Marrano past, but in every way was thoroughly identified with the Catholic Church. In those instances when no memory at all of the Jewish past remained, the decision was that such individuals could not be considered as Jews or as returning apostates, but should be treated as converts. There is some unclarity about this depending on how far from the original Jewish generation the descendants were and whether the maternal line remained "Jewish." We have five different categories.

(1) Apostates were Jews who had sinned but, nevertheless, remained Jewish (Isaac ber Sheshet; Simon ben Zemah of Duran but on some occasions he did not grant this status; Solomon ben Solomon; Zemah ben Solomon).

(2) Those who considered the apostate as Jewish only in matters of matrimony (and so their offsprings were Jewish), but not in any other area (Samuel de Medina).

(3) Marranoes (*anussim*) were non-Jews in every respect including matters of marriage; their children were not considered to be Jews (Judah Berab, Jacob Berab, Moses ben Eliea Kapsali, etc.).

(4) An apostate was worse than a Gentile (ben Veniste, Mercado ben Abraham).

(5) Descendants of the Marranoes who have been baptized were like Jewish children who have been taken captive by non-Jews, and their children are Jewish (Samuel ben Abraham Aboa). A full discussion of the problem may be found in H. J. Zimmel's *Die Marranen in der Rabbinischen Literatur* pp 21 ff. One extreme position was held by Solomon ben Simon Duran (Rashbash *Responsa* #89) who felt that not only the apostate but also the children would continue to be considered Jewish forever into the future as long as the maternal line was Jewish. He also felt that nothing needed to be done by any generation of such apostates when they returned to Judaism. No ritual bath or any other act was considered necessary or desirable. In fact, he emphasized that no attention be given to their previous states, for that might discourage their return. Rabbenu Gershom earlier similarly urged the quiet acceptance of all who returned to Judaism (*Mahzor Vitry* pp 96, 97).

The other extreme has been presented by Hai Gaon as cited in a slightly different fashion by Rashi (in his commentary to Kid 68b and Lev. 24.10). He felt that any returning apostate, or the children of a Jewish mother who had apostatized, were potentially Jewish but had to undergo a process akin to conversion if they wished to become part of the Jewish community. That point of view was rejected by most later scholars, as for example, Nahmanides (in his commentary to Leviticus 24.10; *Shulhan Arukh* Yoreh Deah 268.10 f; Ezekiel Laudau *Noda Biyehudah* #150, etc). We, therefore, have two opposing positions in rabbinic literature; both, of course, represented reaction to particular historic conditions. Solomon ben Simon of Duran wished to make it easy for a large number of Marranoes to return to Judaism; unfortunately this did not occur. Even when it was possible for Jews to leave Spain, the majority chose to remain. Rashi's harsh attitude probably reflected the small number of apostates who were a thorn in the side of the French community. The later tradition chose a middle path and encouraged the apostates return along with some studies, but without a formal conversion process. Even if an apostate indicated no desire to return to Judaism, he would, nevertheless, be considered as part of the Jewish people (San 44a).

In this instance we are very far removed from any Jewish identity even if we take the reference to "noble lineage" in a family tradition as one which alludes to the Falashas. There certainly was no continous maternal "Jewish" line.

My investigation of the origin of American Negroes and the African slave trade to North America, the Caribbean and Central America indicates that virtually all the slaves came from the West African Coast or the hinterland immediately behind it. Occasionally captives were transported a greater distance but the cost of such transportation and the difficulties inherent in a long march over

209

land made this the rare exception. There is no known record of individuals from as far as Ethiopia having been transported to North America nor is there any Falasha tradition of members lost to the Western slave trade. That, of course, does not mean that there might not have been an isolated incident, however, the likelihood is very small.

Clearly it will help the Jewish identity of this Black woman if she considers herself from a Falasha tradition even though that can never be proven. However, her current affiliation with the Jewish community must occur through a conversion as any other convert. We will then gladly accept her into our community.

January 1988

133. JEWISH STATUS AND THE TEN LOST TRIBES

QUESTION: A young man interested in Judaism has stated that he wishes to be considered Jewish through his descent from one of the ten lost tribes. His parents raised him in the Mormon tradition. (Mark Kaplan, Cincinnati OH)

ANSWER: Let us look at the statement on patrilineal descent. "The Central Conference of American Rabbis declares that the child of one Jewish parent is under the presumption of Jewish descent. This presumption of the Jewish status of the offspring of any mixed marriage is to be established through appropriate and timely public and formal acts of identification with the Jewish faith and people. The performance of these *mitzvot* serves to commit those who participate in them, both parents and child, to Jewish life.

"Depending on circumstances, *mitzvot* leading toward a positive and exclusive Jewish identity will include entry in the covenant, acquisition of a Hebrew name, *Torah* study, *Bar/Bat Mitzvah*, and *Kabbalat Torah* (Confirmation). For those beyond childhood claiming Jewish identity, other public acts or declarations may be added or substituted after consultation with their rabbi."

This indicates that if one of the parents is Jewish and the child has been raised as a Jew or has made a commitment to Judaism as an adult, we would consider that individual as a Jew. There is some debate in the tradition about apostasy in a previous generation and how the descendants should be treated (H. J. Zimmels *Die Marranen in der Rabbinischen Literatur* pp 21 ff). Here, however, the individual involved was raised in a Mormon family and it is from that association with the last ten tribes has been derived. Joseph Smith the founder of the Church of Later Day Saints considered America colonized by two groups, both related to the Bible. The first came to this continent after the dispersion of the Tower of Babel, and the second after the destruction of Jerusalem in 587. These as well as other speculation about the American Indians as the ten lost tribes have led to various pieces on the subject (Israel Worsley *A View of the American Indians*, etc).

We can, however, not recognize these individuals as Jews even if their claim were true. Rabbinic Judaism has developed far beyond the Biblical period. The young man, therefore, should be treated as any other convert.

April 1989

134. PRETENDING TO BE JEWISH

QUESTION: A Russian Jewish family arrived in this country a decade ago. They lived a Jewish life, the family belongs to a synagogue and the two children continue to be educated in the Religious School. Now the woman, in order to clear her conscience, has stated that she was not born of Jewish parents, never informed her husband of this fact and pretended to be Jewish in order to preserve family harmony in Russia and to simplify immigration. She has considered herself Jewish for more than a decade and a half. What does she need to do to change her status? (Paul Simon, Boston MA)

ANSWER: We should treat this woman with considerable understanding when she pretended to be Jewish for the sake of family harmony in the Soviet Union. This was not an easy choice. She has since, along with her husband, lived a Jewish life and obviously intended to become part of the Jewish community. We should now accept her with only a minimal amount of additional study and proceed with the usual conversion ceremony. As the couple was married in the Soviet Union and therefore did not have a Jewish wedding ceremony, they wish to have the wedding ceremony or something akin to it now, but this is certainly not absolutely essential. There is no question about the status of the children as their father was definitely Jewish at the time of their birth and they are receiving a Jewish education. This is in keeping with the resolution of the Central Conference of American Rabbis.

"The Central Conference of American Rabbis declares that the child of one Jewish parent is under the presumption of Jewish descent. This presumption of the Jewish status of the offspring of

212

any mixed marriage is to be established through appropriate and timely public and formal acts of identification with the Jewish faith and people. The performance of these *mitzvot* serves to commit those who participate in them, both parents and child, to Jewish life.

"Depending on circumstances, *mitzvot* leading toward a positive and exclusive Jewish identity will include entry into the covenant, acquisition of a Hebrew name, *Torah* study, *Bar/Bat Mitzvah*, and *Kabbalat Torah* (Confirmation). For those beyond childhood claiming Jewish identity, other public acts or declarations may be added or substituted after consultation with their rabbi."

We should wish this family well and will gladly accept the woman formally into the Jewish community.

February 1991

135. PREREQUISITE FOR A *SOFER*

QUESTION: What training or characteristics must a *sofer* (scribe) possess in order to fulfill the traditional requirements? (Rabbi James S. Glazier South Burlington VT)

ANSWER: In the past, two categories of *sofrim* existed. Some acted as notaries and also kept the records for the rabbinic court while others dealt with the text of the *Torah*,, the *tefillin*, *megilot*, and *mezuzot*. We, of course, are dealing with the latter kind of *sofer*. Although every Jew is obligated to write a *Torah* scroll for himself (Ex 15.2; Shab 133b; *Shulhan Arukh* Yoreh Deah 270.1), most have found the personal and technical requirements too difficult. *Sofrim* were therefore engaged for the task and the

213

individual who involved them often wrote a symbolic word or phrase of the last column. In ancient times the community, of course, depended entirely upon the *sofer* for its written material and so a scholar was not to live in a community which did not have a *sofer* (San 17b).

The qualifications of a *sofer* fall into two categories, skill and piety. A *sofer* must reproduce the script of the *Torah* accurately and may never do so from memory but must always follow a written copy which is before him and follow the very precise specifications which govern the shape of the letters, the paragraph divisions, the column length and width, etc. (Er 13a; Meg 18b; *Shulhan Arukh* Yoreh Deah 274:1 ff). In addition he must concentrate on his work and think about the divine name appropriately whenever he writes it, so that the act of writing does not occur mechanically (Shab 104a). This demands an unusual degree of piety. If a *sofer* is a non-believer then the *Torah* which he writes should be destroyed (*Yad* Yesodei Hatorah 6.8).

The individual who writes a *Torah* or prepared the other documents must be an adult male (Git 45b; *Shulhan Arukh* Yoreh Deah 281.3) and Jewish (*M* Git 4.6; 45b; *J* A Z 2.2 *Shulhan Arukh* Yoreh Deah 281.2). Women are excluded from the act of writing many of their ritual objects (Git 45b) by tradition, although the scroll of Esther is not included in that prohibition (*Shulhan Arukh* Orah Hayim 691.2; Meyer Perls *Teshuvah Meahavah* #2).

The *sofer* possessed an honored status within the Jewish community, the Biblical Ezra was known as a *sofer* as were some great *Talmudic* authorities as Meir. In later times that was rarely accompanied by adequate compensation and most *sofrim* were poor.

In addition, the *sofer*, of course, must be technically qualified (*Ezrat Sofer* 1769; *Tikun Sofrim* 1874; *Sefer Midinei Ketib Tefilin* (ed) Dubno; L. Löw *Graphische Requisiten und Erzeugnisse bei den Juden*). The ink, the writing tools and the parchment are all carefully prescribed. Although the *sofer* is not responsible for the preparation of the parchment, he must be able to test its appropriateness. In addition he is responsible for all other ingredients for the ink, utensils, etc.

It would be perfectly possible to train modern *sofrim* both male and female. Many would probably wish to engage in the preparation of more decorative items like *ketubot* as so many couples seek them. We should be certain that this work does not influence their efforts as *Torah* scribes.

June 1988

136. THE CONDITIONAL LOAN OF A *TORAH*

QUESTION: The Nassau Community Temple possesses a *Torah* which was given or lent to a congregation in Connecticut. Subsequently the family agreed to lend this *Torah* to Temple Judea, the congregation to which their children belonged, on condition that the *Torah* follow the children if they disaffiliated. There is no documentation of the terms of this loan. Eventually Temple Judea merged with the Nassau Community Temple and the family left the congregation. They wished to retrieve the *Torah* at that point but as a dedication ceremony had already been scheduled they were willing to participate in that ceremony which took place a decade and a half ago.

Now the family has once more pressed its claims for the *Torah* which they wish to place with their present congregation in Lynbrook. In return for this they are willing to make a substantial gift to the Nassau Community Temple.

They now claim some documentation of the original transaction in the form of a letter from an individual who was present during the conversations with the rabbi of Temple Judea two decades ago.

The *Torah* in question has been in continual use by Nassau Community Temple. What disposition should be made? (Rabbi Linda Henry Goodman West Hempstead NY)

ANSWER: Various issues connected with this problem have been fully discussed precisely as you indicated in your letter by Solomon B. Freehof (*Contemporary Reform Responsa #22*). He concluded (1973) that the *Torah* belonged to the congregation which now held it even though it became part of that congregation through a merger. The transfer by the officers of the original congregation was appropriate and can not be questioned now. We are concerned about the terms of the "loan" which were not entirely clear then, nor has the new evidence brought absolutely certainty to this matter.

The only new factor is the letter of an individual who was present at the initial conversation. She testified to the fact that this was a loan which would continue only as long as the children were members of the congregation. We, of course, honor this testimony and have high regard for the individual involved. It, however, does not answer all the questions which might be raised about this issue. Tradition and Reform would follow the responsum of Joseph Colon (*Responsa Mahariq #159*). He indicated that unless the custom of lending a *Torah*, while maintaining permanent family possessions,

216

was widespread the claim of ownership by the congregation should be followed. In another responsum (#70) he decided in favor of the individual who claimed ownership as the custom of that community was that of an individual lending the Torah to a synagogue. That, however, is not our custom in North America; the vast majority of synagogues own their Torahs as gifts. As the Torah has been in continual use by the congregation for two decades and as the claims of the family remain somewhat in doubt despite the attestation of a new witness. In other words, we do not really know whether the father intended to place long term conditions upon the use of the Torah, especially as the congregation (Temple Judea) to which it was lent was new and was being served by a student rabbi. As its future was in doubt the condition he may have imposed would have been understandable. The removal of the Torah in those early years particularly during the lifetime of the individual, who provided it, would have been permissable, but now two decades later when all of the matters involved are somewhat beclouded it should not occur and we agree with the decision of Solomon B. Freehof.

Let me suggest another solution which may avoid inter-congregational conflict and help the family in question. The two congregations could simply exchange one Torah for another. In other words the congregation to which the family now belongs may wish quietly to provide the Nassau Jewish Community Center with a Torah in an unannounced exchange for the disputed Torah. That might satisfy everyone's honor and avoid further conflict. As indicated in Solomon B. Freehof's responsum such a movement of a Torah from one congregation to another in accordance with the wishes of the congregations or their officers would be perfectly permissable. An alternative solution to the problem might be binding arbitration through a bet din which could be convoked to look into this entire matter. Before, however, moving in that direction we should ask ourselves whether it is really worthwhile, a decade and a half later, to continue a quarrel about the ownership of a *Torah*. Surely there must be enough good will on both sides to either exchange *Torahs* as suggested above or to simply conclude the issue.

April 1988

137. A *TORAH* PERMANENTLY DISPLAYED IN A MUSEUM CASE

QUESTION: May a *Torah* be displayed in a museum case on a permanent basis? The synagogue museum is located in the foyer of the synagogue. It is visited by a large number of Jews and non-Jews. The *Torah* in question has been damaged and can no longer be used at services. It has survived the Holocaust and so is considered as a silent witness to these tragic events. (Charles Goldman, Toronto Ontario)

ANSWER: A *Torah* or any Hebrew book which contains the name of God is considered sacred. When it can no longer serve the original purpose it should be buried or disposed of in such a way that no desecration or inappropriate use of it will be made (Meg 26b; *Shulhan Arukh* Yoreh Deah 282:10; Orah Hayim 154.5). Traditionally *Torah* scrolls, prayerbooks, and Bibles were buried in the congregations cemeteries or in some countries placed in storage areas in the synagogue which were designated for this purpose. For example the *Geniza* in Cairo which contained documents and books spanning a period of more than four centuries. *Torahs* particularly were put away and removed from the synagogue as soon as they became defective so that they would not be read at a service in error. The principle involved was that of honoring the book and the name of God rather than permanently removing the work from circulation. There has never, for example, been any reservations about displaying ancient Hebrew manuscripts in museums either Jewish or non-Jewish, as for example the Isaiah Scroll in the Shrine of the Book in Jerusalem.

We must, however, ask whether a *Torah* is in a special category. Certainly viewed historically it is not. It is simply the earlier form of the book before the invention of books with separate pages. However, through the centuries in which the *Torah* scroll remained virtually the only book in this form it has acquired through custom a special status. It has always been maintained in a separate container, either the permanent ark of the synagogue, the movable container of the *Sephardic* tradition or the still earlier mobile arks. This was an effort to safeguard it; even a *pasul Torah* remained sacred (Sab 115b); it could continue to be kept in the ark though this was usually not done in order to avoid accidental use (Jacob Ettlinger *Binyan Zion* 1.97; *Magen Avraham* to *Shulhan Arukh* Orah Hayim 154.8; Gedaliah Felder *Yesodeh Yeshurun* 2.142). Special rules also evolved about handling the *Torah* and the honor due to it at religious services. Furthermore being asked to participate in the *Torah* service was both a *mitzvah* and a special honor and thereby gave a unique status to the book itself (W. Jacob (ed) *American Reform Responsa* #39).

The display in a museum case would certainly be appropriate as it continues to honor the *Torah*. We should view this as an educational tool which will bring about a better understanding of the *Torah*.

There may be some problems with the museums location in the foyer of the synagogue. After all that is an area generally used for gatherings not only before and after services, but also for many social occasions not of a religious nature and so the behavior in the foyer will not always necessarily be decorous. It would therefore be appropriate to place the *Torah* in such a fashion that it is not directly accessible from the foyer and can only be seen upon entering the museum area itself. If that is not possible than it might be well to construct the case in which it is displayed in such a fashion that a curtain akin to that normally found in a *Torah* ark (*parokhet*) can be closed when the museum is not open or when the synagogue foyer is used for general assembly purposes. In this fashion the continued honor of the *Torah* will be maintained and people's sensitivity toward this *Torah* which has survived the Holocaust will be heightened.

June 1989

138. TRANSPORTING THE *TORAH*

QUESTION: A former member of our temple wishes to purchase one of our *Torahs* and give it to her new congregation in memory of her parents. Are there any restrictions on how the *Torah* is to be transported to the new community and the money which paid for this *Torah*? (Rabbi Leonard Winograd, McKeesport PA)

ANSWER: Let us deal with the matter of the sale of the *Torah* first. A *Torah* may be sold in order to support those who are poor or the educational ventures of the congregation (*Tur* and *Shulhan*

Arukh Yoreh Deah 259). As this *Torah* will simply be moved from one congregation to another the honor of the *Torah* will not be disturbed.

The problem of transportation or storage has not been dealt with extensively as the main consideration is that the *Torah* be treated with reverence and not be dishonored. The *Torah* was to be treated with honor and anyone who despised a *Torah* would also have contempt for human beings (*M* Pirqei Avot 3.2). When the *Torah* was raised individuals always stood (Kid 33b) and when it passed, adults and children either bowed their head or kissed it (*Tur* and *Shulhan Arukh* Even Haezar 115). There were regulations which governed the manner of carrying a *Torah* while in procession.

Nothing disrespectful is to be done in the presence of the *Torah*. The congregation must not leave the synagogue until the *Torah* has been safely stored (Sotah 39; Ber 23b). A *Torah* may not be tossed from one place to another nor may it be placed on or beneath a bed. If, by chance, it is placed on a bed then no one may sit there with it (*Mas Sofrim* 3.11-13). It could also not be stored in a bedroom (*Shulhan Arukh* Yoreh Deah 282). The sacredness of the *Torah* extended to its coverings and the ark in which it was kept should subsequently not be used for a profane purpose (Meg 26b f). A defective *Torah* is hidden away or burned (Meg 26b; Ket 19b).

A *Torah* should therefore be transported personally from one synagogue to another in order to accord it proper reverence. If this is not feasible then it may be carefully packed and shipped.

November 1987

139. THE SECOND PARAGRAPH OF THE *SHEMA*

QUESTION: In our prayer books the second paragraph of *shema* has been omitted. Would it be desirable for the sake of consistency to also omit it from the text in our *mezuzot*? (Ronald Alexander, Detroit MI)

ANSWER: The second paragraph of the *shema* was omitted from various editions of the *Union Prayer Book* and does not appear in the *Gates of Prayer* either. We have omitted it as Reform Judaism for most of the century has placed relatively little emphasis upon ritual, but that has now changed and we find a large number of congregations have adopted the use of the *talit*, the *kipah*, etc. We can see from this that our attitude toward the ritual aspects of tradition has been flexible. We moved in the direction of minimizing ritual as a reaction against the over emphasis at the expense of the underlying values of Judaism. Those objections were valid and appropriate in an age when Judaism for many had become an automatic response with little attention to content. That period now lies behind us and we have seen that a certain number of rituals are necessary in order to provide concrete ways of expressing identity, prayer, sense of community, etc. For these and other reasons we have reintroduced ritual and moved in a different direction. It is perfectly possible therefore to conceive of a later edition of the prayerbook which will contain the second paragraph of the *shema*.

In light of these thoughts there would be no good reason for omitting the text from the *mezuzot*. That might have been suggested early in the century, but it was not and we should not consider this now. Furthermore, the *mezuzot* along with many other matters tie us together as a Jewish people. There is no good reason for introducing a change in the text of the *mezuzot* which would only divide us. This may not reflect consistency but in this matter as a fair number of others, it is probably wise not to be absolutely consistent.

December 1990

140. THE PAPER *MEZUZAH* TEXT

QUESTION: May the gift shop of a congregation sell *mezuzot* which contain the text on paper rather than on parchment as the tradition has mandated? (Rabbi Sue Levy, Houston TX)

ANSWER: The tradition of using parchment for the *Torah*, the *megillah* and the *mezuzah* has already been recorded in the tractate *Sofrim* 1:1 ff; *Mezuzah* 1:1 and all later codes. Despite the use of paper alongside parchment during this and subsequent periods, parchment continued to be mandated probably as it was more durable and was readily available. Irrespective of the reasons involved, tradition has demanded parchment. We must now ask whether there is any good reason for us to change this tradition? For us in the twentieth century the use of a traditional *Torah*, *megillah*, and *mezuzah* serves as a direct link with the past and with fellow Jews. As Reform Jews we are open to suggestions for change, but only for good and valid reasons. No such reasons exist in this instance. We may contrast this with the use of a *Torah* which is very expensive. If a congregation cannot afford a *Torah* then it may simply read from a printed Bible until a *Torah* can be acquired (W. Jacob *Contemporary American Reform Responsa* #69). No great

223

expense is involved with a *mezuzah*. It is possible for everyone to set aside enough money to purchase a *mezuzah* with the proper parchment.

We should be careful about any unnecessary escalation of the costs of this parchment. It might well be possible for congregations to train scribes who can produce *mezuzot* and do so at a minimal charge or perhaps as a gift to the congregation. We at Rodef Shalom years ago trained a high school student who wrote a *megillah* which we still use. This should be encouraged.

There are some unusual conditions under which a paper *mezuzah* may be acceptable. For example, during the recent persecution of Soviet Jews, affixing a *mezuzah* presented an act of courage. As a *kasher* text was difficult to obtain a printed text was acceptable under those circumstances until an appropriate text could be obtained.

It is especially important for a synagogue gift shop to sell only *kasher mezuzot*. Anyone purchasing a *mezuzah* would assume that the text was *kasher*. A printed text violates the prohibition of Leviticus "do not place a stumbling block before the blind" (Lev 19:14). If for some reason a paper text is provided by the supplier, then this should be made absolutely clear to the purchaser. Better yet, a *kasher* text should be substituted.

In summary, therefore, the gift shop of a congregation should sell only *mezuzot* with a *kasher* text. Anything less would be inappropriate.

February 1990

141. *MEZUZAH* ON A TRAILER

QUESTION: A young man has taken a position on an Indian reservation for a period of three months; he will live in a trailer. Is it appropriate to affix a *mezuzah* to the door of the trailer as this is only a temporary home? (Clark Fishman, Tuscon AZ)

ANSWER: If a trailer is to be used for a very short time, as for example for a vacation, as I have seen often on family camping trips, then it is not necessary to affix a *mezuzah*. It is not required on a *succah* or a cabin on a ship, etc. (*Shulhan Arukh* Yoreh Deah 286.11 ff). Here, however, we are dealing with a semi-permanent residence which will be home for a period of time. He should, therefore, treat this as his permanent home and place a *mezuzah* on the door. Perhaps, as these trailers are treated with less care than a normal house, he should not leave the *mezuzah* when he moves (*Shulhan Arukh* Yoreh Deah 291.2) but remove it.

December 1989

142. KISSING A HEBREW BOOK

QUESTION: I have seen many traditional Jews kiss a book which has been dropped. What is the reason for this and what is the origin of this custom? (Lottie Treidel, Pittsburgh PA)

ANSWER: Reverence for books which contain the tetragrammaton has been associated with the reverence for the

Divine name itself.

Sensitivity about the written name of God was partially derived from the command to obliterate names of the idols (Deut. 12.3 ff.) with the subsequent injunction that this was not to be done to "the Lord your God." Our concern with the name of God stems equally from the third commandment: "You shall not take the name of the Lord your God in vain" (Ex 20.7; Deut 5.11), and one interpretation of this commandment (W. Jacob "The Third Commandment" unpublished Prize Essay, Hebrew Union College, 1953). There was some discussion of this matter in the *Talmud* (Arahin 6a) in which we heard of a pagan who gave a large wooden beam to be used in the construction of the Temple. It was incised with the name of God and there was some question whether the beam could be worked and the name of God erased. *Talmudic* authorities decided that this incised name was not sacred as it was not the usual place in which the name of God was written. The medieval authorities agreed with this thought (Rashi *ad loc*; *Yad* Hil Yesodei Torah 6.1 ff).

The *Talmud* continued the discussion and indicated that despite the passage in *Arahin* in most instances the name was to be preserved (Mak 22a) and the later tradition agreed (*Yad* Hil Yesodei Torah 6.1 ff). Our texts dealt with the name inscribed on pieces of metal or tattooed on skin, uses which were not normal. These discussions brought about a later absolute reverence for the name of God which was never to be obliterated or destroyed (*Sefer Hahinukh* #437; B. Jacob *Im Namen Gottes* pp 164 ff). All of this has led to great care with printed texts.

The actual custom of kissing a book which has been dropped arose in the Middle Ages in Germany and was first found among the Hassidim (*Sefer Hassidim* #691). The custom was probably also influenced by the other *minhag* of fasting if a *Torah* Scroll was accidently dropped (*Shulhan Arukh* Orah Hayim 40.2; *Mishpetei Shemuel* #12).

Both of these customs together have emphasized the sacredness of Hebrew books and the respect which they deserve. Such a reverence for books has been an important educational element in our life and should be fostered.

July 1988

143. THE HEBREW BIBLE ON COMPUTER

QUESTION: A disk which contains portions of the Hebrew Bible has been used in our Religious School for some time. Should this disk be treated with the same reverence as a Hebrew Bible? If some computer errors occur, may the disk be reformatted and the text reentered as is the normal procedure with computer text? (Samuel Thompson, San Francisco CA)

ANSWER: A computerized text stores the information in a binary form; in other words, the actual letters of the alphabet and the combinations into sentences have been translated from the Hebrew alphabet into a different form of transliteration. Although it is possible through the electronic means to retrieve the original Hebrew text from that coded transliteration, an actual change must take place in order for the Hebrew text to appear. If one were to see the binary form of the Bible it would be totally incomprehensible. We need, therefore, not consider the normal restrictions on the misuse of the name of God (Ex 20.7; Deut 5.11; Deut 12.3 ff) which do not extend to transliterations or translations.

It is correct that the name of God must never be removed

227

from any place in which it has been written with intent, and this has certainly been done with intent (*Shulhan Arukh* Yoreh Deah 274 and commentaries; Simon ben Zemah of Duran *Responsa Tashbetz* I.177). In this instance we are not dealing with either a Hebrew text or with a recognizable name of God written in the customary fashion. The computer disk, therefore, may be reformatted and the information encoded again properly if the original text was destroyed.

November 1990

144. ERASING THE NAME OF GOD FROM THE COMPUTER SCREEN

QUESTION: The writer is using traditional Hebrew Biblical texts in his studies. They have been entered into his computer screen. He needs to erase them constantly as he moves forward or manipulates the screen. This leads to erasing the divine name. Is this permissible? (Levi Dannenberg, Boston MA)

ANSWER: The tradition was concerned with reverence for the written name of God, the *tetragramaton*. This was one understanding of the third commandment (Ex 20.7; Deut 5.11), and also of the commentaries to an injunction in Deuteronomy (12.3 ff). In the considerable discussion which followed in subsequent literature, we find an emphasis on the sacredness of the name of God whether written in the *Torah,* another book, on a metal vessel, or even as a tattoo on the skin (*Yad* Hil Yesodei Torah 6.1; *Sefer Hahinukh* #437). Ultimately, the decision was made that the name was sacred only if it was written with intent to be sacred (*Shulhan Arukh* Yoreh Deah 274 and commentaries).

The computer disk intends to make the text available for study and not for any sacred purpose. Furthermore, removing a section from the screen is akin to turning the page and does not obliterate the item from memory. If we take this one step further and ask whether such a disk can be reformatted, or must it be buried like a book? We may state that the recorded form is not Hebrew but binary, and it becomes Hebrew only through a transformation which takes place through the computer program. The above mentioned care does not apply to translations or transliterations. It is permissible to utilize the text on the computer and to erase it when the user has finished it.

January 1991

145. THE NAME OF GOD

QUESTION: Our librarian has asked to what extent we treat the name of God as sacred. He is concerned about two different matters: a) the library subscribes to a number of Israeli Hebrew newspapers and magazines which regularly deal with religious matters and use *adonai* (the *tetragramaton*), *elohim* or *el*; b) various classes in the religious school use photo copies of prayers as well as *Torah* portions in order to practice reading. Need any of these Hebrew texts be buried or be disposed through incineration? May they simply be discarded? (Edward Feinberg, Boston MA)

ANSWER: Sensitivity about the written name of God was partially derived from the command to obliterate names of the idols (Deut 12.3 ff) with the subsequent injunction that this was not to be done to "the Lord your God." Our concern with the name of God stems equally from the third commandment, "You shall not take the name of the Lord your God in vain," (Ex 20.7; Deut 5.11) and one interpretation of this commandment. There was some discussion of this matter in the *Talmud* (Arahin 6a) in which we heard of a pagan who gave a large wooden beam to be used in the construction of the Temple. It was incised with the name of God and there was some question whether the beam could be worked and the name of God erased. *Talmudic* authorities decided that this incised name was not sacred as it was not the usual place in which the name of God was written. The medieval authorities agreed with this decision (Rashi *ad loc*; *Yad* Hil Yesodei Torah 6.1 ff).

The *Talmud* continued the discussion and indicated that despite the passage in *Arahin* in most instances the name was to be preserved (Mak 22a) and the later tradition followed this precaution (*Yad* Hil Yesodei Torah 6.1 ff). Our texts dealt with the name inscribed on pieces of metal or tattooed on skin, uses which were not normal. These discussions brought about a later absolute reverence for the name of God which was never to be obliterated or destroyed (*Sefer Hahinuh* #437). This has led to great care with printed texts.

Tradition has, however, also asked about the individual who was responsible for the text and sanctity was limited to texts written by the pious Jews with sacred intent both explicitly stated or in the mind of the writer (*Shulhan Arukh* Yoreh Deah 274 and commentaries). A piece written without such intent could be erased (Tashbetz *Responsa* I.177). Simon ben Zemah of Duran based this line of reasoning on an incident described in the *Talmud* in which he wrote the *tetragramaton* by mistake and so definitely not with intent (Git 20a).

As we look at the reasoning, we see that tradition has leaned toward strictness certainly with the *tetragramaton* and possible also with other names of God. These discussions were mainly from periods in which books were scarce and the printer's piety could be assumed. Matters are different in contemporary Israel. Furthermore we would face an unusual burden if we tried to deal with the ordinary Hebrew newspaper or magazine in this fashion. We may on the contrary assume that no sacred intent was present.

It is a different matter when we are dealing with photocopies of *Torah* portions or prayerbooks. The text of these are educational tools that should be treated as sacred, for this too is part of the religious education of our children. They should learn appropriate respect for prayerbooks, Bibles and other traditional literature. When such loose pages are no longer usable they should not be discarded but either buried or incinerated if that is possible.

December 1990

146. SHREDDING SERVICES TO PROTECT GOD'S NAME

QUESTION: My synagogue is faced with the problem of xerox services and other material for children which contain the Divine name; it is not practical to bury. The congregation would like to purchase a shredder and thereby destroy the material. Is this an acceptable way of dealing with the problem of the sacred name. (Lloyd Silver, New York NY)

ANSWER: The sacredness of the name of God and the care taken with it goes back to the Biblical period when the Divine name itself was pronounced only once by the high priest on *Yom Kippur*. It was not to be misused in any way. Sensitivity about the written name of God was partially derived from the command to obliterate

231

names of the idols (Deut. 12.3 ff.) with the subsequent injunction that this was not to be done to "the Lord your God." Our concern with the name of God stems equally from the third commandment, "You shall not take the name of the Lord your God in vain," (Exodus 20.7; Deuteronomy 5.11) and one interpretation of this commandment. There is some discussion of this matter in the *Talmud* (Arahin 6a) in which we hear of a pagan who gave a large wooden beam to be used in the construction of the Temple. It was incised with the name of God and there was some question whether the beam could be worked and the name of God erased. *Talmudic* authorities decided that this incised name was not sacred as it was not the usual place in which the name of God was written. The medieval authorities agreed with this thought (Rashi *ad loc*; *Yad* Hil Yesodei Torah 6.1 ff).

The *Talmud* continued the discussion and indicated that despite the passage in *Arahin*, in most instances the name was to be preserved (Mak 22a) and the later tradition agreed (*Yad* Hil Yesodei Torah 6.1 ff). Our texts dealt with the name inscribed on pieces of metal or tattooed on skin, uses which were not normal. These discussions brought about a later absolute reverence for the name of God; it was never to be obliterated or destroyed (*Sefer Hahinuh* #437). This has led to great care with printed texts.

Tradition has, however, also asked about the individual who was responsible for the text, and sanctity was limited to texts written by the pious Jews with sacred intent both explicitly stated or in the mind of the writer (*Shulhan Arukh* Yoreh Deah 274 and commentaries). A piece written without such intent could be erased (Tashbetz *Responsa* I.177). Simon ben Zemah of Duran based this line of reasoning on an incident described in the *Talmud* in which a person wrote the *tetragramaton* by mistake and so without intent (Git 20a).

YOREH DEAH

As we look at the reasoning, we see that tradition has leaned toward strictness certainly with the *tetragramaton* and possible also with other names of God. These discussions were mainly from periods in which books were scarce and the printer's piety was assumed

Great care was always taken with the name of God and every effort made to protect texts containing it from misuse. For this reason, we have either placed such documents in a *genizah*, buried them in a cemetery or destroyed them through incineration. Each method did not prevent the ultimate destruction of the texts and no effort was made to preserve it. The real task was that of protecting the text from an improper use which would be offensive. We could well say then that it would be appropriate to shred such texts especially if the shredding machine were able to grind the material into very narrow strips. That would totally destroy their usefulness and it would be almost akin to incineration. We should only be certain that once the text has been shredded it is not used as packing material, but recycled.

This method of disposal is acceptable as it removes such documents from circulation. In our modern society with heavy use of paper for educational purposes, this is probably the most appropriate way of dealing with the problem.

October 1991

147. REFUSAL OF IMMUNIZATION

QUESTION: A family in the congregation, for reasons of it's own, does not wish to have their child immunized. Normally children who attend both religious and public school are immunized unless there is a specific religious reason which prevents the parents from doing so. What is our Reform Jewish attitude toward the parents and their decision, and secondly what should be the attitude of the Religious School in registering this child? (Rabbi J. M. Parr, Atlanta GA)

ANSWER: The Jewish tradition has sought to do everything possible to cure those who are ill and to prevent disease. There is a long honored history of Jewish physicians from Asaph in the early Middle Ages to modern times which has demonstrated that some of our best minds have devoted themselves to medicine. Among them were Moses Maimonides and a host of others who were also great Jewish scholars (H. Friedenwald *Jewish Luminaries in Medical History; Jews and Medicine*). In the twentieth century a large number of Jews have been particularly involved with seeking ways of immunizing in order to prevent diseases. For example, Salk and Sabin with the polio vaccine.

Health has always been considered a primary good, so *pikuah nefesh* has been considered as overriding virtually every religious prohibition in order to cure or save a life. The *shabbat* commandment, those of *kashrut*, and all except the most basic precepts may be violated in order to save a life and restore health. There were some discussions in the literature which dealt with medicines and vaccines prepared from non-kosher substances. Their use is, of course, permitted. I have found no other mention of immunization in the responsa literature.

The rejection of immunization by these parents is certainly outside the basic mood of the Jewish tradition. Unless there is a very specific medical reason, nothing in Jewish thought or *halakhah* would condone this.

Now let us look at the child's enrollment in Religious School. The requirement of immunization by the public school authorities is a way of assuring universal immunization and as a method of protecting the other children. It also, of course, protects an entire population as broad immunization will effectively eliminate certain diseases from the schools. The public schools and the courts have, however, decided that if there is a strong religious objection the child need not be immunized and is nevertheless required to attend public school. That child is equally liable to the laws of school attendance as all others. The school authorities therefore, feel that the failure of a few children to be immunized will not harm the others.

We should follow the same pattern in our religious schools. Although there is no basis in Judaism for the action of the parents, we believe them to be misguided and outside the realm of Jewish tradition. Nevertheless, the youngster should be accepted in the Religious School and enrolled as any other child.

December 1990

148. CONSENT FOR A MEDICAL OPERATION

QUESTION: Does Jewish tradition require consent for a medical operation? Is oral or written consent required for the treatment of the patient by a physician? (Harold Goodman, Houston TX)

ANSWER: When tradition discussed the liability of physicians it felt that the patient had sought out the physician and, therefore, placed himself/herself into his/her hands. It was the individual's responsibility to seek the best physician for a particular ailment (Shab 32a). It was assumed that the physician had been trained appropriately and was licensed (Nachmanides *Torat Haadam* 12b; Simon ben Zemah of Duran *Responsa* Vol 3; *Tur* Yoreh Deah 336; *Shulhan Arukh* Yoreh Deah 336; Eliezer Waldenberg *Tzitz Eliezer* Vol 5 #23). As long as the physician has treated the patient in a responsible manner, no liability was incurred (J. Preuss *Biblical and Talmudic Medicine* p 28 ff).

No specific permission was normally given except for circumcision where the responsibility of the operation rested with the father. He could assign it to another person and it was usually the *mohel* (Gen. 17.11; *Yad* Hil Milah; *Shulhan Arukh* Yoreh Deah 261). Permission in this case was oral.

The permission forms and other papers which are commonly signed in our hospitals are the result of law suits brought against physicians and hospitals for malpractice. They have led to caution. There is, however, no Jewish basis for this kind of caution. When a person had placed himself/herself into the hands of the physician, that indicates the acceptance of treatment which was suggested. The patient always possessed the right to change physicians or to remove himself/herself from any physicians care.

December 1989

149. RESPONSIBILITY TOWARD A DRUG USER

QUESTION: What kind of ethical responsibility do parents have toward their son now in his thirties who is married and on drugs? There is considerable tension between the parents and both son and daughter-in-law. (Errol Canter, San Diego CA)

ANSWER: There is surprisingly little information about the use of drugs in the vast responsa literature. Although hundreds of thousands of responsa exist and many of them from societies in which drugs were widely used this does not seem to have been a Jewish problem in earlier periods. Certainly the use of drugs is prohibited as is anything else which may seriously injure an individual (Deut 4.9; 4.15; Ber 32b; B K 91b; *Yad* Hil Rotzeah Ushemirat Hanefesh 11.4; Hil Shavuot 5.57; Hil Hovel Umaziq 5.1). No one is to endanger their life or permanently effect their health in a negative fashion.

We must, however, ask whether this remains the responsibility of the parents or is it entirely in the hands of the younger generation. The traditional view has parents responsible for the acts of their children to the age of maturity. In an earlier time this was at age thirteen (*Bar Mitzvah* or puberty). In our age, although this remains technically so, parental responsibility in fact continues through the years of further education often to the end

237

of college or certainly until secular legal maturity is reached at age twenty-one. After that time, although parents may advise and often will be called upon to help, their responsibility is limited. They may be much saddened and may feel guilty about what they did or did not do earlier in life. Most of these feelings are misplaced as someone in his thirties is completely independent and should be responsible for his own actions. It would be wise if the parents continue to be helpful and try to get the young man involved in a treatment program but direct responsibility is no longer theirs.

June 1989

150. STERILIZATION

QUESTION: A married couple is physically capable of procreation but prefers to adopt children rather than to produce their own biological children. Their motivation is altruistic and demonstrates a strong sense of ethical obligation to give a good home to a Third World child. Under such circumstances may the the couple undergo sterilization? Would adoption be considered equivalent to fulfilling the *mitzvah* of *peru urvu*? (Rabbi Dena A. Feingold, Kenosha WI)

ANSWER: It is, of course, noble and highly commendable that this young couple will provide a home for some Third World children and thus help those children who otherwise would have a doubtful future. That should be encouraged, however, it need not be connected with sterilization especially as the Jewish tradition feels so strongly on this subject. The *halakhah* which prohibits sterilization is based upon a Biblical verse (Lev 22.24). That was subsequently amplified by the rabbinic tradition (San 70a; Kid 25b; Hag 14b; Shab 10b; ff). The various codes as well as recent works continue to discuss sterilization and rejected it (*Yad* Hil Issurei Biah 16; *Shulhan Arukh* Even Haezer #20; *Noam* Vol 1 pp 257 ff; *Otzar Haposqim* Even Haezer Vol I #68 ff). Our Reform tradition has also emphasized the need to have children, but has approved temporary methods of birth control (W. Jacob (ed) *American Reform* Responsa #156) which would be helpful to the couple. For a discussion of adoption, see other responsa in this and previous volumes.

We should consider another sad factor; it is realistic to note that the instability of marriage today and the rate of divorce may lead the present family unit to collapse and each partner may regret his/her sterilization in the future. For that added reason it would be wrong to move in the direction of permanent sterilization. The Reform Jewish tradition therefore would congratulate the couple on what they plan, but sterilization is inappropriate.

August 1989

151. DRUGS TO RELIEVE PAIN

QUESTION: Does Jewish tradition set a limit to the use of drugs in order to alleviate pain? Frequently, physicians seem hesitant to prescribe drugs due to the fear of addiction or other reasons. What is our attitude toward pain and its alleviation? (Rena T. Hirsh, Santa Barbara CA).

ANSWER: Jewish tradition is not ascetic and does not endorse self affliction through pain. The only exception is *Yom Kippur* along with some of the lesser fast days. On that day we are commanded to "afflict our souls," but that does not entail real suffering, only fasting and abstinence from sexual intercourse. Even fasting is not necessary for those who are physically impaired. We feel no necessity to renounce this world and its blessings and so need not afflict ourselves in order to attain salvation in the next world. This is in vivid contrast to some forms of Christianity.

It is true that rabbinic tradition has interpreted the suffering of the people of Israel and of individuals, as either Divine punishment or as a test (Job; B B 5a; Shab 55a, etc). However, in none of the sources and many others has anyone been asked to seek suffering, rather we try to avoid it. During illness we may use every medical means available to avoid pain (*Shulhan Arukh* Yoreh Deah 241.13 and commentaries).

There are enormous variations in the pain threshold of individuals. Many physicians refuse to consider this or do not appropriately deal with the entire issue of pain. Sometimes this is because specialists, who do not communicate with each other, are treating the patient; each is concerned with a specific organ or system and none is aware of the total effect on the patient. At other times, it is simply due to indifference and a lack of interest in the patient, possibly because the attending physician has never suffered any serious pain. There is certainly nothing within Jewish tradition which would restrain the treatment of pain. We would have a greater fear of continuous pain than addiction.

We must be equally concerned with pain of the terminally ill. There is a fine line of distinction between alleviating pain and prescribing a drug which may hasten death. When the pain is great the physician should alleviate the pain and not be overly concerned about the latter consequence, as death is certain in any case. (W. Jacob (ed) *American Reform Response #79*, etc).

There is nothing within Jewish tradition that would keep pain medication from being given when medically indicated. We would hope that the patient be made as comfortable as possible and that this will help recovery or make the last days of life easier.

August 1991

152. A MEDICAL EXPERIMENT

QUESTION: A patient is afflicted with a fatal disease which leads to an unpleasant death. An effort to control it for a short period of time (less than one year) can be made through using drugs which in the final stages have the following side effects: The body skin peels constantly and this is accompanied by pain which no drug will alleviate. Some researchers feel that the full effects of the medicine can only be studied through such human utilization. Should a physician permit his patient to undergo this treatment? (Rabbi Mark Staitman, Pittsburgh PA)

ANSWER: The general principles governing our question are fully discussed by the modern Israeli authority, A. Abraham (*Lev Avraham* Vol II pp 75-76; Meiri to San 84b; I.Y. Unterman *Noam* Vol 12 pp 5 ff). He stated that no doctor has the right to subject another person to a medical experiment even though such an experiment may eventually help others. The doctor may expose himself/herself to danger (*sofeq sakana*) when she/he attends an infectious patient, as that is her/his duty as a physician, but he cannot ask a patient to submit to danger. The author adds that if the experiment is *not* dangerous, then the patient may participate in it and that would be reckoned as a *mitzvah*. Eliezer Waldenberg (*Ttzitz Eliezer* Vol XIII #103; Moses Sofer *Hatam Sofer* Yoreh Deah #76) disagreed with this view of safe experiments and denied any religious obligation even when there was no danger. At the most, one may permit such participation, but it is in no sense a religious duty (*mitzvah*).

It is a general rule that every person should avoid danger to life. So, the *Talmud* (Ber 3a; Shab 32a) warned people against walking among ruined buildings as a weak wall may collapse. The *Talmud* (Hul 10a) stated that danger to life and health was of greater concern than religious prohibitions (*sakanta tamira meissura*). In other words, one must exercise greater care to avoid danger than a religious prohibition.

This general rule of avoiding danger is, however, confronted with the duty of rescuing a fellow human. Discussion of these issues have continued through the centuries (Lev. 19.16; San 73a; *Yad* Hil Rotzeah Ushemirat Nefesh 1:2, 14, 15; *Shulhan Arukh* Hoshen Mishpat 426). The question then is to what extent we may endanger ourselves in order to help others. There is no doubt that we must assist our fellow human beings, but where are the limits? This question has been discussed in a rather picturesque responsa of the 16th century scholar David ibn Zimri of Egypt (Vol III #627): The Pasha told a certain Jew to allow his leg to be amputated or else he (the Pasha) would kill another Jew. May this man endanger his life through the amputation in order to save the life of a fellow Jew? David ibn Zimri considered this beyond the call of duty.

The medieval *Sefer Hassidim* (#467 (ed) Margolis) described a medicine which cured or killed the patient in nine days. The book prohibited the drug on the basis that it might kill the patient before his time (*qodem simno*). A number of later authorities have agreed with this assessment (*Shevut Yaaqov* I #13, III #85; *Binyan Zion* #111; *Hatam Sofer* Yoreh Deah #76).

In this instance the patient appears to be doomed by the disease, and both patient and doctor have a choice whether to use this experimental treatment which leads to a horrifying death or whether a natural death somewhat sooner and also unpleasant shall be permitted. No one should persuade the patient to undertake this therapy which leads to a terrible death even if the patient may wish to help others and to use the last portion of his/her life in some useful fashion. In this instance the weeks of agony before death are so terrible that we can not justify the "treatment". It is unlikely that the patient or the family will be able to imagine the horrifying nature of this death. We should therefore do everything possible to persuade the attending physician not to suggest this treatment if he/she feels that it must be mentioned then to put it into the bleakest possible context so that the patient is unlikely to choose it.

We cannot justify an experiment which will cause long terrible suffering through the vague hope that it will eventually produce a cure for others. The researchers who are working on this project must devise another means of testing their therapy.

February 1991

153. PATENTING GENETIC ENGINEERING *

QUESTION: May genetically engineered changes in a mouse designed for medical experiments be patented? (Arthur Gershman, Arlington VA)

ANSWER: The members of the Responsa Committee who discussed this question felt a high degree of discomfort with patenting changes in a living creature. The animal itself should not be patented. An animal, in contrast to a plant, possesses an additional element of the sacred, (although the medieval discussion of whether an animal possesses a soul was inconclusive, and was left to the "days of the Messiah"). Animals possess a special relationship with human beings according to our tradition.

Social policy has led to plant patents. This has protected the livelihood of individuals and made a more abundant human existence possible. However, patenting an animal leads us in a direction not conducive to respect for life. The Holocaust has made us aware of the dangers of dehumanization, the process, i.e. the genetic change, may be patented but the mouse itself should not be patented.

If we look at patents and the protection they offer within Judaism, we realize that the notion of protecting an idea or a newly created work is fairly new. There were periods in our history when the originator of a new work sought to make it seem old and thereby give it a greater acceptance. That was true of large anonymous sections of the Bible which have been added to various prophetic books, the apocryphal books and of such works as the *Zohar*. In modern times we have sought to protect the creative efforts of individuals. We may link this to the traditional concern for protecting an individuals livelihood. It was always considered

244

important to assure the livelihood of craftsman, artisans, teachers and tradesmen in the community by limiting the access of others or prohibiting it entirely. This was carefully balanced throughout the ages with a concern for the economic well being of the community and concern about a potential monopoly which might drive prices excessively high (*M* B M 4.5; B B 21a; Kid 59a and commentaries; *Yad* Hil Zekia Umatanah 1.14; *Tur* and *Shulhan Arukh* Hoshen Mishpat 156; Meir of Rothenburg *Responsa* #544; etc).

Even in conjunction with "sacred" areas as the teaching and interpretation of the written and oral law, great care was exercised to protect the jurisdiction and status of rabbis and teachers. Some authorities like Isserlein and Weill permitted competition and felt that it was good for the community (Weill *Responsa* #151; Isserlein *Terumat Hadeshen* #128). Israel Isserlein made his decision on the basis of encouraging the study of *Torah*. Some later authorities agreed with them. Many scholars felt that the appointed rabbi of the community had a right to protect his status, both as a teacher and a judge. He could also protect the income from these and other sources (*Avnei Nezer* Yoreh Deah 312.37; *Meshiv Davar* I 8, 9; *Hatam Sofer* Hoshen Mishpat #21; *Mayim Amuqim* #70). The *Shulhan Arukh* and its commentaries present both points of view (*Shulhan Arukh* Yoreh Deah 245.18 ff). This equivocation on the part of the medieval authorities was intended to encourage strong scholarly leadership.

Matters changed when the modern rabbinate became a profession and the rabbis livelihood depended upon services rendered to the congregation. Under these circumstances, it was forbidden to trespass on another rabbi's territory (Moses Sofer *Hatam Sofer* Hoshen Mishpat #21; Yoreh Deah #32; *Meshiv Davar* #8). Some disagreement remained on the right of a newcomer to teach as this is a *mitzvah* and its fulfillment should not be denied to anyone (Elijah ben Hayim *Mayim Amuqim,* #70; Akiva Eger, *Responsa Tanina* #12; Abraham Mordecai Halevi *Ginat Veradim* Yoreh Deah 3.7). Livelihoods were protected and the matter under discussion is related to this question.

Similarly books of prayer which were in the public domain and which could be considered part of the divine tradition were protected through copyright. So, for example, the first edition of the famous Heidenheim *Mahzor* printed in Roedelheim contained statements by four prominent rabbis granting a copyright. When a printer in Sulzbach proceeded to re-publish the work, a special statement warning against its purchase was issued by Pinhas Horowitz of Frankfurt (final page Heidenheim *Mahzor* 1832). Many responsa subsequently have dealt with copyrights. The main consideration was the effort and investment made in the work; without protection publishers would be unwilling to undertake such risks (Moses Sofer *Responsa* Hoshen Mishpat #41; etc). All of these instances indicate that protection of an invention is permitted and may be considered necessary as well as desirable.

We can see that the pattern of tradition intended to protect someone's livelihood and reflected social policy. As we look at this social policy in connection with medical experiments we must always ask ourselves whether this enhances or diminishes the respect for human life and all life.

In conclusion we have many reservations about patenting an animal and would reject that concept. We also have reservations about the implications of patenting the genetic change. We would tentatively agree to patenting the process.

March 1989

154. JEWISH INVOLVEMENT IN GENETIC ENGINEERING *

QUESTION: May a Jew genetically alter a mouse or may a Jew use a mouse if it has been genetically engineered by a Gentile? What is the status of animals in Jewish law? (Arthur P. Gershman, Arlington VA)

ANSWER: Genetic engineering is a field which is still in its infancy but we can expect major advances in this area in the future. At the moment it is possible to introduce permanent genetic changes in plants, animals and human beings. There are many questions about the control which needs to be exercised and the dangers which may arise from new, altered, or hitherto unknown, substances formed through these methods. Unusual safeguards have been proposed both by the scientific community, national and international agencies. Such caution is wise and we should proceed carefully even when we are dealing with animals. This responsum is not intended to discuss genetic engineering in human beings.

We will, perhaps, begin with the question of the status of animals in relationship to human beings and then turn to genetic engineering.

The Biblical statement in Genesis (2.26) placed people above animals and enabled them to rule them and therefore to use them in any way that seemed appropriate and certainly to save a life (*pikuah nefesh*). So, for example, cattle could be used for food or for various kinds of work (B M 86b; Hag 3b; Meila 13a; A Z 5b, etc). Consumption or sacrifice was limited to those deemed clean (Lev 11.3 ff); the list included both animals, birds, as well as fish. Other animals which were unclean could be used by man in various ways. There were few limits on the manner of catching or housing animals as long as it was humane so a varieties of means of catching birds were discussed in the *Talmud* (B M 42a; *Taanit* 22a; Sab 78b; Ber 9b; etc.) Animals which endangered human beings such as wolves and lions could be destroyed (Ber 13a). This was even more true of pestilent insects such as grasshoppers, mosquitoes or scorpions and ants. Crop eating field mice and rats could also be destroyed (*Taanit* 19a; 14a; Sab 121b; M K 6b). The *Midrash* which sought to find a use for some such animals like fleas and mosquitoes stated that they were created in order to plague evil people (*Midrash Rabbah* Vayikra 189).

Animals could be used by man as long as they were treated kindly. It is prohibited to consume a limb from a living animal (B M 32b). An animal which was threshing may not be muzzled; it must be permitted to eat as freely as a human being (Deut 23.25 f; B M 87b, 90a; *Yad* Hil Zekirut 13.3; *Shulhan Arukh* Hoshen Mishpat 338). Furthermore, one should not consider acquiring an animal unless one has the means to feed it (*J* Ket 4.8) and a person should then feed his animals before feeding himself (Git 62a; *Yad* Hil Avadim 9.8).

Unnecessary pain may not be inflicted on animals (Ex 23.5; B M 32a; *Yad* Hil Rotzeah 13.9; Solomon ben Aderet *Responsa* #252 #257). Some of the medieval scholars who were concerned with the protection of animals felt that those precautions needed to be stricter than with human beings, as animals do not have the intelligence to care for themselves or to take a longer view of matters (*Yad* Hil Zekhirut 13.2; David ibn Zimri *Responsa* I #728; Yair Hayim Bacharach *Havat Yair* #191; *Shulhan Arukh* Hoshen Mishpat 337.2). Biblical law prohibited the killing of a mother with its young (Lev 12.28; Hul 83a; *Yad* Hil Shehitah 13; *Shulhan Arukh* Yoreh Deah 16). The later Jewish codes also insisted that a seller inform a buyer of the relationship between any animals sold so that a mother and its offspring would not be slaughtered together on the same day. A similar kind of provision forbade the taking of both a mother and a chick from the same nest. (Deut 12.6; Hul 138b *Shulhan Arukh* Yoreh Deah 292).

Kindness to animals included the lightening of the load from an overburdened animal (Ex 13.5). Domestic animals were required to rest on *shabbat* as human beings (Ex 20.10; 23.12; Deut 5.14). Provisions were made for animal care on *shabbat*, an animal which was normally milked by a non-Jew. If an animal needed to be rescued it was to be done even on *shabbat* (Shab 128a; *Yad* Hil Shabbat 25.26;1 *Shulhan Arukh* Orah Hayim 305.19).

We should also note that the castration of animals was prohibited and this has always been considered as a form of maiming, which was forbidden (*Shelat Yaabetz* 1.11). We may summarize this by relating that our tradition demands kind treatment of animals. They may be used by human beings but not treated cruelly. We should note that the medieval discussion by some Jewish philosophers about the soul of animals was left as a speculative issue.

Now let us deal with genetically induced changes in mice which are to be used as experimental animals. Systemic genetic changes are a recent scientific achievement. The only area which approached this field in the past was controlled breeding. Our tradition had very little to say about breeding animals as long as no attempt was made to do so with unlike species. There was a great interest in maintaining species of both plants and animals separately, based in part on Biblical verses (Lev 19.19; Deut 22.10). An entire section of the *Mishnah* (Kilaim) dealt with the problem of sowing various kinds of seeds together, grafting one plant onto another and interbreeding of animals. This segment of the *Mishnah* contains eight chapters which dealt with various kinds of mixtures such as the prohibition against interweaving wool and linen and with the cross breeding of certain species of animals or plants. The *Mishnah* and *Tosefta Kilaim* indicated a fascination with mixtures and sought to explain the natural world from this perspective. The *Mishnah Kilaim* presented two points of view according to a recent scholarly volume by Avery-Peck. The circle of Yavneh argued that species were to be kept separate as God created order in the Universe and it was Israel's duty to maintain this separation.

Those of Usha argued that Israel imposed order on the natural world and Israel now had to maintain it. Neither group ultimately included non-edible plants in their scheme. (A. J. Avery-Peck *The Mishnah's Division of Agriculture*)

When the *Mishnah Kilaim* dealt with animals, it was mainly concerned about unlike species harnessed together or interbred. Neither the *Mishnah* nor later Jewish literature prohibited ownership of animals bred in such a manner. Interest in this subject, however, diminished and so there was no Babylonian Talmud to these chapters of the *Mishnah* and later discussion of this material is sparse.

The chief Biblical section which deals with this issue, aside from the legislation mentioned above, is the story in Genesis in which the young Jacob promised to maintain the flock of Laban and as payment asked the speckled, spotted and dark colored sheep and goats. He then proceeded to influence the breeding in that direction. Ostensibly this was done through the placement of shoots of poplar, almond and plane trees but there has been some speculation that he possessed some knowledge of genetics which helped him to his goal of a large flock. That theory has been advanced by Judah Fliks ("Yorashah Usvivah Bemaaseh Yaakov Betzon Lavan" *Tehumin*, Vol III pp 461 ff). We should note that the Biblical commentators do not single this story out for special comment and to the best of my knowledge do not use it as an example of animal breeding.

There were occasional commentaries like Ramban who stated that human beings should not change nature as that would imply imperfection in God's creation (Ramban to Lev 19.19) That medieval view was found frequently in church literature. It has not been followed by Jewish thinkers.

Jewish law said nothing about changing the characteristics of a particular species or breed. Throughout the centuries every effort was made to assist nature and to produce animals suited to specific purposes as well as plants which would yield abundantly. Despite Jewish involvement in agriculture through the centuries, this matter has not been discussed in the older responsa literature, to the best of my knowledge. In modern times these efforts have been accelerated through selective breeding and an understanding of the genetic process. More recently cloning of plant tissues has been used successfully to produce plants which are absolutely true; this method holds great promise as well as potential dangers.

Genetic engineering of plants or animals within a species poses few old *halakhic* problems though it raises many other issues. Human beings have selective bred plants and animals since the beginning of herding and agriculture in order to adapt them to specific human needs and environments. Genetic engineering will vastly accelerate this process. This may eliminate poverty, famine and disease but may also bring scourges and problems which we can not foresee.

We are standing at the edge of a new scientific era. We certainly wish to utilize the potentials of genetic engineering for the benefit of humanity. That may be partially within our power. It is not within our power to stop the scientific experimentation. The human yearning to understand the divine creation and everything in it as fully as possible cannot be halted, nor can the desire to alleviate the problems of hunger, disease, and poverty.

As we learn more about the nature of genetic engineering we must discuss its moral implications both with regard to animals and human beings. We realize that the line between plants, animals, and human beings is thin and in some ways does not exist at all. So we must proceed with caution. In consort with others we must set limits and provide direction. We have, of course, become especially sensitive to all of these issues since the Holocaust and the terrible medical experimentation which occurred during the Holocaust.

We may be ready to accept genetic changes made for medical purposes and experimentation as *pikuah nefesh* is an overriding consideration (Shab 132a; Yoma 85b; *Tosefta* Shab 17 and Alfas; *Shulhan Arukh* Orah Hayim 328.1; Hatam Sofer *Responsa* Hoshen Mishpat #185). Human life must be saved if it is at all possible and even some pain to animals is permitted for this purpose. Economic reasons, however, could not justify such a course of action. These should always be reviewed carefully.

When dealing with experimental animals we should be quite certain that they are not subjected to pain or used for frivolous reasons as for example cosmetic experimentation.

A mouse engineered genetically for a specific set of experiments, which will eventually help human beings, lies within the boundaries of utilizing animals for the benefit of human beings. Naturally the humane treatment of the animals in accordance with our tradition must be observed. It would be appropriate for Jews to be involved in this kind of genetic engineering and to use the animals that they themselves have genetically changed.

March 1989

155. THE ABORTION OF AN ANENCEPHALIC FETUS

QUESTION: Can an anencephalic fetus be aborted? (Rabbi Lane Steinger, Oak Park MI)

ANSWER: An anencephalic fetus may be aborted under certain circumstances. The principal consideration, however, should be the condition of the mother and any danger, psychological or physical, which this fetus may pose. Some mothers may opt to carry the fetus to full term as they may not feel that the diagnosis is absolutely reliable although it is generally considered so. Our feeling about when abortion is permitted is summarized in a fairly full responsum (W. Jacob *Contemporary American Reform Responsa* #16). We are willing to permit abortion in the first trimester along with traditional authorities and would permit it later for serious reasons.

If the fetus is brought to term it would be considered a person. This status is attained as soon as the child has left the womb (*M* Oholot 7.6; *Shulhan Arukh*, Hoshen Mishpat 425.2; *Yad* Hil Rotzeah Ushemirat Hanefesh 1.1). Such an infant possesses all the rights of a human being although its life span may be doubtful. That has been the traditional attitude toward all newborn infants.

An anencephalic infant cannot survive for long. After it is clinically dead, vital organs may be taken for transplantation provided, of course, that the parents agree to this and that the other legal procedures have been followed. The human dignity of this child must be preserved as of any other infant.

September 1988

156. LIVING WILL *

QUESTION: What is the Jewish attitude toward a "living will"? (Loren Roseman, Norcross GA)

ANSWER: The "living will" provides a legal method in some thirty-seven states for terminating life support systems in the case of individuals who are dying because of serious illness or accident. The pain of family members or friends in comas over long periods of time and in a "persistent vegetative state" while attached to life preserving machinery has led to the consideration of such documents. At that juncture often no one will agree on what should be done. In some occasions the courts have intervened; in others eventually a family member or physician intervenes, but at the risk of subsequent legal action.

Those who wish to spare their family from this agonizing decision may decide on a "living will", a form frequently used with a proxy designation statement reads as follows:

Living Will Declaration

To My Family, Physician
and Medical Facility

I,..........., being of sound mind, voluntarily make known my desire that my dying shall not be artificially prolonged under the following circumstances:

If I should have an injury, disease or illness regarded by my physician as incurable and terminal, and if my physician determines that the application of life-sustaining procedures would serve only to prolong artificially the dying process, I direct that such procedures be withheld or withdrawn and that I be permitted to die. I want treatment limited to those measures that will provide me with maximum comfort and freedom from pain. Should I

254

become unable to participate in decisions with respect to my medical treatment, it is my intention that these directions be honored by my family and physicians)s) as a final expression of my legal right to refuse medical treatment, and I accept the consequences of this refusal.

Signed..................................Date....................Witness..............
............Witness...........................

Designation Clause (optional*)

Should I become comatose, incompetent or otherwise mentally or physically incapable of communication, I authorize....................
presently residing at...
to make treatment decisions on my behalf in accordance with my Living Will Declaration and my understanding of Judaism. I have discussed my wishes concerning terminal care with this person, and I trust his/her judgment on my behalf.

Signed..................................Date...................
Witness...........................Witness...........................

*If I have not designated a proxy as provided above, I understand that my Living Will Declaration shall nevertheless be give effect should the appropriate circumstances arise.

The various statutes specifically exclude chronic debilitating diseases such as Alzheimers which are not life threatening and attempt to deal with other problems as well.

This approach raises many questions about traditional and modern Jewish perceptions of life and death. Is this akin to suicide or euthanasia? Suicide has always been considered a major sin (A Z 18a; Semahot 2.2; *Shulhan Arukh* Yoreh Deah 345.2) and even its contemplation was considered wrong. We have also felt that euthanasia is not consistent with our tradition (W. Jacob (ed) *American Reform Responsa* #78, 79). We may see from the arguments presented in these two responsa that nothing positive

255

may be done to encourage death, however, the "Living Will" is not euthanasia, but an instrument of antidysthanonic. Our tradition has felt that a *goses* (dying person) should also not be kept from dying after all hope for recovery has passed, and so the *Sefer Hassidim* stated that if the steady rhythm of someone chopping wood kept a *goses* alive, the wood chopping should be stopped (#723; Isserles to *Shulhan Arukh* Yoreh Deah 339.1). Some rabbinic statements limit the definition of *goses* to persons who will not live for more than three days, however modern medical technology has made these limitations obsolete. Earlier Biblical statements clearly indicated that no positive acts to abbreviate life even when there was not hope were permitted (I Sam 31.1 ff; II Sam 1.5 ff). In a later age Solomon Eger indicated that medicine should also not be used to hinder a souls departure (comment to *Shulhan Arukh* Yoreh Deah 339.1). We may then safely say that at the critical juncture of life when no hope for recovery exists the soul should be allowed to drift away peacefully. We have become even more sensitive to issues of euthanasia through our own experiences with the Holocaust.

Love of life in all its forms is very much part of our tradition. Even when conditions of life are rather doubtful and when there might have serious questions about the "quality of life" we cannot encourage euthanasia (W. Jacob *Contemporary American Reform Responsa* #83) nor can we make assumptions about "the quality of life."

The modern development of medicine has brought wonderful cures and provides additional years of life even to those in advanced years. On the other hand its technology may leave us in a permanent coma or a persistent vegetative state in which we are neither alive nor dead. Such individuals may be completely dependent upon life support machinery. While this is acceptable during periods of recovery, we fear a permanent coma when the mind has ceased to respond and a plateau of mere physical existence has been reached.

When the Harvard criteria of death have been satisfied, life support machinery may be removed. This state of "brain dead" has been defined by an ad hoc committee of the Harvard Medical School in 1968 (*Journal of the American Medical Association* Vol 205, pp 337 ff). It recommended three tests: (1) Lack of response to external stimuli or to internal reed; (2) absence of movement and breathing as observed by physicians over a period of at least one hour; (3) absence of elicitable reflexes; and a fourth criterion to confirm the other three; (4) a flat or isoelectric electroencephalogram. The group also suggested that this examination be repeated after an interval of twenty-four hours. Several Orthodox authorities have accepted these criteria while others have rejected them. Moses Feinstein felt that they could be accepted along with shutting off the respirator briefly in order to see whether independent breathing was continuing (*Igrot Mosheh* Yoreh Deah #174). Moses Tendler has gone somewhat further and has accepted the Harvard criteria (*Journal of American Medical Association* Vol 238 #15 pp 165 ff). David Bleich (*Hapardes* Tevet 5737) and Jacob Levy (*Hadarom* Nisan 5731 Tishri 5730; *Noam* 5.30) have vigorously rejected these criteria as they feel that life must have ceased entirely with the heart no longer functioning, a condition belatedly established by Hatam Sofer in the eighteenth century (Responsa *Hatam Sofer* Yoreh Deah #338). We can see that although the question has not been resolved by our Orthodox colleagues, some of them have certainly accepted the recommendations of the Harvard Medical School committee. We are satisfied that these criteria comply with our concern that life has ended. Therefore, when circulation and respiration only continue through mechanical means, as established by the above-mentioned tests, then the suffering of the patient and his/her family may be permitted to cease, as no "natural independent life" functions have been sustained. We would permit a physician in good conscience to cease treatment and to remove life giving support systems. The "persistent vegetative state" is more difficult as "brain death" has not yet been reached. Such an individual would be considered a *goses* who is considered to be a living human being in all respects (Semahot 1.1; Yad Hil Evel 4.5; *Tur* and *Shulhan Arukh* Yoreh Deah 339.1 ff.). One may desecrate the Sabbath to help him according to Jacob Reischer (*Shevut Yaakov* 1:13), though others (*Kenesset Hagadol*) disagreed.

The long discussions about a *goses* indicate that no positive actions to hasten death may be taken, so he/she is not to be moved or his/her eyes closed, etc. As stated above there is no prohibition against diminishing pain or increasing the person's comfort or initiating new treatment which will not change the condition of the patient. Under these circumstances a "Living Will" may be helpful although we realize that we know little of the "inner life" of people in this state; we do not wish to terminate what may still be significant to them.

It would be permissible according to this point of view to help and assist those who may need to make these kinds of judgments for us in the future through a "Living Will". This may be especially important if there is no one present who can be counted on to make an appropriate decision in keeping with our verbally expressed wishes. The document must be worded so that it deals with the "persistent vegetative state" without moving toward euthanasia. The document should be sufficiently recent to assure that it reflects the wishes of the patient.

All of us wish for a reasonable exit from this world and would also like to make that period as bearable as possible for ourselves and our surviving family. The positive outlook on life which governs Judaism prohibits any drastic steps toward death but it does not insist that life continue when the person is a *goses*. At that point a peaceful release is permitted. The "Living Will" provides one possibility; the appointment of a proxy provide another.

March 1989

157. AN ELDERLY PATIENT WHO REFUSES DIALYSIS

QUESTION: An intelligent, articulate, eighty-three year old widow has renal disease which can be treated by kidney dialysis. She was diagnosed eight years ago and refused dialysis. Since then her health has generally deteriorated with a hip fracture, incontinence and heart disease. She has now entered a nursing home and suffers from end-stage renal disease as well as congestive heart failure. She has made it clear to her brother as well as those at the nursing home that she wishes no drastic treatments (CPR, mechanical ventilation, feeding tubes, etc.) but wants to die *peacefully and without pain*. One of the attending physicians feels a strong obligation to save this patient's life. He argues that he cannot let her die of renal kidney disease and wants to impose dialysis upon her. Should she be forced to undergo dialysis? What are her rights and obligations and what are those of the physician in this case. (Rabbi Dayle Friedman, Philadelphia PA)

ANSWER: A good deal has been written about the obligations of a physician to heal. Our tradition from *Talmudic* times onward has encouraged the use of every possible medical procedure in order to save lives. The discussions were based on "He shall cause him to be thoroughly healed" (Ex 21.20) and "You shall not stand idly by the blood of your fellow" (Lev 19.16). Even risky procedures may be undertaken if the physician thinks that there is a reasonable hope for recovery (San 73a; A Z 27b; J. Reischer *Shevut Yaakov* III #85; Eliezer Waldenberg, *Tzitz Eliezer* 10 #25 Chap 5 Sec 5; Moshe Feinstein *Igrot Mosheh* Yoreh Deah 2 #59; I. Y. Unterman *Noam* 12 p 5; W. Jacob (ed) *American Reform Responsa* #75, 76, 77, 79; W. Jacob *Contemporary American Reform Responsa* #77, 85). We have gone somewhat further and permitted a patient who understands the risks, to be part of a dangerous medical experiment in which the chances of recovery are slim (W. Jacob *Contemporary American Reform Responsa* #17).

Patients have always been encouraged to use physicians and to follow the Biblical dictum "Heal yourself". Physicians have been held in high regard from early times onward (*Ben Sirah* 38.1; *Tobit* 2.10, *Midrash Rabbah* Exodus 21.7; see also I. Jakobovits *Jewish Medical Ethics* pp 201 ff). On the other hand skepticism about physicians has also played its role in Jewish life; the *Mishnah* quotes R. Judah: "The best among physicians is destined for hell", (*M* Kid 4.14). All of these sources establish the physicians duty to heal as well as the patient's obligation to maintain good health and to do whatever is considered reasonable to regain health.

It has been established that nothing positive may be done to hasten death even in a terminal patient, yet, there is also no obligation to intervene in a hopeless situation to minimally prolong life (S. B. Freehof *Modern Reform Responsa* #34 and 35). In most instances in which this has been discussed the terminal patient is no longer capable of making rational decisions and must rely completely on those who are providing treatment. In this instance we are dealing with an individual who has made her wishes known.

We may understand the role which the patient and the physician play in their inter-relationship by looking at the frequently discussed theme of treatment for illness overriding various religious obligations. It has long been permitted to violate the Sabbath laws not only in order to save a life but even for someone who is dying (Yoma 84b; I. Lampronti *Pahad Yitzhaq Holeh Beshabbat* etc). The general principle is that if either the physician or the patient believe that a treatment is required and there is some risk to life then the normal religious legislation is suspended (*Shulhan Arukh* Orah Hayim 328.5 and commentaries). The decision favored the patient who considered a treatment necessary even if a hundred doctors considered it not sufficiently urgent to override religious obligations, "because a heart knows its own bitterness." This and other discussions indicate that the patient is heavily involved in the treatments and not merely a quiet and subservient recipient.

In the instance of our patients, proper persuasion might have brought the widow to dialysis eight years ago. The fact that she lived eight years without dialysis at this advanced age may indicate that she chose the appropriate path for herself. Now as she is suffering from end stage renal disease as well as congestive heart failure, it is not a question of saving her life, but possibly prolonging it at the expense of her dignity and with some pain both physical and psychological.

This patient rejected dialysis while living independently at home; and should not have dialysis imposed upon her now that she is dependent upon the services of a nursing home. Her attitude has led to a full, long life. Additional medical attention which she does not wish should not be forced on her; it is only likely to shorten her life. The physician has done his duty by suggesting the treatment. The patient who knows that she is close to the end of her life with or without the treatment and is not obligated to accept the suggestion.

November 1988

158. INFORMING A DYING PATIENT

QUESTION: The children have been informed that their mother is dying, and the physician believes that it is his responsibility to inform their mother of the hopelessness of her condition. The children have insisted that this news be kept from her as they feel it will hasten her death and make the last period of her life miserable. Which path should be followed? (Norman Levin, Cleveland OH)

ANSWER: It is our principle task during illness, including the final illness, to maintain an attitude of hope in the patient. Therefore, the rabbinic tradition rejected the approach of the prophet Isaiah to King Hezekiah in which he demanded that the king "set his house in order, for you will die and not live." (II Kings 20.1), actually the king was healed and survived. The *Talmudic* discussion of such situations felt that prayer and hope should not cease even when the outlook was bleak (Ber 10a). In another Biblical story which the rabbis quoted, the prophet Elijah was asked whether Ben Hadad the Aramean King would recover, and he lied to encourage him (II Kings 8.10 f). We may therefore stretch the truth to engender hope. This mood of hopefulness was carried even further by the injunction not to inform a seriously ill patient of the death of a relative as that might change her mood (*Shulhan Arukh Yoreh Deah* 377).

We must, of course, weigh this attitude against that of giving the patient sufficient time to prepare her affairs before death and also the opportunity to make confession (Sem 4.1; *M* San 6.2; 32a). In this instance there are no pressing business affairs which need to be settled. Personal confession can occur at any time; it need not be formalized into an occasion which will frighten the mother. The physician has done his duty by speaking of the condition to the children. If the mother inquires repeatedly from the physician and indicates that she wishes to know the truth, then she should be told to her. If that does not occur we should follow the path of tradition and the inclination of the children and allow the mother to retain her currently hopeful attitude.

July 1988

159. NUTRITION AND INCURABLE CANCER

QUESTION: Should nutrition in contrast to medicine be continued for a comatose patient who is suffering from incurable cancer? (Stanley Landman, San Antonio TX)

ANSWER: We need to make some distinctions immediately between a terminal cancer patient and a victim of stroke or an accident. In the latter cases, the prognosis is not at all certain and death may not be indicated in the foreseeable future. In the case of the incurable cancer patient, a time is reached when medicine can no longer be considered as healing and when the suffering patient is being kept alive artificially with no potential of improvement. When we have reached this point and nothing more can be done, then we may justifiably state that we are dealing with *goses* and should remove obstacles which may lead to an easier death (Ket 104a; Ned 40a; *Sefer Hassidim* #723; Isserles to *Shulhan Arukh Yoreh Deah* 339.1; *Even Haezer* 121.7; *Hoshen Mishpat* 221.2 and commentaries). We are willing to utilize modern medical criteria to determine when this stage has been reached (W. Jacob (ed) *American Reform Responsa* #79 etc). We realize that these criteria will be refined as medicine is making rapid strides. Medical and technical means need not be continued when the patient is dying and is only being kept alive through these means.

Now let us look at nutrition specifically. We should not think of it in terms of the meals which we normally eat but rather of nutrition provided intravenously or through a stomach tube. Both of these methods are certainly appropriate when they are part of the healing process and help the patient toward a cure. They should, however, be discontinued, just as medication when only they and medicine are artificially keeping the patient who is dying (*goses*) alive. Such feeding does not help the patient and at best must be debilitating, uncomfortable, if not painful. We should also realize that diminished interest by those patients normally capable of eating is another sign that life is ebbing and that the last stages have been reached. Our main goal should be the patient's comfort.

Nutrition artificially introduced at the last stage of life should be seen as a hinderance to death and may be stopped, along with medication. At the appropriate time, the family should be able in clear conscience, in line with Jewish tradition, to make this decision together with their physician.

August 1991

160. CPR AND THE FRAIL ELDERLY *

QUESTION: When elderly patients in a nursing home or hospital are in need of CPR is it advisable to initiate it among the frail elderly who are less likely to survive hospitalization subsequent to CPR than a younger person and who may even if they recover, be more frail and debilitated with a poorer quality of life? Should the patient or the official representative of the patient be able to indicate whether CPR should be initiated? What should the policy of long-term care institutions be in connection with Jewish patients? Should we make a distinction between patients who are likely to survive a year or more and those whose life span will be less? (Rabbi Lennard R. Thal, Los Angeles CA)

ANSWER: Traditional Judaism has been very careful about judgments of life and death. In earlier times and at the present it remains difficult for the medical profession to predict the length of life. We have all seen cases in which the general prognosis is poor but the spirit or physical condition of the patient enables that individual to survive considerable longer. Furthermore while some diseases rapidly take their toll among the elderly, others move much more slowly among them.

It is also virtually impossible to assess such matters as "the quality of life" and so Judaism has refrained from doing so. What might seem a very poor quality of life for some may be acceptable to others. In addition we must reckon with longer or shorter periods of depression which may strike such individuals either in the natural course of events or due to medication.

For these reasons and the general respect for life we have made no judgments on "quality of life" and would not consider that as a factor in instituting CPR or any other medical measures.

We should make a distinction between the frail elderly and a *goses* (a dying individual). Nothing needs to be done for someone who is clearly and obviously dying and whose death is close. At that stage we may not remove life support systems, but we also need not institute any procedures. There is a long tradition for allowing individuals not only a return to health but also a peaceful death.

Already in *Talmudic* times the pupil of Rabbi Judah Hanasi stopped his colleagues' prayers so he could die more comfortably (Ket 104a) and one may pray for death (Nisim Gerondi to Ned 40a). While in another instance a servant stopped the chopping of wood as the rhythmic beat of the axe disturbed the passage of the individual from this world (*Sefer Hassidim* #723).

The chief problem with a *goses* lies in the final stages when family, medical personnel, and hospitals may not know how to proceed and may fear legal or other consequences. This situation may be helped through some form of a "Living Will" which would describe the condition under which no further direct medical assistance should be provided. There are problems with the "Living Will" too. They have been described and discussed in another responsum in this volume. This is probably the best vehicle we now posses to deal with these issues.

The frail elderly should understand that they may amend or totally reject this document at any time. That is particularly important for individuals in an nursing home who may not have relatives nearby. In this way they will feel in control of their future rather than having the nursing home staff control their lives.

Under normal circumstance CPR should be given to the frail elderly if it can prolong their life. It should not be given to a *goses*.

April 1989

161. RESPONSIBILITY OF AN "AIDS" CARRIER *

QUESTION: An individual has been diagnosed as having AIDS, the testing has been positive, there is little room for doubt as he has developed some initial symptoms. Years may pass before other symptoms appear. It is currently estimated that at least thirty percent of carriers of AIDS will be affected by the syndrome. As a carrier he is also a transmitter of the syndrome; he is aware of the fact that the active stage of AIDS is fatal. The young man in question insists on continuing to be sexually active and is careless about using preventive measures like condoms. Would Judaism consider him a danger to society or if married, to his wife? Would Judaism label his transmission of AIDS as murder? What are his responsibilities to society? (D. R. Pittsburgh PA)

ANSWER: We sympathize with anyone struck by this illness and must help them in every way possible. AIDS victims must be protected from needless discrimination yet society must also protect itself from obvious dangers. Let us view this question from two different perspectives. First, let us look at the matter of his sexual activity and Judaism's attitude toward this. The question does not indicate whether the individual is homosexual, heterosexual, single or married. Let us initially assume that he is heterosexual, not married and that his sexual activities are conducted with a number of different partners. Traditional and Reform Judaism have, of course, rejected promiscuous sexual activity and we would reject his behavior on these grounds. In fact the *Talmud* assumed that if a man had intercourse, with a woman, that it was intended to be serious and would lead to marriage (*eyn adam oseh beilato bilat zenut* Yeb 107a; Ket 83a; Git 81b). There were many statements which prohibit sexual relations outside marriage (Prov 6.29,32; Lev 19.29, 20.10; *Tos* 1.4; etc) this applied to both men and women. All unmarried individuals were to refrain from sexual intercourse (Pes 113 a ff; Shab 152a; San 107a; Ket 10a; etc). Any male who violated this prohibition could be flogged (Ket 10a); more severe penalties were applied to females. The efforts of traditional Judaism to segregate men and women sought to remove the temptations of sexual intercourse outside of marriage. Men and women were to be separated on all festive occasions in public places; a man was even prohibited from walking behind a woman for this reason (*Yad* Hil Yom Tov 6.21). There are numerous similar citations in the *Talmud*, the codes and the responsa literature. Despite this, such extra-marital sexual relationships did exist and were sometimes defended as a human weakness. Looser standards were tolerated in some ages, for example in Judea in the *Talmudic* period (Ket 7b); in the Byzantine Empire and in various Balkan lands in the last centuries (L. Epstein *Sex Laws and Customs in Judaism* p 128). Yet consistent efforts were made to restrict sexual intercourse to marriage. In marriage, human sexuality was considered a positive experience. The tradition, of course, said much more on the subject. We would therefore reject this man's promiscuous behavior and state that Judaism demands restraint and would punish violations when possible.

Now let us ask that what would our attitude be if the individual in question is married; we must ask whether he can continue sexual relations with his wife. If he remains careless about his use of condoms he will probably transmit AIDS to his wife. No one is permitted to endanger the life of a fellow human being; one must die rather than endanger another human life even if one's own life is in danger (San 60 b ff; A Z 43b; 54a; Ket 33b; Shab 149a; *Sefer Hamitzvot* Lo Taaseh #2 ff, 10, 14; *Shulhan Arukh* Yoreh Deah 157.1). As every source of *saqanat nefesh* must be removed (Deut 4.9; 4.15; Ber 32b; B K 91b; *Yad* Hil Rotzeah Ushemirat Hanefesh 11.4-5 *Hil* Shevuot 5.7; Hil Hovel Umaziq 5.1) this individual should *not* permit himself to continue sexual relations with his wife. This may ultimately provide grounds for divorce which could be enforced by a *bet din*. A woman has always been able to seek a divorce if her husband was afflicted with leprosy (*M* Ned 11.12) or similar diseases. For that matter she could seek it if her husband engaged in a new field which was noxious to her as tanning of hides. (*M* Ket 8.9) Certainly if the danger is great as with AIDS, grounds for divorce exist. We would discourage a divorce and rather encourage the wife to support her husband in this difficult period, when he needs her help. The couple must, however, refrain from intercourse or use stringent precautions.

We should also view this situation entirely from the point of view of transmitting a fatal disease. Traditional literature has dealt with dangerous contagious diseases through quarantine from the Biblical period onward ("Jewish Reaction To Epidemics - AIDS" W. Jacob *Contemporary American Reform Responsa* #82). Every effort was made to isolate the individual and to protect the general society in Biblical times from the dangerous but not fatal *zoraat*. In this instance we are dealing with a fatal disease whose effect is felt over many years. This means that a false sense of security may be given to both the carrier and the recipient. It also remains possible for the carrier to hide her/his condition from the recipient in the early stages of the symptoms.

We are aware of the tragic consequences for any individual who has AIDS and must sympathize with his/her plight. Every possible support and help must be extended to such individuals. His/her right to work and to function in a normal manner in our society must be protected as long as such individuals are willing to do their share in protecting society. We must also differentiate between absolutely positive testing for AIDS and those whose status is doubtful. Such individuals should undergo further tests. Yet such a respect for individual rights cannot be permitted to endanger others through reckless behavior.

Our present knowledge of AIDS and the lack of any cure or immunization leads us to see a known carrier who is aware of his/her condition and engages in sexual relations without the regular use of condoms as guilty of endangering another human life. This must be made absolutely clear to such individuals; society can demand that they refrain from all sexual activity or to protect their partner with great care. Such partners must be adequately warned. We should in turn also warn *everyone* against promiscuous sexual behavior as it is considered morally wrong and may endanger their lives.

If such demands cannot be met by known carriers of AIDS then society must protect itself by isolating individuals who are known carriers and utilize every means at its disposal to protect the remainder of society. No individual has the right to endanger the life of another. It is incumbent on all members of society to protect themselves against such reckless and dangerous behavior.

July 1987

162. AIDS AND A DENTIST

QUESTION: A dentist has tested HIV positive. He is not yet suffering from any of the symptoms of AIDS, and now wishes to know whether he can continue his practice as long as he takes proper precautions. Must he inform his patients? (P.R. Phoenix AZ)

ANSWER: AIDS is a serious illness for which there is no known cure or vaccine, so we must take the infection of the dentist very seriously. We should be concerned with this AIDS victim as the disease is fatal; he needs our compassion.

The fear of the general population is understandable as little is known about the disease, its incubation period or a potential cure. We must be concerned with both the individual and the larger community, and in this instance with the danger which may exist. It is true that the dentist can protect his patients through the constant use of gloves; the danger would then be minimal. The dentist, of course, wishes to protect his livelihood and realizes that any notification to his patients would destroy his dental practice, and that is probably an accurate assumption.

We must be concerned with *pikuah nefesh*, the potential danger to the patient. If a patient feels that there is no risk, or is willing to assume a very slight risk, then that is fine, but the patient must be informed that a remote possibility of infection exists. Furthermore, unless the dentist informs his patients now, any patient later tested as HIV positive will blame the dentist rather than any other possible source. By withholding this information he will find himself accused and sued. We would agree with the tradition based on the Biblical statement "Do not place a stumbling block before the blind" (Lev 19.14; Pes 22b; MK 5a; *Yad* Hil Rotzeah 12; *Sefer Hamitzvot*, Lo Taaseh 299) and the obligation of avoiding unnecessary danger (Deut 4.9; 4.15; Ber 32b; B K 91b; *Yad* Hil Rotzeah Ushemirat Hanefesh 11.4; Hil Shevuot 5.57; Hil Hovel Umaziq 5.1). A patient would be well advised to be cautious about using this dentist even if the risk of HIV infection is small.

As the dentist must inform his patients of his condition, the dentist should be encouraged to sell his dental practice while that remains possible. He may not be able to continue some aspects of dentistry in a setting where his condition will be known, but will not effect patients, or simply retire from the field.

January 1990

163. FETUS KEPT ALIVE AS A SOURCE FOR ORGANS

QUESTION: When an infant possesses only a brain stem and no other functionary brain, may it be kept alive by machines, etc, as a source for future organ transplants? (Walter Jaslow, Beechwood OH)

ANSWER: A fetus which possesses life of its own is considered a human being; that status is reached as soon as the child has been born or a major part off it has left the womb (*M* Oholot 7:6; *Shulhan Arukh* Hoshen Mishpat 425.2; *Yad* Hil Rotzeah Ushemirat Hanefesh 1.1). This child, therefore, possesses all the rights of any human being. In this instance it is clear that the child can not survive without artificial means and can never have any independent life as it lacks vital organs. We should, therefore, permit the child to die peacefully and possibly allow the machinery to maintain normal bodily functions for a short period necessary to transfer the organs, which will be transplanted and used to help others. Such a short period of artificial life will not impinge upon the human dignity of this infant nor will it cause undue additional suffering to the mourning parents. It would be inappropriate to keep this infant alive for a longer period of time.

May 1988

164. AIDS AND FREE NEEDLES FOR DRUG ADDICTS

QUESTION: The spread of AIDS takes place in a number of ways. Among them is through infected needles shared by drug users. Among the suggestions of public health officials has been the providing of free needles for drug users. This somewhat curtails the spread of AIDS. Is it ethical to utilize this method which after all enables drug addicts to continue their habit? Ultimately that habit may be as destructive as AIDS. (Leonard Silberman, New York NY)

ANSWER: As noted in some previous responsa there is surprisingly little material in the vast responsa literature about the use of addictive drugs (W. Jacob *Contemporary American Reform Responsa* #82). As you have indicated this is a matter of public policy rather than a specifically Jewish issue. We must ask ourselves what are we trying to accomplish. The free needles may somewhat curtail the spread of AIDS. They do, however, continue the problem of drug abuse, and do nothing to help the addict overcome his/her addiction. Can we in good conscience move along this partial path and ignore the larger question of drug addiction and its harm to the individual as well as the broader society?

The use of drugs whose harmful effect is known has, of course, been prohibited by Jewish law (Pes 113a; Eruv 54a; Nid 30b). No person is to endanger his/her life in any fashion (Deut

4.9; 4.15; Ber 32b; B K 91b; *Yad* Hil Rotzeah Ushemirat Hanefesh 11.4; Hil Shevuot 5.57; Hil Hovel Umazig 5.1). Even the use of experimental drugs whose benefit is uncertain has been permitted reluctantly, and only with the full consent of the ill person, and if there is reasonable chance that healing will occur. In this instance an additional factor is created by the involvement of health authorities in the use of drugs. In other words making it easier for those addicted to continue their habit.

Those considerations are negative and would lead us to a negative conclusion. There is, however, another side to this question. AIDS is a fatal disease for which no cure is now known. Individuals who suffer from this syndrome can be helped for some time, but eventually death is certain. Use of drugs may also kill, but it is possible to be cured of this habit and only a serious overdose or very long term use will kill. Most deaths result from side effects of the drugs or crimes connected with drugs. Therefore drugs, although a major evil in our society, are the lesser evil for the individual.

We may therefore defend the providing of free needles to known drug users on the grounds that we are helping them to preserve their lives. They will be less likely to be afflicted by AIDS, and so will not spread this disease to others. Furthermore the possibility of a cure from their drug problems, although unlikely, exists. We may therefore say that in order to prevent a greater evil we will condone a lesser evil, and we do so on the grounds that saving a life permits anything accept murder and adultery. In this instance the life saving factor becomes predominant, and we would condone, albeit reluctantly, the distribution of free needles for this purpose.

June 1989

165. FUNERAL ON TU BESHEVAT

QUESTION: May a funeral be held on *Tu Beshevat*? The question has been asked by environmentally conscious teenage grandchildren who feel that this holiday is important to them? (Charles Lehman, Chicago IL).

ANSWER: This day, the New Year of the trees, is one of the very minor commemorative days mentioned by the *Mishnah* (R H 1.1) which has hardly been noted through the centuries. In ancient times it was customary to plant a cedar for every male child and a cypress for each female baby on that day. When the child was to be married the trees were cut down and the wood used for the *hupah* poles (Git 57a).

It was celebrated more widely by some kabbalists including Nathan Benjamin of Gaza who provided a liturgy for the night. Hayim Vital of Safed in the 16th century developed a full *seder* for the holiday (*Sefer Peri Etz Hadar*) of readings from many different sources. Hayim Vital also specified thirty species of fruit and nuts to be consumed during that night. He divided them into three groups of ten, each for ten *sefirot*. Consuming these fruit was considered atonement for the sin of eating from the Tree of Knowledge in Paradise.

In northern Europe where fruit and nuts were not as plentiful and the population much poorer, carobs from Israel where consumed as a symbol of the festive day.

In more recent times this holiday has been associated with our ecological concerns and some congregations has developed their own *seder* for the night. Judaism has historically expressed concern for the environment (W. Jacob *Contemporary American Reform Responsa #* 12); as our interest in this increases, the minor

275

holiday will become more important. This has happened during the last century with *Hannukah*.

Despite such emphasis there would be no reason for avoiding a funeral on this day. There are no such prohibitions connected with any of the minor holidays. The grandchildren should combine their concern for ecology with the honor due to their grandfather; it may make the day even more memorable for them in the future.

January 1989

166. FUNERAL ON YOM HASHOAH

QUESTION: May a funeral be held on *Yom Hashoah*? Do we consider this a holiday or a commemorative day? (Bernard Kaufman, Newark NJ)

ANSWER: *Yom Hashoah* is a commemorative day added to our calendar to honor those who died in the Holocaust. A brief liturgy appropriate for a special service has been created for this day. Some congregations add commemorative readings to their normal service. In other communities there is a communal program of rememberance which often involves the non-Jewish community as well. The commemoration of the day should be encouraged.

The day is not a holiday, but a commemorative day, so none of the prohibitions connected with holidays are applicable. It would be permissable to conduct a funeral on this day.

March 1989

276

167. JEWISH FUNERAL DIRECTORS

QUESTION: My congregation is located in a distant suburb, and we wish to know whether it is obligatory for us to encourage the use of a Jewish funeral director in the inner city versus a non-Jewish funeral director nearby. (Arlene Cowan, Los Angeles CA)

ANSWER: Traditionally each community had a special *hevrah qadishah* which took care of the arrangements connected with the burial of the dead. Participation in this *hevrah* was considered a *mitzvah* and members of the group were accorded special honors within the community. The preparation of the deceased for burial such as guarding the corpse, and the burial itself were carefully regulated (*Shulhan Arukh* Yoreh Deah 361 ff; J. Greenwald *Kol Bo al Avelut* pp 85 ff; *Gesher Hahayim*). This group of men and women saw to it that the deceased was appropriately honored. In contemporary America, this *hevrah qadishah* works in conjunction with a funeral director and provides for the ritual elements necessary, but only rarely has been involved with the details of the funeral. This has become a profession and the funeral director looks after the arrangements, complies with state laws, and is able to transport bodies from a distant place of death to the city in which the funeral and burial will take place. It is certainly preferable to use a Jewish funeral director who, although is not the equivalent of a *hevrah qadishah*, is nevertheless more akin to it. One might say that he/she represents the professionalization of this ancient group.

A few cities have communal funeral arrangements which encourage lower cost funerals and give their profits to communal institutions. This is much more akin to the *hevrah qadishah* and would be the most preferable.

A non-Jewish funeral director may, of course, be used if no Jewish funeral director is available, in keeping with the tradition which states that on the first day of *yom tov* non-Jews should be engaged for the burial (*Shulhan Arukh* Orah Hayim 526.4). Generally, however, a Jewish funeral director should be utilized and your congregation should encourage that. We would not require the involvement of a *hevrah qadishah* as we are willing to rely on the Jewish funeral director for proper care and guardianship of the deceased.

January 1990

168. LINEN SHROUDS OR A GARMENT

QUESTION: A family has asked whether it is necessary to purchase expensive linen shrouds for their dead grandfather. The family has limited means and would prefer to use some ordinary garments for burial. What is a attitude of tradition? (Kate Goldsmith, Houston TX)

ANSWER: Tradition has emphasized simplicity for funerals. Rabban Gamliel, who was wealthy, insisted that he be buried in only a linen shroud in order to set an example (M K 27b). Another scholar R. Hezkiah asked that the shrouds used for his burial be limited in number (*J* Kelaim 9.4). Linen shrouds, often eight in number came to be used (*Shulhan Arukh* Yoreh Deah 352; Tekushinsky *Gesher Hayim* Vol 1 p 102f). The number may have arisen under kabbalistic influence. Shrouds could be omitted for a known sinner as a sign of disparagement (Joel Sirkes to *Tur* Yoreh Deah 362).

YOREH DEAH

There is a well established tradition for the use of shrouds, but we should remember that they were used to avoid extravagence and unnecessary expense. In keeping with tradition it should be possible to obtain inexpensive linen shrouds or shrouds of any other material. It would also be permissable to use the garments which the deceased wore and so avoid any additional expense. This is appropriate and in the spirit of tradition.

May 1989

169. *TAHARAH* AND AIDS

QUESTION: At the present time the funeral director of the local Jewish funeral home refuses to permit *taharah* for AIDS victims. Are there circumstances under which *taharah* may be withheld? For example, dangerous infectious disease or should we insist that he treat AIDS victims like all other dead? (Rabbi Norman M. Cohen, Hopkins MN).

ANSWER: The fact that this question is asked at all indicates the progress of modern medicine in removing the danger of most infectious diseases. Through most of our long history the grave danger of plagues and major epidemics was, of course, recognized even while the danger of infectious diseases was not. Special precautions were occasionally initiated during major epidemics, but those who died from any disease were treated alike and were provided with the same preparation before burial. In fact crises like epidemics and plagues led to the creation of new burial societies and to renewed devotion to proper burial (I. Abrahams *Jewish Life in the Middle Ages* pp 355 ff). Special burial preparations were only

279

made for those who were murdered or those who died in childbirth (For a summary see Grunwald *Kol Bo al Avelut* p 49 ff; and *Sedei Hemed* IV (Avelut #141).

There was, of course, considerable discussion in the rabbinic literature about the reaction to plagues. Flight from the affected areas was encouraged (*Shulhan Arukh* Yoreh Deah 116.5; and commentaries; see also J. Preuss *Biblical and Talmudic Medicine* pp 151 ff. Solomon ben Simon Duran (*Responsa* Maharil #195) approached the whole matter from a philosophical point of view and asked whether flight would be successful if an individual had already been destined for death. Isaac Luria devoted an entire chapter to the question (*Yam Shel Shelomo* 6.26). There were a large number of responsa which deal with contagious diseases and ways to escape epidemics (H. J. Zimmels *Magicians, Theologians, and Doctors* pp 99 ff, 193 ff). Flight was the principal remedy.

Those who were not fortunate enough to escape and died were to be buried in the appropriate manner. It might be possible to throw quicklime on the grave in order to avoid the spread of the plague (*Shulhan Arukh* Yoreh Deah 374 Pithei Teshuvah; Jacob Reischer *Shevut Yaakov* II #97). Furthermore, the laws of mourning could be modified or suspended in these sad times (*Shulhan Arukh* Yoreh Deah 374.11 and commentaries).

Although these modifications were readily undertaken, the basic rites of burial were followed as closely as possible. In other words there is no doubt that in times of mass deaths, when a large proportion of the community had fled, some normal honors accorded to the dead were no longer possible. Yet there was no question about *taharah* or any matter connected with burial or the preparation for burial.

The local funeral director is obligated to perform *taharah* and to treat AIDS victims as all other dead in accordance with local custom and the specific wishes of the family. The funeral director would be encouraged to take all possible precautions to prevent infection by AIDS.

April 1988

170. THE BURIAL OF HUMAN ORGANS

QUESTION: Is it necessary to bury organs which have been replaced through a transplant operation? How would Jewish tradition dispose of these portions of the human body? (Rabbi Norman Cohen, Hopkins MN)

ANSWER: Organ transplants are a very modern medical remedy. However, the problems of disposal of amputated limbs is ancient. Traditionally they were interred and that was required for two reasons. It was considered important to show respect for all parts of the human body and so limbs could not simply be discarded. In addition the ritual uncleanliness, which a corpse or an amputated limb caused priests (*kohanim*), presented an important consideration. Any priest who came in contact with a dead body or a portion of such a body would be considered defiled (Ket 20b; *Yad* Hil Tumat Okhlin 16.8; *Shevut Yaaqov* II #10).

Limbs were buried without formal ritual and simply interred in a portion of the cemetery (*Tur* Yoreh Deah 266; *Shulhan Arukh* Yoreh Deah 266; Moses Feinstein *Igrot Mosheh* Yoreh Deah I 231). We would suggest that major organs be similarly buried or treated in some other respectful manner as incineration.

We, of course, face not only the disposition of major organs as heart, kidney, liver, etc., but also with the disposition of innumerable smaller fragments as pieces of bone, arteries, veins, skin, etc. It is the normal procedure of hospitals to dispose of these fragments in a sanitary and safe manner, frequently through incineration at high temperatures. This reduces the segments to virtually nothing and assures no misuse of these fragments. We would agree that this method of disposition is appropriate and does not dishonor these fragments of the human body nor does it present other problems to us.

May 1988

171. BURIAL WITH A BATON

QUESTION: The widow of a man very fond of music would like to bury him with his baton. Is this appropriate? (Regina Rosen, Greensburg PA)

ANSWER: The main emphasis with our funerals has been simplicity and helping the mourners overcome their sorrow. Rabban Gamliel already stressed simplicity by having himself buried in a plain shroud although he was wealthy (Ket 8b; M K 27b). Normally nothing was buried with the deceased with the exception of sacred writings which could no longer be used (W. Jacob *Contemporary American Reform Responsa* 108). Such books were buried not to honor the deceased, but to guard the name of God from improper use.

Often some items normally associated with the deceased such as a ring or glasses have been buried with the individual, so it would be permissable to bury a baton which meant a lot to him. This should be done especially if it provides some additional comfort to his family.

November 1991

172. BURIAL WITH CANDELABRA

QUESTION: The children of a woman who has just died are divided over the desire of one of them to bury her mother's antique silver *shabbat* candelabra with her. She made no such request. Another child understood that she was to receive the candelabra. Is this appropriate to bury a Jewish ritual item? (Selma Horotwitz, Boston MA)

ANSWER: The main emphasis with our funerals has been simplicity and helping the mourners overcome their sorrow. Rabban Gamliel already stressed simplicity by having himself buried in a plain shroud although he was wealthy (Ket 8b; M K 27b). Normally nothing was buried with the deceased with the exception of sacred writings which could no longer be used (W. Jacob *Contemporary American Reform Responsa* 108). Such books were buried not to honor the deceased, but to guard the name of God from improper use.

Here we are dealing with a ritual item of considerable emotional and monetary value. The struggle over this issue undoubtedly covers some deeper hostility and older rivalry. The will may specify the disposal of the candelabra and they should be given in accordance with that document or any understanding reached. As they seem to have been promised to one child, they should not be buried.

Often some items normally associated with the deceased such as a ring or glasses have been buried with the individual, but this has usually been limited to items of daily, personal use and would not include candelabra.

June 1988

173. BURIAL WITH A KIPPAH

QUESTION: Is it necessary to provide a *kippah* for a more traditional deceased? Should this be added to the shrouds? (Esther Leibowitz, Miami FL)

ANSWER: Tradition has emphasized simplicity for funerals. Rabban Gamliel, who was wealthy, insisted that he be buried in only a linen shroud in order to set an example (M K 27b). Another scholar R. Hezkiah asked that the shrouds used for his burial be limited in number (*J* Kelaim 9.4). Linen shrouds, often eight in number came to be used (*Shulhan Arukh* Yoreh Deah 352; Tekushinsky *Gesher Hayim* Vol 1 p 102f). The number may have arisen under kabbalistic influence. Nothing was mentioned in these sources about a *kippah*. It was probably assumed that the entire body was wrapped in the shrouds and so the head was not left uncovered or visible. If the family feels more at ease by providing a *kippah* it should be done. It is, however, not necessary.

February 1989

174. JERUSALEM SOIL INTO THE GRAVE

QUESTION: A relative of the deceased has brought some soil from Jerusalem which he wishes the family to place into the coffin. The burial took place some months earlier; should the grave be openned in order to do this? What is the origin of the custom of burying with a vial of such soil? (Hannah Smith, Seattle, WA)

ANSWER: Burial in the land of Israel has been sought by the pious through the ages. Jacob, the patriarch, and later his son Joseph were taken from Egypt to be buried in Israel (Gen 49.31; 50.13). When this was not possible, some pious individuals travelled to Israel in their old age, so that they might die and be buried there. As resurrection of the dead will begin with the land of Israel according to some speculations, burial there would assure earlier resurrection.

In our century burials may be arranged in Israel and some Orthodox families have done so. Others have sought to emphasize their ties with Israel by including a vial of soil from Jerusalem in their coffin. I have not found any traditional sources which mention this custom.

A body may be exhumed for a variety of reasons, including reburial in Israel (*Shulhan Arukh* Yoreh Deah 363.1 ff), but this would not include the placement of a vial of Israeli soil into the coffin. It would be appropriate to sprinkle that soil onto the existing grave, without disturbing it, and thereby satisfying the wishes of the visiting relative.

June 1989

175. DECORATED COFFIN

QUESTION: An aunt in a small southern town will be buried by a Christian funeral director. He has provided a wooden coffin in accordance with tradition; it is heavily decorated with carved figures. Should this coffin or a simple metal coffin be used for her burial? (Dorothy Cohen, Birmingham AL)

ANSWER: We along with tradition have emphasized simplicity in all funeral arrangements. This included the service, coffin, and tombstone. The deceased was better honored through gifts to charity. Rabban Gamliel sought to set this pattern by being buried inonly a shroud although he was a wealthy man (Ket 8b; M K 27b).

The older tradition assumed burial in the ground and understood the decay of the body as atonement (*M* San 5.6; 46b; *Tur, Shulhan Arukh* Yoreh Deah 362). Coffins were, however, used in ancient times as we know from the *Jerusalem Talmud* (Kel 9.4) and from those excavated at archeological sites. Maimonides preferred wooden coffins (*Yad* Hil Avel 4.4) and many authorities have followed him. Stone or pottery coffins were used in ancient Israel (*M* Oholot 2.3; *Shulhan Arukh* Yoreh Deah 362.5); a metal coffin was used to bury Joseph according to tradition (Sotah 13 b; Jacob Levinson *Hatorah Vehameda* pp 65 ff). Both wood and metal deteriorate in contrast to stone or pottery.

This discussion demonstrates that the primary consideration for a coffin was simplicity. A wooden coffin has been preferred by many, but is not essential. The simpler and less expensive coffin should be used. Charitable donations should be made with the funds which remain.

176. A PLASTIC COFFIN

QUESTION: May a plastic coffin be used to bury our dead? (Roland F. Kantor, Los Angeles CA)

ANSWER: Originally the dead were buried directly in the ground and there was some question whether a coffin of any kind was appropriate (*Shulhan Arukh* Yoreh Deah 362.1 and commentaries). However, a coffin was permitted as long as it was placed directly in the ground. Of course, at an earlier time burial in caves and niches cut into the walls of the cave was quite common in ancient Israel, and this meant that burial in coffins of stone was also considered appropriate (*Tos* Oholot 2.3; I. Goodenough *Jewish Symbols in the Greco-Roman World*; *Semahot* 13; *Shulhan Arukh* Yoreh Deah 362.5). Generally coffins were made of wood and often with loose boards on the bottom so that there would be some direct contact with the ground (*J* Kelaim 11.4; *Shulhan Arukh* Yoreh Deah 362.1 and commentaries). We should note that one *Talmudic agadah* indicated that Joseph was buried in a metal casket and that casket was then preserved in the Nile River until taken to the land of Israel when the Israelites left Egypt (Sota 13a).

We can see that a variety of caskets were used in the past. Two considerations were important. Everything connected with the deceased such as the shroud and coffin were to be simple. In addition it was felt that the physical decay of the dead served as an atonement. We too seek to curb excesses connected with funerals. If, therefore, a plastic casket is less expensive, then we may use it

Jewish burials. For those who feel that contact with the soil is important, holes might be drilled in the bottom of the casket as has been done earlier with metal caskets.

October 1988

177. VERTICAL BURIAL

QUESTION: My father has expressed a desire to be burial vertically rather than horizontally. We have discussed this a number of times but he insists and I would like to carry out his wishes if that is in keeping with Jewish practices (Norma Weigel, Berkeley CA).

ANSWER: Jewish tradition assumes that burial will be horizontal. This is true both for burial in the ground which is our customary practice and the ancient burial in caves as we find at Bet Shan and in other sites in Israel. My search through the *halakhic* literature has not come across any statements about vertical burial. It is unlikely that this would have been discussed in an earlier age, as horizontal burial is much easier and requires less digging into the ground. Vertical burial would demand a considerable excavation. That is readily possible for us with our mechanized equipment, but as my cemetery superintendent has told me may cause practical problems as well with neighboring graves which might cave in. Furthermore, the coffin because of its construction may collapse if placed vertically.

As long as there is no damage to nearby graves or other technical difficulty, the vertical burial which this individual has requested should be considered appropriate. The grave marker should be placed in the usual position and nothing connected with the grave need indicate that this burial was somewhat different.

August 1991

178. FILING THE GRAVE IN HOT WEATHER

QUESTION: In this congregation with its mixture of more traditional and more liberal minded families, the bereaved family at the funeral often wishes the grave to be filled or partially filled after interment. As the temperature in the summer may reach as high as 118, the *minyan* which normally gathers at the graveside resists doing this in such excessive heat. What is the traditional response to filling in the grave under these circumstances? (Rabbi Albert Michels, Sun City AZ)

ANSWER: As you quite properly state it is not our custom to fill the grave at all while the mourners are present, as this is especially difficult for them and at least in our present mood does not help them recover from their grief. The general feeling of tradition, of course, is that mourning begins once the grave has been filled (*Shulhan Arukh* Yoreh Deah 371). I do not know of any question which arose akin to yours in which burial was difficult because of excessive heat. In ancient Israel a fair number of burials took place in caves and so, of course, the problem did not arise as the site was cooler and as rolling a stone completed the burial (*M K* 27a; Matt 28.2). Of course, under your circumstances this could be done in the evening by individuals working in the cemetery, or even in the daytime after the mourners had left, using machinery.

Under special circumstances when it was not possible to bury, as for example when there was a grave diggers strike and graves could not be prepared for burial, then mourning began once the coffin was sealed and placed in storage rather than waiting for the strike to be over (Solomon B. Freehof *Reform Responsa* #36). The other occasion when burial was not possible incurred in Russia and Poland with its harsh winters which sometimes froze the ground so that it was not possible to bury anyone, and the deceased were placed in a coffin and stored until weather conditions had changed. In both of these instances we are dealing with the entire burial not simply with the filling in of the grave.

Although it has become customary in traditional circles for relatives and friends to fill in the grave, this is not required. The custom stems from a time when all such work was done on a voluntary basis. The presence of a large number of individuals at the graveside assured that the task would be shared and be done rather quickly. These are not considerations for us, and under the circumstances you describe it would be perfectly proper and within the bounds of tradition to have the same people who dug the grave fill it with their mechanical equipment after the mourners had left. Those present at the interment could throw a few handfuls of dirt onto the coffin (*Shulhan Arukh* Yoreh Deah, 375.1).

In any case because of *pikuah nefesh* (Deut 4.0; 4.15; Ber 32b; B K 91b; *Yad* Hil Rotzeah Ushemmirat Hanefesh 11.4; Hil Shavuot 5.57; Hil Hovel Umaziq 5.1), it would be wrong to impose the obligation of filling the grave upon the *minyan* which attends the graveside services.

August 1989

179. CRIMINAL PAST

QUESTION: How much detail about the unsavory past of a parent must be told to his children? A mother of young children would like to continue to portray her deceased husband as a normal father, although he served a prison sentence. How forthright should she be with her children? (D.K. New Orleans LA)

ANSWER: We generally tend to embellish the memory of the deceased, and some of our funeral rites are intended more for the survivors than the deceased. For this reason we provide a normal funeral for suicides (W. Jacob (ed) *American Reform Responsa* #89 and #89). For the same reason virtually no congregation now buries criminals or others considered wicked in a special section as the tradition demanded (San 49a; *Shulhan Arukh* Yoreh Deah 362.5). Extenuating circumstances have usually been discovered even by the most traditional Jews.

Eulogies were normally not given for the deceased, but some words of praise were spoken (Shab 105b; *Shulhan Arukh* Yoreh Deah 344; *Shevut Yaakov* II #25); it has always been considered appropriate to praise the deceased more fully than deserved.

In this case, we are faced with a more difficult situation. We should note that a *midrash* portrayed even God as stretching the truth occasionally, in order to keep peace between Abraham and his wife Sarah (Yeb 65b). The mother should always indicate that their father cared for them and was concerned about them. In this instance as long as the children are very young nothing need be told them. She need not, at this young age, deal with his criminal status in the general community. It would, however, a little later be good for her to deal with it and to make clear that he was punished for some specific wrongs. It is better for the children to hear this

291

from their mother than to receive this news from someone else in the community. As long as they live in the community where their father was known, it would be wrong to withhold this knowledge from them as they grow up.

November 1989

180. INCENSE FOR MOURNING

QUESTION: A group of Jews interested in meditation wish to use incense as part of their funeral ritual at the grave. Their liturgy is normative Jewish. They meditate and feel that incense might help them and be appropriate as it was used in ancient times. Would this be acceptable at a graveside service? (Barry Gold, Berkley CA)

ANSWER: Incense is used continuously in the worship in the Bible. We find lengthy descriptions and they even provide details of precise mixtures as well as all of the ingredients. This material is further expanded subsequently in the *Mishnah* and the *Talmud*. A good deal of modern work in studying the plant material has been done. However, the interest in incense and its use ended with the Temple. This was a form of worship which was related to the sacrifices and therefore could not be replicated in the synagogue except through readings, and these occurred in various points of the service as for example in the prelimary readings of the *shaharit*. In other words, this along with all other matters associated with the Temple was limited to Temple worship and not considered transferable.

There is nothing which would prohibit the use of incense for this Jewish meditation group as part of a funeral ritual as long as they made no effort to copy the ritual of the ancient Temple, but simply did whatever they felt appropriate for their meditation.

The use of incense by various oriental religions has undoubtedly influenced this group; there is an element of *huqat goyim*, so we must view the practice with caution.

Although we would not recommend the use of incense, it would be permitted if the cemetery rules allow it.

October 1991

181. THE FUNERAL OF A NON-JEWISH SPOUSE OF A MEMBER

QUESTION: The non-Jewish spouse of a member has died and her husband has requested that the funeral be conducted in the synagogue. The woman has not converted, however, all the children have been raised as Jews and she had involved herself somewhat in congregational activities open to her as a non-Jew. Should this funeral be permitted in the synagogue? (Rabbi Joseph P. Weinberg, Washington DC)

ANSWER: Funerals in the synagogue were restricted to leaders in the community. This was the pattern in a former generation. That also was the view expressed by Solomon B. Freehof (*Reform Responsa for Our Time* pp 95 ff). In recent years we have, however, proceeded along a somewhat different line and relaxed the restrictions on the use of the synagogue for funerals so that virtually any member who is a good Jew may request the use of the synagogue for a funeral though it remains an honor (W. Jacob *Contemporary American Reform Responsa* #89).

The non-Jewish spouse cannot become a member of a synagogue so he/she should not have a funeral in the synagogue (W. Jacob (ed) *American Reform Responsa* #161).

We have been generous in permitting burial to non-Jews in our cemeteries. This is based on the rabbinic injunction that we bury the gentile dead (Git 61a; Yeb 15a; *Yad* Hil Evel 14.12) *Shulhan Arukh* Yoreh Deah 367.1; S. B. Freehof *Current Reform Responsa* pp 175 ff).

We have no problem with the internment of gentile dead or for the matter in officiating at funerals for non-Jews (W. Jacob *Contemporary American Reform Responsa* #99), but such a funeral should not be conducted in the synagogue.

March 1989

182. LOCATION OF TOMBSTONE

QUESTION: May a grave be marked by a stone placed at the foot rather than at the head of the grave? (Rabbi Selig Salkowitz, Brooklyn NY)

ANSWER: Only a few grave markers were mentioned in the Biblical period, such as the pillar which Jacob erected over the grave of his beloved Rachel (Gen 35.20), and the tombs of a number of kings (II Kings 23.17; I Mac 13.27). Numerous later Jewish tombstones and sarcophagi have recently been discovered by archaeologists both in Israel and throughout the Roman Empire (E. Goodenough *Jewish Symbols in the Greco-Roman Period*).

In the *Mishnaic* period ordinances dealt with the erection of tombstones as a form of warning priests away from a grave so that they would not become ritually impure (*Tos* Ohalot 17.14). It had become customary to erect tombstones for all those who had died (Shek 2; Er 5.1).

There is relatively little further discussion of tombstones until the Middle Ages (*Sefer Hassidim* #738; *Or Zarua; Hagohot Asheri*; Solomon ben Aderet *Responsa*; etc). Tombstones eventually became obligatory, and the heirs of the deceased could be forced to erect a stone (*Tur* Yoreh Deah 348; *Shulhan Arukh* Yoreh Deah 348.2; Even Haezer 89.1). The subsequent commentaries to this passage emphasized the need for simplicity in the stone.

Local *minhag* seems to have determined the position of the stone and so Greenwald simply stated that "in some communities the stone was placed at the foot of the grave and others at the head while it was the custom in Jerusalem to lay the stones horizontally over the grave rather than have upright stones" (*Kol Bo al Avelut* p 379 *Hedrat Qodesh* p 21). There is, in other words, no clear *minhag* on this matter, however, uniformity has been sought in each cemetery. This was done to avoid walking on the graves unnecessarily, and that is only possible if one knows whether the stone has been placed at the head or at the foot of the grave.

The specific regulations of the cemetery should, of course, also be consulted especially as Jewish law and custom remain vague. The rules of the cemetery would prevail in this matter.

August 1990

183. A WOODEN GRAVE MARKER

QUESTION: The deceased has requested that the grave marker used for her grave be a simple wooden one. This is in keeping with the simplicity of her life. She would like the fund nromally used for a tombstone be spent charitably? What is the attitude of tradition to this request? (Mark Greenbaum, Dallas TX)

ANSWER: The first mention of marking a grave was with Rachel as the patriarch Jacob set up a pillar in her honor (Gen 35.20); similarly the graves of the ancient Israelite and Judean kings were provided with monuments. In the later period graves were marked so that the priests could avoid contact with the dead (*M* M K 1.2). Generally these gravemarker were made of stone as this is a durable material (Greenwald *Kol Bo al Avelut*), but there is no absolute requirement. We should also remember that the tombstones in many older cemeteries decay despite the effort at permanence. Furthermore wooden markers were used in various European countries when stone could not be afforded.

A wooden marker may be used if it is in keeping with the rule of the congregation. The congregation must be concerned with maintenance and the general appearance of the cemetery. There is nothing in the tradition which would object to this request.

November 1990

184. A COLORED TOMBSTONE

QUESTION: The deceased, a well known local avant garde artist, has asked that a bright yellow imported stone be used as a tombstone. This is in keeping with some of the material which he used for his sculpture. The cemetery committee wishes to know whether we must accede to his request as this would be out of keeping with the rest of the cemetery. (Ross Kagan, Chicago IL)

ANSWER: The first mention of marking a grave was with Rachel as the patriarch Jacob set up a pillar in her honor (Gen 35.20); similarly the graves of the ancient Israelite and Judean kings were provided with monuments. In the later period graves were marked so that the priests could avoid contact with the dead (*M M K* 1.2). Generally these gravemarker were made of stone as this is a durable material (Greenwald *Kol Bo al Avelut*), but there is no absolute requirement. In reading through the literature I have found nothing about tombstones of unusual material or of any colored tombstones. Normally the locally available stone was used.

The cemetery committee has the power to set the rules for everything connected with the cemetery and its care. They may reject this request.

April 1990

185. METAL TOMBSTONE

QUESTION: The deceased has requested that a metal grave marker be used. He was engaged in aluminum fabrication and designed and produced some fine decorative work. Should this request be honored by the cemetery committee as there are no metal markers now in the cemetery? (Richard Cohen, New York NY)

ANSWER: Tradition has required that graves be marked for the honor of the dead (Gen 35.20) and to prevent *kohanim* from straying onto them (*M M K* 1.2). A durable material was used so that the descendents would not need to replace it. Usually the local stone has been used; although in the poorer sections of Europe wooden markers were used. There is nothing in the literature which would prevent the use of a metal marker.

The cemetery committee must decide whether it is appropriate and whether it will need unusual maintenance. They may reject this request or accede to it.

June 1989

186. UNMARKED TOMBSTONE

QUESTION: The deceased has requested that the tombstone set upon his grave be a large piece of granite, uncut and without any markings. No name or date is to be placed upon it. What is the attitude of tradition to this request? (Dora Nelkoff, Philadelphia PA)

ANSWER: The first mention of marking a grave was with Rachel as the patriarch Jacob set up a pillar in her honor (Gen 35.20); similarly the graves of the ancient Israelite and Judean kings were provided with monuments, but nothing was said about inscriptions. In the later period graves were marked so that the priests could avoid contact with the dead (*M M K* 1.2). Generally tombstones were marked with the name of the deceased and there was some discussion of inscriptions (Greenwald *Kol Bo al Avelut* pp 380 ff), but there is no absolute requirement. We should also remember that the tombstones in many older cemeteries have become illegible, but the graves are nevertheless honored.

The request for marking the burial site with a simple natural marker should be honored.

June 1989

187. ISAIAH VERSE ON A TOMBSTONE

QUESTION: May a verse from Isaiah which has also been used in the *New Testament* be inscribed on a tombstone? It was the favorite verse of the deceased who was a convert to Judaism. (Saul Nathanson, Dallas TX)

ANSWER: Except for the fact that this woman converted to Judaism we would have absolutely no hesitation about using any Biblical verse, irrespective of the later use of such a verse as that is irrelevant for us. The only restriction for us is that we would not put anything on a stone which would mock the inability of the dead to praise God (Ber 18a; *Shulhan Arukh* Yoreh Deah 367.2). In this instance we must ask ourselves whether the Biblical verse carried

Christian connotations for the woman in question. It may very well be that her first acquaintance with this verse came through the *New Testament*, and so it may have childhood memories, however, she has virtually lived her whole adult life as a Jewess, participated in the synagogue, raised her children as Jews and in every way was part of the Jewish community. We should, therefore, treat her wish to have this verse inscribed on her tombstone as the wish of any other Jew and ignore the fact of her conversion many years ago. The verse from Isaiah is appropriate and we should use it without hesitation.

February 1989

188. A WIDOW'S INSCRIPTION

QUESTION: A woman has been married twice. She did not have children from either marriage and both husbands have predeceased her. She was married to her first husband for twenty-five years and her second husband for twenty-three years. She will be buried with her second husband, but would like to have the marriage to her first husband permanently remembered. May she have her name placed on the tombstone of both men? (Rabbi Robert L. Lehman, New York NY)

ANSWER: The original purpose of a tombstone in a Jewish cemetery was simply to make *kohanim* aware of the location of the grave so that they would not inadvertently come in contact with the dead and be defiled (*M* Ohalot 7.1). Tombstones were mentioned in connection with the patriarchs (Gen 42.23) and elsewhere (Ez 39.15). In these instances and subsequently, the honor of the dead was a major motivating factor (Y. M. Tukzinski *Gesher Hayim* Vol I pp 303 ff). The inscriptions on tombstones from Hellenistic and Roman times were simple and usually contained the name of the deceased and occasionally the name of the father (*Gesher Hayim* Vol II p 205 ff). Subsequently the name of the husband was frequently included on the wife's stone, but that was not mandatory (Greenwald *Kol Bo al Avelut* pp 381 ff). There was little discussion about tombstone engravings except for lengthy debates about the secular versus the Hebrew date. In the last century there was some discussion about the Hungarian custom of affixing photographs of the dead to the tombstone.

Biographical statements and the Biblical verses now found on some tombstones have not been mentioned in the literature. They have arisen as a folk custom.

In this instance there would be nothing wrong or novel about indicating on the tombstone of each husband that he was the husband of ... and so remembering the marriages on the stones.

July 1988

189. UNMARKED GRAVES

QUESTION: At the Jewish community cemetery in Winston-Salem, Mt. Sinai Cemetery, a new grave was being dug this past spring in an area in which the maps, in the possession of the Cemetery Committee, indicated that no one was buried. However, an old unmarked grave existed there. How should this old grave be marked and what should be done with that grave and the area around it? (Rabbi Thomas P. Liebschutz, Winston-Salem NC)

ANSWER: We know from Scriptural sources that markers were erected over graves even when the specific person buried there was not known (Gen 38.20; II K 23.17; Ez 39.15). The reference in Ezekiel was taken by the *Mishnah* (M K 5a) to indicate that grave markers represented a continuous tradition since Biblical times. Yet some doubt about this was shown by the statement in *Sheqalim* which stated that graves were marked with a white plasterlike substance on the first of *Elul* annually. This was done so that priests would not inadvertently come in contact with the grave and defile themselves (*M* Sheqalim 1.1). However, another section of the *Mishnah* stated that sums of money which remained after a funeral could be used for a permanent grave marker (2.5). We also have a statement about the earlier Simon, the Maccabee, who built a rather elaborate tomb (I Mac 13.27 ff). This may have been done because of his position as a ruler. Whatever uncertainties exist about the earlier period by *Talmudic* times, grave markers were commonly used (Hor 13b; San 96b; *J* Sheq 47a). These tombstones undoubtedly served a dual purpose: they honored the deceased and warned the priests away from this site of potential uncleanliness (M K 1.2, etc). In the later tradition tombstones became mandatory (*Shulhan Arukh* Yoreh Deah 348.2; Even Haezer 89.1; Greenwald *Kol Bo al Avelut* 370 ff). By the nineteenth century this *minhag* had become universal and was considered an essential part of each funeral (Abraham Benjamin Sofer *Ketav Sofer* Yoreh Deah 178).

In this instance there has been an interment, but the deceased is now unknown, therefore, a simple tombstone should be erected with a traditional inscription. This would be appropriate even though we do not know whether the grave is that of a Jew or a Christian. The fact that the individual is unknown should not disturb us. After all, names on many older tombstones have become illegible. The stone, itself, reminds us that someone is buried there and that we should treat this area with respect.

September 1987

190. REUSE OF A GRAVE

QUESTION: An individual was recently buried on our cemetery in the wrong grave. The person will soon be interred in the proper grave, but the question arose whether the grave in which the individual was briefly interred may be used or must it remain vacant. (Rabbi Thomas Liebchutz, Winston Salem NC)

ANSWER: There is a broad and sweeping general rule which indicates that no benefit must be received from the deceased. This referred, for example, to grazing animals near graves, etc. This principle of *hanaah* (Meg 29a; San 47b) would seem to prohibit such a reuse along with the statement of the *Talmud* (San 47a b; *Tur* and *Shulhan Arukh* Yoreh Deah 364.7), which declared that if a man prepared a grave for his father he, the son, may not be buried in it even though the grave was never used for the father. However, the discussion indicated that other matters were at issue; this referred to a *kever shel binyan* (in other words a grave that had been constructed of stone or possibly a grave built in a cave, and not a grave simply dug in the soil). The *Talmud* also indicated that its prohibition was limited to father and son because of the respect and devotion due from a son to a father, but that the grave could have been used for someone else. Furthermore, the *Talmudic* section also indicated that although no benefit of any kind may be received from a grave, i.e. it could not be sold, but it could be used for burying another individual. This whole matter was developed further in a responsum by Moses Sofer (*Ketav Sofer* Yeah Deah 177) who indicated that although one may not benefit from the dead, for example by using an empty grave as a storage site, one may bury another body in it. The same decision was reached by Abraham Glick (*Yad Yitzhaq* Vol III #295).

It would therefore be perfectly permissible in this instance to rectify the error, and rebury the body in the proper location. Then the individual who originally owned the grave or to whom it had been assigned may utilize it at the appropriate time. May that time be distant.

October 1989

191. THE ASHES OF A COUPLE IN A SINGLE URN

QUESTION: Is it appropriate for the cremains of a husband and a wife to be mingled in one urn? (Rabbi Jonathan Brown, Youngstown OH)

ANSWER: Reform Jewish practice permits cremation. This matter was discussed at some length a century ago (W. Jacob (ed) *American Reform Responsa* #100). In a note to that responsum added a decade ago, the committee stated that although we permit cremation we would, after the Holocaust, generally discourage it because of the tragic overtones. Orthodox Jews would, *bediavad,* generally bury cremains although they would not consider this an obligation (David Hoffmann *Melamed Lehoil* Yoreh Deah 113; S. Deutsch *Or Hamet*; etc).

In this instance, however, the husband and wife wish their ashes to be intermingled. This raises a whole series of questions. It is unlikely that the husband and wife will die at the same time. This means that one set of ashes may remain unburied for a considerable period or it would be necessary to disturb the buried ashes later. It is not permitted to disturb a grave once burial has taken place and it would make no difference whether we are dealing with cremains or a buried body. Exhumation is only permitted under very special circumstances, as for example when a cemetery can no longer receive proper care or has been condemned or when certain legal matters must be determined (Ezekiel Katzenellenbogen *Keneset Yehezkel* Even Haezer 46; I. Fleckeles *Shivat Zion* #64; S. B. Freehof *Current Reform Responsa* #37). Solomon B. Freehof also provided some additional reasons.

It would be acceptable to bury the two urns close to each other as tradition only requires six handbreadth between bodies buried side by side, and three handbreadth if they are buried on top of each other. This became necessary in the crowded cemeteries of Central Europe as in Prague. This solution of burial side by side or with one urn on top of the other would be acceptable if it is in accordance with congregational cemetery policy. The ashes should, however, not be intermingled.

February 1990

192. SCATTERING ASHES OF THE DEAD

QUESTION: On two separate occasions a husband and wife have left instructions that their cremated remains be scattered. In one instance, over a high mountain which meant a great deal to them. In the other, along the banks of the Potomac River as the family had been dedicated to the protection of this river basin. Should a rabbi participate in a funeral if he knows in advance that the cremated remains are not to be buried but will be scattered? May he participate in a memorial service after the remains have been dispersed in accordance with the wishes of the deceased? (Rabbi Arnold S. Task, Greensboro NC)

ANSWER: Burial of the dead was taken for granted by our forefathers and there were no discussions about whether burial should take place, but rather how soon it must occur. In addition the burial of individuals of doubtful status (criminals, apostates, etc.) was discussed. We Reform Jews have had no hesitation about burying the ashes of those who have been cremated (W. Jacob (ed) *American Reform Responsa* #100). Although there have been many Orthodox objections to cremation and a number of Orthodox authorities would not officiate at a funeral of those who were to be cremated (*Dudaeh Hasadeh* #16; Meyer Lerner *Hayei Olam*; Michael Higger *Halakhot Veaggadot*). However, the English Orthodox rabbinate permits rabbis to officiate both at a funeral and at the burial of the ashes of those who have been are cremated (*Rules of the Burial Society of the United Synagogue*). The American Conservative rabbinate permits a rabbi to officiate at the funeral but not at the cemetery in order to discourage cremation (*Proceedings, Rabbinical Assembly* 1939 p 156). In each of these instances as well as our own the burial of the ashes has been assumed.

Burial has traditionally been seen as a form of atonement (*M* San 6.6; 46b; *Tur* and *Shulhan Arukh* Yoreh Deah 362; Moses Feinstein *Igrot Mosheh* Yoreh Deah #143). Furthermore, burial permitted appropriate honors to be extended to the dead through the various rituals connected with the funeral and in subsequent years through visits to the cemetery. The large number of recent Reform responsa which have dealt with burial, funerals, *qaddish*, tombstones, and *Yahrzeit*, indicate the religious and psychological value of these rituals and customs.

Scattering the ashes removes one source of comfort which may help the surviving family overcome their grief and resume a normal life. We would, therefore, discourage the scattering of ashes and encourage their burial in an appropriate fashion in the cemetery. Furthermore, as cremation possesses new and different overtones for us, after the Holocaust, we have discouraged the practice.

There is nothing within Reform Jewish practice or custom which would prohibit a rabbi from officiating at a funeral or a memorial service of those who are to be cremated even when the ashes will not be buried.

April 1988

193. A TOMBSTONE FOR SCATTERED ASHES

QUESTION: A man who recently died requested that his ashes be scattered and the family has executed his wishes. Now, however, they would like the tombstone placed in the cemetery although there is no grave. They are willing to buy a grave space and simply set a stone. Is this in keeping with our tradition? (Rabbi D. N. Gluckman, Olympia Fields IL)

ANSWER: As we look at the history of tombstones in our tradition we will note that the patriarch Jacob marked the tomb of his wife Rachel (Gen 35.20). Then we find various other references to two markings in other sections of the Bible particularly the graves of the kings (II Kings 23.17; 1 Mac 13.27). When the tombs were discussed again in the *tanaitic* literature, we find that they were used principally to warn priests against the ritual uncleanliness associated with the dead (Tos Ohalot 17.4). The responsa of the Middle Ages indicated that tombstones were customarily placed on every tomb and that tradition was followed by Joseph Caro (*Shulhan Arukh* Even Haezer 89.1; Yoreh Deah 348.2).

Solomon B. Freehof has pointed out that there were few references until modern times about setting a tombstone in the absence of a body, but it has been discussed a number of times earlier in this century and, of course, following the Holocaust (W. Jacob (ed) *American Reform Responsa* #112). He stated that when a body could not be found it was perfectly permissible to set up a tombstone to honor the memory of the deceased. Such occasions have arisen in times of war, through accidents at sea and, of course, through the tragic destruction of European Jewry during the Holocaust.

Our case is somewhat different for we are dealing with an individual who specified that he not be buried and the ashes should be scattered. This is certainly not a matter which we wish to encourage. Since the Holocaust we have viewed cremation in a different light as the overtones of cremation have certainly changed for us. Scattering the ashes deprives the succeeding generations of a way to honor the dead which often is useful not only during the period of mourning, but subsequently.

In the spirit of discouraging this practice I would suggest

that we always ask such a family to obtain a plot in the cemetery and to erect a tombstone. This will indicate that the practice of scattering of ashes will complicate the period of mourning rather than simplify it and will increase stress. A stone may be erected and it would be unveiled in the normal manner.

December 1990

194. A CEREMONY FOR BURIAL OF BOOKS

QUESTION: The congregation wishes to have a ceremony for the burial of old books and a worn *Sefer Torah*. What kind of ritual would be appropriate? Is there anything in tradition about the burial of these objects? (Morris Teitelman, Toronto Ontario)

ANSWER: Traditionally a *Torah* or books which contain the name of God and were no longer fit for use were buried or set aside in a safe place (Rashi to Ket 19b; *Shulhan Arukh* Orah Hayim 154.5). Those sources indicated that they were frequently buried with a scholar. This was done in order to prevent the desecration or erasure of the name of God (Deut 12.3 *Sifrei* (ed Friedman p 87b; *Sefer Hahinukh* #437). In glancing through the literature I have not found any ceremony connected with the burial of books or their placement in a *genizah*.

We may wish to stimulate reverence for sacred texts through such a ceremony. It might begin with an explanation of the nature of the sacred in Judaism and the special place which the *Torah* and Hebrew books have had for us. This could be accompanied by readings or some form of study, perhaps utilizing the texts now to be buried. We might conclude with the *qaddish derabanan* normally recited at the conclusion of study. There are, of course, many other possibilities and the nature of the group with whom this is done should determine the form of the ceremony.

July 1990

195. AN OLD ISRAELI FLAG

QUESTION: An Israeli flag which has stood on our pulpit for some time is now worn-out. How should we dispose of it? (Morton Kramer, Los Angeles CA)

ANSWER: Special honors have been accorded to the various appurtinences of the synagogue which possessed different degrees of sacredness. Sacred texts and the *Torah* were buried or set aside in a safe place (Rashi to Ket 19b; *Shulhan Arukh* Orah Hayim 154.5). They were sometimes interred with a scholar. Items which were a little more distant like the cover of a *Torah* and binder were also sometimes buried with a scholar. Still other synagogue decorations, as for example the cover of the *bimah*, could be renewed, and the old item discarded.

Although the Israeli flag may stand on the *bimah*, it does not possess any degree of sacredness. It is a symbol of the State of Israel, but has no specific religious connotations, so we need exercise no unusual care for religious reasons. Of course there are the normal reasons for disposing of a flag in an appropriate way. We do so with the American flag in accordance with specific regulations about the flag, and would accord similar respect to the

310

flag of Israel. The attitude toward flags has changed in various periods as we have seen from recent discussions about the burning of the American flag, as well as its use on shirts and jackets, etc.

There is no degree of sacredness connected with the Israeli flag despite its place on the pulpit. We should dispose of a worn flag in a dignified manner, but not as a sacred object.

December 1989

196. CONTROL OF A CEMETERY

QUESTION: Our cemetery is part of a general cemetery. We now need to obtain new burial space, however, the general cemetery is unwilling to sell us any additional land. They would, however, provide an adjacent section and permit the Jewish community to control who may be buried there as well as the burial procedures. The land, however, would remain part of the larger general corporation which would set the fees and own the property. (Rabbi Richard B. Safran, Fort Wayne IN)

ANSWER: Burial grounds were owned by families or Jewish communities through most of the Jewish past. This tradition began with Abraham when he purchased a burial site for his wife, Sarah (Gen 23). Subsequently other cave tombs generally owned by families were used (M K 17a; B B 58a; etc), while communities established Jewish communal cemeteries. In some instances in which the number of Jews in a country was small a single cemetery sufficed for the entire nation. So, for example, medieval English Jewry possessed only a single cemetery in London. When efforts to enlarge the cemetery through purchase of additional ground failed or this was refused, Jewish communities were forced to add soil to the existing cemetery and bury anew atop of the old graves (Ariye Lev *Shaagat Ariye* #17; Abraham Danzig *Hokhmat Adam* Matzevot Mosheh #10; *Tur* and *Shulhan Arukh* Yoreh Deah 362.4; 363). Fortunately, that problem no longer arises.

In the nineteenth century it became customary for various European cities to control the land used for burial by establishing a single large municipal cemetery with sections for each religious body. I am under the impression that the land itself remained in the hands of the municipality though they permanently allocated a section to the Jewish community and stipulated that all matters connected with burial were to follow the practices of that community. Certain general matters such as security, the maintenance of roads, paths and walls were in the hands of the general cemetery. The details varied from place to place but such a pattern was established and accepted (*Shulhan Arukh* Yoreh Deah 363 ff and commentaries; Ezekiel Landau *Noda Biyehudah* #89).

The principal concern is the permanence of the graves sites as we do not wish to disturb the graves of those dear to us. If the land is permanently designated as a Jewish section and not a lease for a specific amount of time there is no problem. Nor would there be in your case. It is true that theoretically the owners could change their rules and at some time in the future use some of the land in a different manner. However, this might also occur with the cemetery entirely owned by the Jewish community. The construction of a public road forced the relocation of hundreds of graves in several instances (Greenwald *Kol Bo al Avelut*). In other words, even outright ownership of the cemetery does not guarantee the perpetual safety of the graves.

We should note one other distinction between the arrangements which you have discussed and those of Europe. In the

European case the municipality actually owned the cemetery, while in the United States it is likely to be a private corporation. That type of corporation despite regulations is more likely to suffer instability in the future than a municipality. As the Jewish cemetery in Fort Wayne has been part of the general cemetery for a long time, and as a good relationship with the general cemetery has existed through the years, there should be no problem about the new arrangements through which a Jewish area with the controls which you have stipulated is designated, but not purchased. It is important that this area be clearly delineated and that the agreement stipulate that this land be so designated permanently. Furthermore, all control over burial procedures, tombstones, memorial services, plantings, etc. must follow your congregational practices. It will be necessary to write a carefully worded document to guarantee that this will indeed be a Jewish cemetery although the land will not actually be owned by the Jewish community.

March 1988

197. NAMING A CEMETERY

QUESTION: An individual or family is considering the gift of a considerable sum of money so that the congregation can establish a cemetery. May the cemetery be named for an individual or a family? Does tradition mandate any particular wording for such a dedication? (Rabbi Michael M. Remson, Naperville IL)

313

ANSWER: Although there is a good deal of literature about death, burial and mourning, there is nothing about the name which a cemetery may bear. Traditionally cemeteries have either been named for the sponsoring congregation or simply for the neighborhood in which they were located. The latter name was often assigned by the people as they wished to describe the location; it was not part of an official document. In other instances the cemetery was merely designated as "old" or "new" and bore no name other than the name of the city.

I suppose that several considerations kept congregations from naming cemeteries for particular individuals. In ages past, and to some degree nowadays, there are superstitions connected with the cemetery and with death, so individuals feel that it is bad luck to have the cemetery bear the name of a living person or for that matter even the name of a family which survives in that community. Such considerations are of minor importance to us.

The second reason may be the fact that the cemetery is the final resting place for all individuals in a community and some bad feelings toward a particular family may make it difficult for some individuals to be buried in a cemetery which bears the name of that person. However, the same considerations would play a role with classrooms or meeting halls in synagogues which frequently bear the names of both living and dead donors.

There is also a third consideration if the cemetery is named after a family, will others be willing to provide funds to maintain it. Some funds, of course, are mandated by law; others are designated for individual graves, however, additional funds may be necessary and difficult to obtain when the cemetery bears a particular name. It may be wise, therefore, to attempt to include an endowment in the original gift and thereby avoid this problem in the future.

None of these considerations are of great significance. If an individual wishes to provide the funds so that the congregation may obtain a cemetery then it may in gratitude be named after that individual.

March 1990

198. JEWISH CEMETERY IN A GENERAL CEMETERY

QUESTION: Our congregation will establish its own cemetery through the purchase of a section of a municipal non-sectarian cemetery. Let me ask the following questions connected with it? (1) How should the Jewish section be separated from the general section as it will not be possible to erect a fence? (2) A number of our members are intermarried and therefore burial of gentile family members will occur from time to time, this will involve requests that non-Jewish clergy officiate. As this Jewish cemetery is part of a larger general cemetery, can we be more lenient and permit non-Jewish clergy to officiate or perhaps can we do so on the principle that each family lot is really a small individual cemetery, and that *betokh shelo* this would be permitted? (3) The general cemetery prohibits burial on Sunday or holidays. That would mean a potential delay of three days for burial on certain holiday weekends. Would that be permitted or should we reject the use of this cemetery for that reason? (Rabbi David F. Sandmel, Bangor ME)

QUESTIONS AND REFORM JEWISH ANSWERS

ANSWER: Let me turn to each of these questions separately. There is no difficulty in establishing a Jewish cemetery as part of a general municipal cemetery especially if the land is acquired through purchase. The Jewish section must be appropriately separated from the non-Jewish sections. This may be done through a fence or a permanent, continuous series of plantings. A fence line may be created through a permanent hedge, of hardy evergreen which will indicate clear boundaries at all seasons of the year. Tradition merely indicated that five feet should separate one cemetery from the other and that the barrier between the two cemeteries should be four feet high, sometimes a wide path was considered sufficient (W. Jacob (ed) *American Reform Responsa* #96). We would recommend a wall or a hedge (Greenwald *Kol Bo al Avelut* p 163). Tradition has few restrictions on cemetery plantings although they were generally avoided so that there would be no temptation to benefit from them and to provide maximum use of space for the actual graves (*Shulhan Arukh* Yoreh Deah 368.2; *Tzavnat Panea* I #74; *Minhat Elazar* IV #61 etc.).

We should follow the existing practices regarding the burial of non-Jews in the Jewish section. These are undoubtedly specified by your congregation. Such graves may not be marked with any non-Jewish symbol nor may Christian clergy officiate. If for some reason they do officiate they should restrict themselves to psalms or prayers of the *Rabbi's Manual* (W. Jacob (ed) *American Reform Responsa* #99). There is no reason to change this ruling as the cemetery is a Jewish cemetery and is to be so considered in every way. The fact that it forms a part of a larger entity is irrelevant. In fact in order to guard ourselves against any efforts in this direction, on the part of our laity, we should be especially strict in such matters.

The question of timely burial will have to be considered in

316

the light of local practice. In other words, a few Reform congregations are strict about burial on the same day or the next day, however, the vast majority will permit a delay so that more distant family members may arrive; that often means two or three days. Furthermore, union regulations frequently make it difficult to bury on Sunday or holidays and various congregations have had to adjust themselves to these conditions.

You might also inquire about potential restrictions by the general cemetery of memorial services as for example, between *Rosh Hashanah* and *Yom Kippur* or on *Yom Hashoah*, although these days may not pose a problem.

On balance it seems that the potential problems of the arrangement you propose may be overcome and you should be able to go ahead with those arrangements.

March 1988

199. A SECTION ADDED TO A JEWISH CEMETERY

QUESTION: The congregation owns a cemetery which has been used for several generations. Burial has been restricted to Jews. Now the congregation has purchased an adjacent section and wishes to change the bylaws of the cemetery so that the non-Jewish spouse of a congregational member may also be buried in the cemetery. They will restrict that right to the new section as they do not wish to impose on the more traditional members of the congregation. Need that section be divided from the rest of the cemetery? Would a walkway or set of plantings suffice? (Rabbi Gary Klein, Palm Harbor FL)

ANSWER: It is surprising that despite a good bit of discussion about burial customs relatively little appears in the literature about cemeteries aside from the mandate that every community should setup its own cemetery and thus honor its dead (Meg 29a; *Shulhan Arukh* Yoreh Deah 34). As a result in many communities the first act of the Jewish settler was the purchase of a piece of ground for a cemetery. That was true here in Pittsburgh as well and antedated my congregation by more than a decade. Once an area had been designated as a cemetery it was considered holy and the land could not be sold or rented out for other use as for example for grazing (Meg 29a; San 46a; *Shulhan Arukh* Yoreh Deah 368.1). Those who visited the cemetery were to behave in a dignified manner.

In some European countries it was not possible to obtain a separate Jewish cemetery so a section of the general cemetery was specifically set aside for Jewish burial (*Dudaeh Hasadeh* #66 and #89). This has also occurred in smaller American communities as for example in Springfield, Missouri, where I grew up. If the government imposed restrictions or condemned the land or if circumstances made it impossible for the community to properly look after a cemetery then it was possible to vacate it, move the graves and let the government have the site (Moses Sofer *Hatam Sofer* Yoreh Deah #353; Moshe Feinstein *Igrot Mosheh* Yoreh Deah 246 f). It was, then, possible according to tradition to abandon a cemetery for these reasons it was not, according to Orthodox practice, possible to set aside a section for non-Jewish burial. Although in *Mishnaic* and *Talmudic* times the command to bury gentile dead undoubtedly sometimes meant interment in a Jewish cemetery. Furthermore general Reform Jewish practice would permit the burial of a non-Jewish spouse in our cemetery (W. Jacob (ed) *American Reform Responsa* #98 ff). We have done so throughout this century.

The solution which you have described is appropriate both for the traditional members of your community and the others. By enlarging your cemetery and changing the rules for the new section you will be able to satisfy both the groups. A walkway or a series of plantings would be quite sufficient even between a Jewish and a Christian cemetery so that would certainly suffice for your purposes.

June 1989

200. SELLING A PORTION OF A CEMETERY

QUESTION: The congregation has owned a large tract of land as designated for use as a cemetery and a major segment of it has been developed. Approximately half of that has been used for burials. Now the congregation wishes to know whether the undeveloped tract of land may be sold. Is this considered sacred ground and part of the cemetery? (Dorothy Weiss, Colorado Springs CO)

ANSWER: Cemeteries and the places in which our dead were interred long held a special sacred place in Judaism. This began with the family burial site which Abraham selected for Sarah. The Cave of *Makhpelah* (Gen. 23; 25.9; 49.31; 50.13). Later on we find that the Kings of Israel had their own burial plots (II Kings 13.13; 15.7). The custom of family burial sites continued on into the period of the *Talmud* (B B 100a, B; San 47a; M Shek 2.5; Erub 5.1). Throughout this period communal grave sites were also used (II Kings 23.6; Ger 26.23; Hag 3b; Nid 17a; Sem 49b). All of these

319

cemeteries and those discussed in later literature were communal and it was the obligation of the entire community both to establish the cemetery and then to care for it appropriately (Ezekiel Landau *Noda Biyehudah* I, Yoreh Deah #89; Isaac Spector *Ein Yitzhoq* Yoreh Deah #34). The land was considered sacred and no profane use of it could be made. However, it was only matters directly related to graves from which no one was allowed to benefit (*Shulhan Arukh* Yoreh Deah 368.2 and commentaries). Of course, the cemetery was to be protected and even if Jews moved away from the community it was to be looked after by a neighboring community (Greenwald *Kol Bo al Avelut* pp 164; Moshe Feinstein *Igrot Mosheh* Yoreh Deah #246). Furthermore, we should note that there are many customs which have risen around the cemeteries care and most of the tradition which surrounds cemeteries is *minhag*.

The sale of a section of a cemetery was very rarely discussed. Generally once a piece of land had been acquired for use as a cemetery and an internment had taken place, it acquired a special status and so needed to be treated with respect. This was true of both the area in which internments were taking place and sections which remained vacant (Meg 29a *Shulhan Arukh* Yoreh Deah 368; Moses Sofer *Responsa* #335). There is some disagreement among the more recent Orthodox authorities but the sale of a cemetery or sections of it which will not be used for burial. Abraham Gumbiner permitted it (*Magen Avraham* to Orah Hayim 153.12), while the German authority David Hoffmann prohibited it (*Melamed Lehoil* Yoreh Deah #125).

In a large number of American cities we are faced with a somewhat different situation than those of Central Europe. In many communities small congregations, founded late in the nineteenth or early in the twentieth century by groups of immigrants, quickly established cemeteries. As they often were able to acquire only the cheapest and most inaccessible pieces of land, these cemeteries are on hillsides and steep ravines or in other areas difficult to reach. Furthermore, many of these congregations were forced to move as neighborhoods changed, and if they did not have the means to do so were simply closed and the cemetery abandoned. It is clearly the responsibility of the rest of the community to look after these cemeteries, but it is not their responsibility to retain all the land originally designated for cemeteries. As the American cities have grown and as modern technology has made formerly inaccessible sites available for use, the land originally designated for these cemeteries has frequently risen in value. It would be perfectly appropriate to sell unused segments of these cemeteries in order to provide necessary care for the sections in which burials have taken place. This is an appropriate use of the cemetery land and would be in keeping both with tradition and with the original intent of the founders of the cemetery.

In your instance you are faced with other American phenomenon with congregations acquiring large tracts of land, and then discovering for a variety of demographic reasons that they may now wish to dispose of it in order to maintain the remainder of the cemetery, to help with congregational projects, and to limit the amount of land for which they must care. Those areas in such cemeteries which have remained wild and totally undeveloped may be sold while those areas which have already been developed and therefore really designated for cemetery use are to be considered part of the actual cemetery and may not be sold.

Generally if the congregation is substantial and the cemetery is in a protected area where there is no danger to the graves, then even large plots of land should continue to be held for the more distant future. My own congregation in Pittsburgh holds such a very large area, probably sufficient for burial for several centuries, and it would be appropriate unless circumstances change drastically to continue to retain this land and use it for burial sites as originally intended.

We may then summarize that it is preferable for a congregation to continue to use lands designated for that use unless there is a very good reason for the sale of a portion of this land. It may then be sold and the funds derived from it should be used for the care of the cemetery or an allied religious purpose.

January 1991

201. HOLOCAUST MEMORIALS AND THE JEWISH TRADITION

QUESTION: Does the Jewish tradition encourage permanent Holocaust Memorials? Are there any negative overtones or problematic aspects to such a memorial? (James Katz, Vancouver BC)

ANSWER: Our tradition has always tried to combine an adequate respect for the past and the memory of martyrs alongside a positive outlook toward the future and the world around us. We know very little about monuments of any kind in ancient times. It was reported that some of the kings of Israel built monuments on their tombs and certain historic events were marked by monuments. So for example when Joshua crossed the Jordan he placed some stones as a memorial to this occasion. However, the other grand events of the past were not marked in any fashion. That was true for military victories, the crossing of the Sea of Reeds, etc. Even in the Hellenistic period of our history, the days of the Maccabees, we find no monuments to their heroic struggle. It is interesting that this is so as the entire Near East is littered with monuments usually to victories and often covered with long inscriptions as well as magnificent art work.

In subsequent Jewish history there were grave markers for individuals or sarcophagi with inscriptions upon them. We possess these from the later Hellenistic and Roman periods in Israel, the rest of the Near East, as well as Italy (E. Goodenough *Jewish Symbols in the Greco-Roman Period* Vols 1 & 3; Lee I. Levine (ed) *Ancient Syngagogues Revealed,* etc). However, none of these were memorials are to any group of individuals or a specific event.

It was only in the Middle Ages at the time of the Crusades that mass martyrdom was noted in elegies as well as historical chronologies. Some of these have survived synagogue poetry or in other forms. Although they were not physical monuments they represented a step in that direction. Even if those Rhineland communities in the twelfth and thirteenth century had wished to memorialize in a concrete fashion it would not have been possible as their lives were too uncertain and they were frequently driven from one community to another. In subsequent centuries major tragedies were commemorated not only in literature, and syngagogue poetry, but also in special monuments or plaques. So, for example the old Jewish cemetery in the cities of Worms and Prague contain memorial tablets to commemorate tragic persecutions over the centuries. Such plaques may be found in synagogues also.

Where it was possible sad events of the past were remembered in a permanent form within the Jewish community. So for example those Jewish soldiers who died in the first World War, either on the Allies side or on the side of the Central Powers, have been memorialized in fountains and statutes as well as whole buildings. For instance the great synagogue in Augsburg had a memorial fountain to those who died in that war while the Budapest Jewish community built an entire synagogue as a memorial.

It was only rarely possible to erect a memorial in the general community. That, of course, is possible nowadays in the Western world. It would be entirely appropriate to do so and to remember the Holocaust in this fashion. There is a long tradition which slowly moved in this direction.

We should, however, exercise some caution for a number of reasons. The resources even of the American Jewish community are not unlimited and so monuments should serve a useful purpose as well as a commemorative one. A museum, educational center or something else along those lines would for that reason, in my mind at least, be preferable to a statue or a fountain. Such facilities could take many forms all of which would be appropriate as memorials.

Further more we must ask ourselves what we wish to accomplish by such a memorial. On the one hand it is necessary for us and for the entire Western world to remember the Holocaust so that nothing like it will occur again to us or to any other group of people. However, we certainly do not wish to look upon ourselves as primarily survivors of this tragedy. There is a great deal which is positive which we have accomplished in the modern world and much in our tradition that has nothing to do with suffering and persecution. So it is important that monuments, memorials, museums, and educational institutions not only recall the tragic days of the past but also the positive and hopeful outlook of Judaism.

June 1989

202. MEMORIAL FOR POLISH FAMILY GRAVES

QUESTION: Several families have recently returned from a visit to Warsaw where their family lived before World War II. Their forebearers were buried in the large city cemetery which is now heavily overgrown. They located some of their graves and will maintain them, but they would also like to erect a series of monuments to their ancestors here and encourage others to do the same. Is this appropriate? (Charles Smith, Washington DC)

ANSWER: From our earliest beginnings, we have recalled the pious figures of the past. *Zehut avot* has played an important role in our lives. This was already followed by Jacob, our patriarch (Gen 32.10), and we have continued that tradition through *Yahrzeit* and in other ways. The latest generation has always done its best to care for family graves. These families will not be able to visit Warsaw on a regular basis, so their wish to honor the family dead in in Washington should be encouraged.

We must, however, remember that our tradition has emphasized simplicity in funeral rites and tombstones as mentioned in earlier responsa of this volume. The memory of previous generations should be honored primarily through acts of *tzedaqah*. The proposed monuments should be simple and not place a burden on the families.

January 1990

203. YEWS IN A CEMETERY

QUESTION: May yews be planted in our Jewish cemetery? Some individuals have objected stating that this plant has specific Christian connotations. (David Weill, Albany NY)

ANSWER: Our Jewish tradition is very specific about customs of non-Jews which are prohibited, and those which are permitted. *Avodah Zarah* (11a) made it clear that only customs which are directly connected with idolatrous worship were prohibited (*Shulhan Arukh* Yoreh Deah 178.1). For this reason, it would not be wrong for a Jew to wear garments akin to those on non-Jews, but he should not wear garments which are specifically used in church ritual. The same would be true of the use of non-Jewish music in Jewish services. As long as it is folk music, and not specifically associated with a Christian service, it would be appropriate as shown by Joel Sirkes (*Bayit Hadash* #127).

Yews and other evergreens such as junipers, hemlocks and cedars have frequently been planted in cemeteries throughout the world as they are evergreens and, therefore, enhance the cemetery in all seasons. Some individuals have associated these evergreens with the promise of eternal life. We have no specific association between that thought and any kind of plant, although the hope remains part of the Jewish tradition.

There would be no reason for avoiding any kind of evergreen in a Jewish cemetery. Any Christian symbolism may be associated in the popular mind is vague and is not universal. Such plantings would not be an imitation of the non-Jewish world around us. They are permitted.

September 1988

204. CEMETERY PLANTINGS

QUESTION: Is it prohibited to plant trees and shrubs in our new Jewish cemetery? May individual plantings on graves be undertaken by various families? (N. Goldman, New York NY)

ANSWER: There are extensive discussion of plantings in the cemetery and their potential use. Low plants as well as shrubs and trees were generally found in Jewish cemeteries. The tradition has stated that grasses and flowering plants which grow within the cemetery, but not on graves may be used (Mahari Weill *Responsa* #94; Isserles to *Shulhan Arukh* Yoreh Deah 368.2). However, greenery which is on the grave itself must be used for the benefit of graves, or it should be burned (*Ibid*). Similar stipulations have been made about fruit trees. We can see from this that trees as well as other plantings have often been found on cemeteries.

Some responsa have discussed whether the fruit of such trees on the cemetery could be used to feed the poor in the community or its wood used to build a *miqveh* (Maharam Schick Yoreh Deah 358; Maharsham *Responsa* Vol 3 #257; *Imrei Yosher* Vol 1 #33; *Shoel Umeshiv* Vol 1 #336; Rivad *Responsa* #42). The more recent authorities have prohibited this; their stance reflects a general mood of restrictiveness. It may also show diminished economic pressures which made it less necessary to use anything from the cemetery for the welfare of the community.

A few Orthodox authorities have stated that it is improper to plant on the graves or in the cemetery (*Responsa Avnei Nezer* Yoreh Deah 476), and the wood or fruit from such plantings which existed from an earlier time could be used only in a very limited fashion (Greenwald *Kol Bo al Avelut* p 170).

We see, from these discussions, that there is little which prohibits the planting of trees in the cemetery. The lack of trees in some Orthodox cemeteries may be due to the space limitations of European cemeteries.

We should note a number of Biblical references to individuals buried under trees (Gen 35.8; I Sam 31.13) or in a garden (II Kings 21.18; 21.26).

Let us now turn to plantings on individual graves; we should be concerned about the uniformity of graves so that there is less distinction between the poor and rich members of a congregation (M K 27b; *Shulhan Arukh* Yoreh Deah 352.1). Let me suggest that if it is the general custom in the community to have some simple plantings on the grave and if the cemetery provides a choice among these which would add no great burden on the survivors, it would be permissible. We should continue to encourage some uniformity in the graves both in the markers as well as in the plantings on the graves.

March 1990

205. WHO IS TO LIGHT A YAHRZEIT CANDLE?

QUESTION: The family has traditionally lit a *Yahrzeit* candle to commemorate the death of their father. A recent divorce has divided the family and so husband and wife have continued to light the *Yahrzeit* candle. The husband wishes to prohibit his former wife from doing so as it was his father who died. Does he have the right to do so? Can the wife continue to light a memorial candle for her former father-in-law? (Arnold Friedman, Trenton NJ)

ANSWER: Commemoration of the dead on the anniversary of their death is a custom which grew more important through the centuries. The custom is of German origin therefore the German name; it was first mentioned by Isaac of Tyrnau in the sixteenth century. It spread to *Sephardic* Jewry over considerable opposition due to the influence of Isaac Luria, the *Kabbalist* of Safed. Among *Sephardim* it is called *Nahalah*. It has been the practice for the male children to recite a memorial prayer on the anniversary of the death (*Shulhan Arukh* Orah Hayim 568.8 Yoreh Deah 402.12).

From the Middle Ages onward *Yahrzeit* candles were also lit. This is probably under the influence of the North German Catholic environment (M. Güdemann *Geschichte* III). Such a flame was usually lit and the fuel was designed in such a way that it would burn for twenty-four hours whether it was a wax candle or oil was used as in earlier periods. Strictly speaking it is not incumbent upon anyone to light such a candle. Generally the surviving children both sons and daughters did so even if the duty of reciting the *qaddish* is only incumbent upon the male children.

There would be no objection for a former daughter-in-law, grandchildren or for that matter anyone else who feels that they wish to honor this man to light a *Yahrzeit* candle. The observance is a fine custom. It is private, not done in the synagogue, and so is no one's specific prerogative. In fact it is commendable that the former daughter-in-law wishes to continue to honor her former father-in-law. She hould be encouraged to do so.

June 1989

206. A YAHRZEIT DATE FOR A HOLOCAUST VICTIM

QUESTION: A family of a Holocaust victim does not know the precise day of his death and now wishes to choose a date for the *Yahrzeit*. Is there any guidance which tradition may provide? Can they select any date of the year? Should it be *Yom Hashoah* or another date? (Rabbi Arnold Fink, Alexandria VA)

ANSWER: The desire to honor the memory of the deceased has been expressed in different ways during various periods of our past. In the *Talmudic* period no wine was drunk or meat consumed on that day (Ned 12a). In the Middle Ages it seems to have been customary to fast as a way of commemorating on the anniversary of a father's death (*Bet Yosef* quoting *Hagohot Asheri* to *Tur* Orah Hayim 568; Caro to *Tur* Yoreh Deah 376; *Shulhan Arukh* Orah Hayim 568.7 ff). The *Yahrzeit* as we now commemorate it arose as a German Jewish custom which slowly spread throughout the Jewish world (*Shulhan Arukh* Yoreh Deah 376.4 and Isserles).

The day for *Yahrzeit* is set by the date of death (*Shulhan Arukh*, Orah Hayim 568.8; Yoreh Deah 402.12). There is some controversy about the observance during the first year. Should *Yahrzeit* be observed to commemorate the day of death or the day of burial. The latter was suggested by Maharil (*Responsa #7*; *Shulhan Arukh* Yoreh Deah 402.12 and commentaries for a discussion).

If the date of death was not known then a date was simply chosen (*Shulhan Arukh* Orah Hayim 568.7 and commentaries). For that purpose any date might be chosen. In this instance one could make a good case for and against the selection of *Yom Hashoah*. It is certainly appropriate as it combines the memory of an individual with all the other dead. On the other hand, as this is a general day of mourning, it may not provide enough specific honor for a particular individual. Tradition provides us with no guidance and my personal inclination would be to choose another date and to set that aside specifically for this victim of the Holocaust.

August 1990

207. YAHRZEIT FOR A NON-JEW

QUESTION: May an individual observe *Yahrzeit* for a non-Jewish leader in the community? The individual was very close to that person throughout life. (Richard Adler, Montreal Quebec)

ANSWER: In the long periods of our history during which relationships between non-Jews and Jews were good, we frequently honored them. So, non-Jews were welcome to worship in the Temple (I Kings, 8.41 ff) and participated in its construction as did Hiram, King of Lebanon. Furthermore, non-Jewish sacrifices were acceptable (Meg 73b), as were gifts by pagans unless made with idolatrous intent (Ar 7b). Much later the famous Bevis Marks synagogue (1702) in London contained a roof beam which was the gift of Queen Anne. There was no mention of specific memorials requested with these gifts, but they were publicly acknowledged as the gift of non-Jews. So, gifts by non-Jews to the synagogue are acceptable as long as they are used in accordance with the desires of the congregation (*Yad* Hil Matnat Aniyim 8.8; *Tur* Yoreh Deah 258; *Shulhan Arukh* Yoreh Deah 254.2 and Isserles, 259.4).

We were, of course, also obligated to bury the dead of non-Jews (Git 60a) and to deal with them in every way as Jews through the *hevrah qadishah*. The usual memorial prayers may be recited for non-Jews and this was done frequently through the ages.

When a non-Jewish ruler who was good to our people died, we mourned him with the appropriate services and several such services from the last century have been preserved. As we honor the dead in these ways there would be nothing wrong with commemorating their *Yahrzeit* in the customary fashion.

June 1989

208. *YAHRZEIT* BONFIRE

QUESTION: A family always finds itself at its country house when the *Yarhzeit* for their father occurs. They normally light bonfires several times during the week and would like to dedicate one of them to their grandfather each year,. May this be done in place of the *Yahrzeit* candle? (Rachel Cohen, New York NY)

ANSWER: *Yahrzeit* is an *Ashkenazi* custom which began in the Middle Ages (W. Jacob (ed) *American Reform Responsa* # 127). The custom of lighting a *Yahrzeit* candle was first mentioned by Solomon Luria (*Responsa* 46; Joseph Schawrtz *Hadrat Qodesh* p 18). When candles or oil were not available or impractical, an electric light may be used (*Gesher Hahayim* I p 343). The *Yahrzeit* candle is lit on the evening when our days normally begin and continues to burn throughout the day of the *Yahrzeit*. On *shabbat* or festivals, it is lit before the festive candles. If one forget to light it, then one lights it upon remembering after *shabbat* or the festival has ended.

The commemoration should last twenty-four hours, from one evening to the next. It would be impractical to keep a fire burning for that length of time. Whatever the children intend to do as a memorial around the bonfire, they should also light the *Yahrzeit* light.

February 1989

209. HEBREW YAHRZEIT DATES

QUESTION: My congregation for many years notified individuals of the date of their *Yahrzeit*, but has chosen to do so with the English dates. We have now switched to the Hebrew dates, but there has been some protest. Is one preferable over the other? (Harry Rubenstein, New Jersey)

ANSWER: As we look at the history of the Jewish calendar we realize that the base year for numbering the years has changed through the ages. In the Biblical period the numbers were reckoned according to the reign of a particular king. As this method proved cumbersome in a more complex society, especially one which dealt with individuals outside of the Jewish kingdom, the Seleucid system of numbering was adopted. Later still the destruction of the Temple was used as the base year, and sometime in the *Talmudic* or *Gaonic* period numbering the years according to the creation, the system now generally used, was introduced. For centuries several systems existed side by side. We should note that when the Seleucid system was adopted it carried no religious overtones, simply the practical implications of Seleucid rule over a large area; it was the system by which contracts had to be dated (*minyan shetarot*). There were which contracts had to be dated (*minyan shetarot*). There were authorities in the *Mishnaic* period who felt that the date according to this system had to be included in a divorce in order to validate it (*M* Git 8.6). Although Joseph Caro much later indicated that this system of dating was used simply "for the sake of peace" (*Bet Yosef* to *Tur* Even Haezer 127). We still find some remnants of this Seleucid dating up to the sixteenth century in Egypt.

Through the entire Middle Ages the Christian and Muslim calendar had strong religious overtones, and so they could not be used. However in the last centuries the Christian calendar has become secularized and is generally utilized for practical and commercial relationships. Leading rabbinic authorities have not hesitated to use it, so for example Moses Isserles in some of his responsa (#51), or much later the extremely conservative Moses Sofer (*Igrot Mosheh* Even Haezer #43). The Jewish calendar remained especially for life cycle events and, of course, the religious seasons. All of this indicates that there is little hesitation about using the secular calendar for practical affair. However, it is important to use the Jewish calendar for *Yahrzeit* and in religious documents. Our people will be aware of the Hebrew calendar only if they are regularly reminded. We do this through announcing the new month, through Hebrew dates in our bulletins and personal correspondence.

The *Yahrzeit* notification should use the Hebrew date. Furthermore why would it be necessary to inform a family of the *Yahrzeit* date as they are unlikely to forget the secular date? They may, however, have trouble assigning the proper Hebrew date. It is appropriate to use the Hebrew dating system.

April 1988

Even Haezer

210. PREMARITAL COUNSELING

QUESTION: What is the status of premarital counselling in the Jewish tradition? (Jerry L. Bloch, Toronto Ontario)

ANSWER: Those who conduct a wedding ceremony, the *mesader qidushin*, must be knowledgeable in the laws of marriage according to the tradition. Nothing in the literature of the past dealt specifically with counselling the couple or discussing potential problems which the couple may have. In other words, the officiating individual should know enough not to marry individuals who are disqualified from marrying each other for a variety of reasons. Nothing else was demanded of him. This pattern may have come about as most marriages up to modern times were arranged by the parents for very young brides and grooms. It was a parental duty to prepare children for marriage and to deal with problems in the new relationship. This was never formalized, but we can assume that it occurred. There is, therefore, nothing in the tradition which deals directly with premarital counselling and the role of the rabbi in it.

Premarital counselling is a modern innovation which should be encouraged especially as the former role of parents in this area has diminished. The rabbi is in a good position to be helpful. Such counseling may help the stability of marriages and will involve the young couple in Jewish life. This type of counselling is important and should become part of all preliminaries to a marriage.

April 1989

211. MARRIAGE BETWEEN *MEHUTAMIN*

QUESTION: The father of the groom and mother of the bride who recently married in my congregation have been seeing each other on a social basis. May they marry? How does this effect the relationship of the children? (Rabbi Alan H. Greenbaum, Thousand Oaks CA)

ANSWER: The forbidden degrees of marriage were listed in the Bible (Lev 20.11-21; Deut 23.3; 27.20-23). The *Talmud* extended these prohibitions either by direct extension or analogy. Sometimes it also did so in order to carry out the intent of the Biblical statement which may not have been clear (Yeb 21a; 49a; 62b; *J* Yeb 2.4).

These forbidden degrees of relationships are further clarified in the later codes (*Yad* Hil Ishut 1.1 ff; Hil Issurei Biah 2.7 ff; *Tur* and *Shulhan Arukh* Even Haezer 15.1 ff; 2.1 ff). Marriages between prohibited degrees which took place despite the prohibition were considered invalid (*en tofsin*) and were dissolved through a divorce (Kid 67b; *Yad* Hil Ishut 4.12 f; *Shulhan Arukh* Even Haezer 15.1; 44.6 f). As one reads through the lengthy discussion of these marriages, the question which you asked has also been discussed. Such marriages were specifically mentioned by the *Talmud* and the later codes, and for that matter a marriage between children of a widower and a widow, who had married each other and thereby became step-brother and step-sister, was also permitted (Sota 43b; *Shulhan Arukh* Even Haezer 15.11). There was some discussion among Palestinian scholars as to whether such a marriage between step-brother and step-sister should be permitted as it might not appear proper, but the law agreed that it was permissible.

336

It is clear from this *Talmudic* discussion that the marriage which the couple in question contemplate has always been considered appropriate and I hope that these individuals have a happy future together.

February 1989

212. A WEDDING AND THE ESTRANGED PARENTS

QUESTION: A bride and groom have disagreed with their parents over the wedding arrangements. The disagreement led to hostility, and eventually the couple asked that the grooms parents and friends not attend the wedding. The parents have asked the rabbi to postpone the wedding. He felt that the couple agreed with each other and there was no reason for postponement. The wedding was held with some additional security to assure no disruptions. Was this the proper path? (Rabbi H. B. Waintrup, Abington PA)

ANSWER: Tradition, of course, stated that the father had complete jurisdiction over his daughter until she reached the age of puberty (*M* Kid 2.1; 41a), although he was asked to fulfill her wishes whenever possible particularly in matters of matrimony. We should note that the father had no such control over his son, although there were instances in which the father nevertheless seized control (Moses Mintz *Responsa* #98). In the Middle Ages some of the synods expressed the feling felt that children were becoming too rebellious and so tried to control them through a variety of ordinances (Friedmann *Toledot Erusin Venisuin* pp 138 ff). There were, of course, responsa which dealt with these kinds of disagreements about marriage. In most instances they decided in favor of the children as they were the ultimate concerned party. One of them put it beautifully and said that the couple was best able to judge the heavenly verdict in this area. Sometimes they stated that marriage would most certainly succeed for those who were in love, and so no compulsion should be introduced (Solomon ben Aderet *Responsa* Vol I #272; Joseph Colon *Responsa* #174.3).

Parents were able to exercise some control over their children. They sought to guide them through whatever means were available, but ultimately in matters of matrimony the decision rested with the couple.

In this case, I presume that the argument over arrangements conceals deeper disagreements. It would be wise if both parties were to see either the rabbi or some counselor who could help them and bring about reconciliation. The path, however, which you have chosen of going ahead with the wedding is certainly very much in keeping with tradition.

May 1990

213. SECOND MARRIAGE CEREMONY

QUESTION: I was recently asked to officiate at the marriage ceremony of congregants who had already been married to each other for more than twenty years. He is Jewish by birth, she converted to Judaism, but without *tevilah*. The idea of the second marriage emerged because the woman in question has undergone a more traditional conversion with *tevilah* under the auspices of a liberal Orthodox rabbi. Should there be a second wedding ceremony in accordance with the wishes of this woman? (Rabbi Daniel S. Alexander, Charlottesville VA)

ANSWER: This question demands that we look at the nature of our conversion ceremony and at the implications of a repetition of the *berakhot* for our marriage ceremonies.

Conversion within Reform Judaism has placed less emphasis on ritual and more on a course of study required of the converts. Through our courses we familarize prospective converts with Jewish life, liturgy, history, literature, Hebrew, and the *mitzvot* which are incumbent upon us as Reform Jews. The course of study has changed over the generations, but not significantly as we have sought to emphasize both ideas and practice. Ultimately, of course, it is the commitment of the respective convert which is decisive.

The ritual for conversion has changed through the years. As a general practice both *miqveh* and circumcision were not customary in the United States by the latter part of the last century. Sometime colleagues, nevertheless, continued to require both, and neither were ever officially abolished; they simply fell into disuse. At the present time judging by congregations with which I am familiar in the United States and in Canada, *tevilah* either in a *miqveh* or in an appropriate body of water is widely practiced and in many communities it has become mandatory for conversion. We would, however, not consider a conversion conducted in the past or present without *tevilah* or *tipat dam* as invalid. That is true even in communities where these rituals have been mandated. Anyone coming from another community would, *bediavad*, be considered as having a valid conversion. For that matter this kind of question should never be asked by any of our colleagues. Such inquiry would be dangerous not only for us, but for everyone within the Jewish community for there are always individuals who consider themselves "more pious." Even among the Orthodox, the conversions of a whole group of traditional colleagues have been rejected by other Orthodox rabbis. Our approach would state that immersion in a *miqveh* has gained new meaning for us and therefore many among us have re-adopted this practice, however, we honor the mood of a former generation which understood it differently.

This line of reasoning would preclude a second wedding ceremony as that would be tantamount to stating that the former conversion was invalid, something which we certainly do not wish to do.

We should also remember the nature of the Jewish wedding. There are three ways of effecting a marriage:

(a) The most common form featured a document witnessed by two competent individuals and handed by the groom to the bride (Kid 9a; *Shulhan Arukh* Even Haezer 32.1-4). This has remained the essential covenant of the modern wedding. The document is the modern *ketubah* signed by two witnesses.

(b) In addition, it was possible to effect a marriage through the transfer of an item of value (*kesef*) in the presence of two competent witnesses. This remains as part of the modern wedding in the form of presenting a ring with the formula "*harei at mequdeshet...*" (Kid 2a, b; *Shulhan Arukh* Even Haezer 27.1).

(c) Finally, marriage can be effected through intercourse (*biah*) preceded by a statement indicating the wish to take this woman as wife in the presence of two witnesses who saw the couple leave for a private place (Kid 9b; *Shulhan Arukh* Even Haezer 33.1). The last method was severely frowned upon by the rabbis, but, *bediavad*, it was valid. Marriage simply through intercourse with proper intent would be akin to "common law" marriage.

Even if we discounted the first two of the three above it is clear that this couple intended to be married and their intention has been witnessed by the community, and so the marriage would be recognized on these grounds alone. This would present an ancillary reason for not having a second wedding ceremony, however, the primary reason remains that of not invalidating the Reform conversion which occurred some years ago.

The wishes of the couple may, perhaps, be accommodated in a different fashion through a ceremony of rededication which often nowadays accompanies an important wedding anniversary. There is no Jewish tradition for such ceremonies, but neither is there anything which would prohibit our going in this direction. We should encourage this as nowadays family life is frequently in jeopardy. Whatever we can do to strengthen family ties and to bring successful marriages to the attention of our people is welcome. A simple ceremony without the original *berakhot* would be appropriate and would fulfill the wishes of the couple without creating the problems mentioned above.

February 1990

214. SIBERIAN WEDDING

QUESTION: A couple recently emigrated to the United States from the Soviet Union and have asked whether they need a Jewish wedding ceremony. They were married in a Siberian prison camp simply by declaring their intent to marry each other. Two Jewish witnesses were present, they exchanged a small object of value, but there were no written documents and no traditional ceremony. (Sylvan Schwartz, Miami FL)

ANSWER: There are three ways of effecting a marriage: (a) The most common form featured a document witnessed by two competent individuals and handed by the groom to the bride (Kid 9a; *Shulhan Arukh* Even Haezer 32.1-4). This has remained the essential covenant of the modern wedding. The document is the modern *ketubah* signed by two witnesses. (b) In addition, it was possible to effect a marriage through the transfer of an item of value (*kesef*) in the presence of two competent witnesses. This remains as part of the modern wedding in the form of presenting a ring with the formula "*harei at mequdeshet...*" (Kid 2a, b; *Shulhan Arukh* Even Haezer 27.1); a *minyan* was required from the Middle Ages onward to avert some specific problems. Yet a marriage is valid *bediavad* without a *minyan*. (c) Finally, marriage can be effected through intercourse (*biah*) preceded by a statement indicating the wish to take this woman as wife in the presence of two witnesses who saw the couple leave for a private place (Kid 9b; *Shulhan Arukh* Even Haezer 33.1). The last method was severely frowned upon by the rabbis, but, *bediavad*, it is valid. Marriage simply through intercourse with proper intent would be akin to "common law" marriage.

In this case we have a couple who lived together with the intent of marriage. They were both adults and knew what they were doing. They sought to make it as Jewish as possible by transferring an item of value in the presence of two adult Jewish witnesses. Since that time they have lived together as man and wife both in the Soviet Union and now in the United States; nothing further is necessary. If they wish to participate in one of the numerous communal "Jewish weddings" created for the benefit of Russian Jewish immigrants in various American cities, that is fine, but such a ceremony is not essential for their marriage to be Jewishly recognized.

September 1990

215. MARRIAGE WITH A UNITARIAN UNIVERSALIST

QUESTION: A young Jewish couple wishes to marry. The woman is of Jewish parentage and was raised as a Jew. She was married for twelve years to a non Jew and has two children age seven and fourteen. For the past four years she has been affiliated with a Unitarian Universalist Fellowship and for eighteen months has been employed as their Director of Religious Education. She is active in this fellowship as are her children yet all of them consider themselves to be Jews and conduct some Jewish rituals in their household. The couple is also active in a Jewish congregation and they intend now to raise their children as Jews and send them to the Jewish Religious School. Is it within the framework of Reform Judaism for me to officiate at the wedding? (Rabbi Richard D. Agler, Boca Raton FL)

ANSWER: The background and pattern of life of this young woman indicate doubt, searching, and a measure of confusion. Tradition would consider her a Jew, but an apostate. As the children have been enrolled in a "religious school" program of this fellowship, and as she has served as Director of "Religious Education", this indicates more than a casual affiliation, but a well thought out religious response.

You mentioned in your letter that the young couple has now

decided that the children would attend the Jewish Religious School. This shows us the future path of the next generation and should be welcomed. However, the young woman's continued service as Director of Religious Education of the Unitarian Universalist Fellowship would exclude her from the Jewish community. She has left us willingly, without duress, and so we must look upon her and others who have joined various Christian groups in the United States as willing, conscious converts and honor their new religious affiliation. Technically according to our tradition such individuals would continue to be considered as Jews by descent (W. Jacob *Contemporary American Reform Responsa* #66, 68), but we would not include them in our congregation. Although Unitarian Universalists are not in the same category as Messianic Jews who frequently misrepresent their true affiliation, the Unitarian movement also poses some danger to us. We should therefore not confuse our congregants by creating the impression that members of a Unitarian Universalists group may at the same time be members of our congregation. This is not a philosophical discussion group which provides intellectual stimulation, but a religious fellowship which seeks to continue its tradition into the next generation.

The young lady has taken an initial step toward Judaism through the enrollment of her children in the synagogue school. That step should be honored and applauded. However, as long as she remains Director of Religious Education of the Unitarian Universalist Fellowship, a rabbi should not participate in her marriage. Perhaps she can be persuaded to give this up and to return fully to the Jewish community where her new husband and her children, by a former marriage are now affiliated.

January 1989

344

216. WEDDINGS ON *HOL HAMOED* AND THE TEN DAYS OF REPENTANCE

QUESTION: Should a rabbi perform a wedding during *hol hamoed* or the Ten Days of Repentance? (James N. Pearlstein, Albany NY)

ANSWER: Tradition has stated that no wedding should be held during the days of *hol hamoed* (*Shulhan Arukh* Orah Hayim 546.1) as we shall not mix one joy with another. However, we have not been particularly strict in this matter as most congregations and most Reform Jews do rather little to celebrate these intermediate days of the festival. We would therefore permit weddings during them. This also was the decision of Kaufmann Kohler early in this century (W. Jacob (ed) *American Reform Responsa* #134).

There is no prohibition against a wedding during the Ten Days of Repentance (W. Jacob (ed) *American Reform Responsa* #135). Jacob Lauterbach provided references; we might add a responsum of David Hoffmann (*Melamed Lehoil* III #1).

May 1988

217. WEDDING ON *YOM HASHOAH*

QUESTION: May weddings be conducted on the Holocaust Memorial Day *(Yom Hashoah)*? (Annette Feinstein, St. Louis MO)

ANSWER: Tradition has a long list of days on which marriages are prohibited. Among them are various fast days as well as days of mourning. So, for example, weddings are not conducted from the first of *Av* to the ninth of *Av* (*Shulhan Arukh* Orah Hayim 551.2). Among Central European Jews it has been customary to extend this time to include the period from the seventeenth of *Tamuz* to the ninth of *Av*, as the walls of Jerusalem were breached on the seventeenth of *Tamuz* (Isserles to *Shulhan Arukh* Orah Hayim 551.2).

As far as other public fast days were concerned there was some controversy. Abraham Gumbiner indicated that a groom is not obligated to fast on a public fast day which was, of course, an obvious indication that marriages were conducted on those days (*Magen Avraham* to *Shulhan Arukh* Orah Hayim 551); other authorities decided that the groom should fast on that day, a similar indication. On the other hand, more recent Orthodox authorities tended to be stricter, and Marcus Horovitz felt that marriages should be prohibited in order to get people to take those days seriously once more (*Responsa Mateh Levi* Vol II #32).

Tradition also prohibited the marriages during some days of the *Omer* period. Yet Joseph Caro indicated that a marriage on the thirty-third day would not lead to any punishment (*Shulhan Arukh* Orah Hayim 493.1). Isserles and Gumbiner disagreed whether marriages may take place after the thirty-third day of *Omer*. The reason for these prohibitions during the *Omer* period is not clearly established. Tradition has stated that we remember a plague which struck the *yeshivah* of Akiba (Yeb 62b).

Yom Hashoah is, of course, a modern commemorative day. As yet there are few traditions connected with it. It has become a major occasion and reminds us of the millions who died during the Holocaust in the middle of this century. It is, therefore, linked with one of the saddest periods in Jewish history. This tragedy is on an equal plane with the destruction of the first and second Temple. It would be inappropriate to conduct a wedding on this day which should be commemorated by all Jews throughout the world.

August 1990

218. HAND HELD *HUPAH*

QUESTION: Does traditional Judaism have a preference for the hand held *hupah* or may the *hupah* be placed in a series of poles held in place by a base? (Laura Pollock, Philadelphia PA)

ANSWER: Let us begin by looking at the origin of the *hupah* and its placement. The *hupah* was originally the room to which the bride and groom retired after the marriage ceremony in order to consummate the marriage (Psalms 19.7; Sotah 49b; *Midrash Rabbah* Genesis 114; *Yad* Hil Ishut 10.10; *Tosefot* to Sukah 25b and Yoma 13b, etc). Usually this was in the house of the groom. Therefore, the act of bringing the bride to the *hupah* indicated the transfer of the bride into the groom's household. This is the generally accepted meaning. Some have considered the ceremony of veiling the bride as *hupah* for it established a new relationship between bride and groom (Isserles to *Shulhan Arukh* Even Haezer 55.1; Ezekiel Landau to *Shulhan Arukh* Yoreh Deah 342.1; see Taz to Yoreh Deah 342 for a contrary opinion).

It is clear that the older usage of the *hupah* did not refer to the simple canopy now used during wedding ceremonies. This was introduced in the late medieval period, possibly just before the time of Moses Isserles as he mentioned it as something used "nowadays"

(Isserles to *Shulhan Arukh* Even Haezer 55.1). The custom itself may have come from the earlier medieval *minhag* of spreading a *talit* over the bride and groom during the wedding ceremony, or of the groom simply spreading his *tallit* over the bride during the ceremony (*Hamanhig* 91b ff).

The placement of our type of *hupah* within the synagogue has not been accepted by all authorities. Moses Sofer objected to it as a Gentile custom (*Hatam Sofer* Even Haezer #65). Isserles knew of its use in the synagogue courtyard. We see, therefore, that this symbolic use of the *hupah* during the wedding ceremony is relatively recent. A *hupah* may be beautifully embroidered. This has been done through the centuries especially by *Sephardic* communities.

The texts said nothing about any person holding the *hupah*. It is likely that weddings in small communities, in the courtyard of the synagogue, or in the synagogue itself saw the *hupah* hand held. When a *tallit* was used it was probably simply spread over the bride and groom and rested upon them directly. When this led to the use of four poles is not known; this certainly was more practical and possibly more aesthetically pleasing. There is nothing which would demand one pattern or another. The hand held *hupah* involves four friends of the couple; that may be a positive factor. Of course, they may tire of the task and find it difficult to continue through the entire ceremony.

March 1990

219. *EL MALEI RAHAMIM* AT A WEDDING

QUESTION: Occasionally some families ask whether the *el malei rahamin* may be recited at the beginning of a wedding ceremony. What is the origin and significance of this custom? What is Reform Judaism's attitude to such a request? (Rabbi Minard Klein, Flossmoor IL)

ANSWER: The origin of this custom as so many others is obscure. We know that the *el malei rahamim* itself began to be recited as a memorial prayer after the Crusades, first in Germany, and then also in Italy. Eventually it was also recited at the time of *Yahrzeit* (I. Elbogen *Gottesdienst* p 203). It was not mentioned for example by Maharil or Moses Isserles. The first written statement about this prayer is found in *Maavar Yabaq*. Although Elbogen noted that it may have originated in the twelfth century, it was not transferred to the synagogue or funeral service until the seventeenth century in Eastern Europe. It has become the custom in some traditions to recite the prayer on *shabbat* for those commemorating *Yahrzeit* (Greenwald *Kol Bo al Avelut* p 399).

We do not know when the custom of reciting it at a wedding arose: it was mentioned by Elzet (*Miminhagei Yisrael* p 357). The prayer was recited at the cemetery for the deceased mother or father of the bride or groom or at the beginning of the wedding ceremony in the presence of the immediate family, and so before the public ceremony began. I can only guess that this began in the nineteenth century. As this is not a custom of long standing the recital at the wedding should be discouraged. The couple should visit the cemetery whenever that is possible before the wedding and may recite the *el malei rahamim* then. This also has the advantage of removing the recital from the festive day as that will cast a shadow on the happy atmosphere.

If the couple insists, then one may recite *el malei rahamim* for the couple privately before the wedding and then change the mood into one of festivity.

This prayer, of course, encourages children to remember their parents at a crucial time in their life. It is appropriate to do so, but this pious act must not destroy the moment of their greatest happiness. If it is at all possible, we should discourage the recitation in conjunction with the wedding ceremony.

March 1990

220. NECKLACE OR RING AT A WEDDING

QUESTION: A couple about to be married has asked whether they must use a ring during the ceremony. The bride in this instance cannot for health reasons wear a ring upon her finger. May the groom give her a brooch, necklace or some other item of jewelry? (Nancy Adelson, Pittsburgh PA)

ANSWER: The wedding ring is symbolic of the object of value exchanged in order to legalize the wedding. This was one of the ways in which the marriage according to tradition could be entered.

The three ways of effecting a marriage cited by the Talmud are: through a document, through money, or by intercourse (Kid 2a; *Shulhan Arukh* Even Haezer 25.4). (a) The most common form featured a deed witnessed by two competent individuals and handed by the groom to the bride (Kid 9a; *Shulhan Arukh* Even Haezer 32.1-4). This has remained the essential covenant of the modern wedding. The deed is the modern *ketubah* signed by two witnesses. (b) In addition, it was possible to effect a marriage through the transfer of an item of value (*kesef*) in the presence of two competent witnesses. This remains as part of the modern wedding in the form of presenting a ring with the formula "*harei at mequdeshet....*" (Kid 2a, b; *Shulhan Arukh* Even Haezer 27.1). (c) Finally, marriage can be effected through intercourse (*biah*) preceded by a statement indicating the wish to take this woman as wife in the presence of two witnesses who saw the couple leave for a private place (Kid 9b; *Shulhan Arukh* Even Haezer 33.1). The last method was severely frowned upon by the rabbis, but, *bediavad*, it is valid. Marriage simply through intercourse with proper intent would be akin to "common law" marriage.

The transfer of an object of value now usually takes the form of a ring; it is normally plain in order to avoid the problems of determining the precise value of a stone (Kid 9a; *Tur* and *Shulhan Arukh* Even Haezer 31.2). Any other object of value may also be used; it need not be in the form of jewelry. A silk garment was considered appropriate according to Rabenu Tam (Tos to Kid 9a). Earlier sources accepted perishables too. A brooch or necklace is perfectly appropriate for the wedding even without health considerations which I have not felt necessary to discuss.

December 1990

221. ORCHESTRA AT A WEDDING

QUESTION: My synagogue seeks to establish some rules concerning weddings and other festivities. Is it appropriate to engage an orchestra for weddings? I presume that it makes no difference whether the musicians are Jewish or Gentile. (Bruce L. Klein, Philadelphia PA)

ANSWER: Rules such as your congregation contemplate are important in our continuing attempt to restrain extravagance. Many efforts at sumptuary regulation have been made through the centuries (Jacob R. Marcus *The Jew in the Medieval World* pp 193 ff; I. Abraham *Jewish Life in the Middle Ages* pp 295 ff; L. Löw *Die Lebensalter*; Louis Finkelstein *Jewish Self Government in the Middle Ages*). These regulations were designed to curb extravagant displays which were wasteful and often aroused the jealousy of non-Jewish neighbors. Policy decisions, therefore, on the nature of festivities such as *Bar/Bat mitzvah*, weddings, etc., held in the synagogue are very much in keeping with tradition.

Music has been reported at Jewish weddings from ancient times (*Midrash Rabbah* Gen 23.50). Although nothing was said about the nature of the music or the musicians, during the Middle Ages we hear of non-Jews playing at weddings and for that matter even being hired specifically to play on the *shabbat* of a wedding week (Mordecai to Alfasi Betzah 5). The practice was cited favorably by later authorities (*Tur*; *Shulhan Arukh* Orah Hayim 338.1 ff). There were, of course, those who disagreed with this practice and tried to stop it, but as it was exceedingly popular it proved difficult to halt (Radbaz *Responsa* #6, #132; "Maarehet Hatan Vekalah" *Sedei Hemed* #13). There is a long tradition of engaging non-Jewish musicians for a wedding. Nothing is said about the number of musicians or even the nature of their music, however, the sumptuary regulations which appeared often in the past would encourage us to keep such music within the boundaries of good taste.

October 1990

222. VIDEO TAPING A WEDDING

QUESTION: A couple who are contemplating divorce have presented a video tape of their marriage which seems to show that the traditional words *harei at...* were not spoken by the groom. The rabbi's words may be heard clearly but the groom seems to have said nothing. The groom now claims that therefore no marriage existed and it should be annulled and no divorce is necessary. (Sandra Berkowitz, Baltimore MD)

ANSWER: Let me begin by stating that there is considerable doubt whether the traditional words *harei at...* must be spoken. The codes and the earlier Talmud provide a variety of texts which may be recited (*Shulhan Arukh* Even Haezer 27. 1 f and commentaries). This question also leads us to look at what constitutes a valid Jewish marriage according to tradition. There are three ways of effecting a marriage:

(a) The most common form featured a document witnessed by two competent individuals and handed by the groom to the bride (Kid 9a; *Shulhan Arukh* Even Haezer 32.1-4). This has remained the essential covenant of the modern wedding. The document is the modern *ketubah* signed by two witnesses.

(b) In addition it was possible to effect a marriage through the transfer of an item of value (*kesef*) in the presence of two competent witnesses. This remains as part of the modern wedding in the form of presenting a ring with the formula *"harei at mequdeshet..."* (Kid 2a, b; *Shulhan Arukh* Even Haezer 27.1).

(c) Finally, marriage can be effected through intercourse (*biah*) preceded by a statement indicating the wish to take this woman as wife in the presence of two witnesses who saw the couple leave for a private place (Kid 9b; *Shulhan Arukh* Even

Haezer 33.1). The last method was severely frowned upon by the rabbis, but, *bediavad,* it is valid. Marriage simple through intercourse with proper intent would be akin to "common law" marriage.

These three acts together or separately, if properly witnessed constitute, a Jewish marriage. In this instance there were many witnesses who were at the wedding, and who either saw the exchange of an object of value, or heard the traditional words, or saw the couple subsequently leave together. It should not be difficult to establish that all of this took place. In addition, of course, two witnesses signed the *ketubah.* That would be the first resource to be tested, but if the *ketubah* has been lost or willfully destroyed then the other forms of evidence would be adequate. The wedding is valid and cannot be questioned on the basis of the video-tape which may not have recorded one aspect of the ceremony.

March 1990

223. AN ANNIVERSARY CEREMONY

QUESTION: A couple is going to celebrate their thirtieth wedding anniversary and their children have arranged appropriate festivities. As part of the celebration they would like the rabbi to conduct a ceremony which re-affirms the couples dedication to each other and proclaim their love for each other. What is the attitude of tradition toward such a ceremony? What kind of *berakhot* may be included? (David Weisberg, Los Angeles CA)

ANSWER: There is nothing in the tradition which bears directly on this question. Although, undoubtedly, anniversaries were appropriately celebrated in the past, the religious portion of it was carried out differently. For example, by honoring the husband through participation in the *Torah* reading or other synagogue honors and at that time an appropriate *misheberakh* would be recited. The woman would, of course, have no direct part in this, but would be equally proud and content. There is a good deal to be said for the public celebration of a special anniversary as it emphasizes marriage and the family within the setting of the broader community. In the late twentieth century with its numerous family problems this is especially desirable. Irrespective of other plans we should encourage such a couple to be honored at a synagogue service in accordance with the traditions of the congregation. For many families this will be enough. If such celebrations occur regularly, then the members of the congregation will be constantly reminded of successful happy marriages.

The children of this couple, of course, wish to go further and want to incorporate some religious feelings into the general festivities. This too should be encouraged as it brings an additional religious element into family life. We should, however, be cautious about the manner in which this is done. The general tenor of the party needs to be in good taste.

The various editions of the *Rabbi's Manual* published by the Central Conference of American Rabbis contain anniversary prayers. The *sheva berakahot* have not been used and have been reserved for the wedding ceremony itself. However, any other prayers recited at a wedding may appropriately be used again at the anniversary. This is a good occasion for new and personal prayers. It would be appropriate for the children and grandchildren to participate in such a rededication service and to express their thoughts about the happy marriage of their parents. There are also many readings from the Bible, *Midrash* and the classical Jewish poets which can be utilized on this occasion.

In summary then, such a special wedding ceremony should use the prayers found in the various editions of the *Rabbi's Manual* which may include a blessing over wine, as well as the thanks to God for having reached this happy day, and other appropriate prayers created especially for the occasion by the rabbi and the family.

February 1990

224. OFFICIATING IN A CIVIL CAPACITY

QUESTION: May a rabbi officiate in a civil capacity in a wedding involving two Catholics? What is our Reform response to such a request? (Peter Schweitzer, New York NY)

ANSWER: There is nothing in the tradition which deals with a situation even remotely akin to this. The procedure used by Jewish military chaplains in the wartime emergency of giving last rites to Catholics was limited to that emergency. In this instance, although it may be legally possible for a rabbi to perform a civil marriage of two Catholics, it would be wrong to do so because of *marit ayin*. As most rabbis do not marry a Jew to a non-Jew, this kind of participation would be bizarre. A rabbi should not conduct such a ceremony for it appears as if he/she is willing to marry anyone without religious considerations.

A rabbi should be involved only in *qidushin* and not in the marriages of other religions or civil marriages. It would be difficult because of our orientation to avoid some religious overtones in such a wedding ceremony and that would be inappropriate.

The rabbi may, of course, give a toast or something akin to that at the festivities following the wedding. That would clearly indicate to everyone that the rabbi is present as a friend and not participating in the actual marriage ceremony. We should not engage in a civil marriage.

October 1990

225. DECORATIONS ON A *KETUBAH*

QUESTION: Are there any limitations on the decorations which may be placed upon a *ketubah*? A couple recently had a *ketubah* prepared with decorations which are almost pornographic. May this document be used for the wedding ceremony? (Martin Kaplan, San Mateo CA)

ANSWER: A great deal has been written about the text of the *ketubah* and studies have indicated that the wording has changed through the ages (Mordechai Akiva Friedman *Jewish Marriage in Palestine*; J. Neubauer *Geschichte des biblisch-talmudischen Eheschliessungsrecht*; Z. W. Falk *Jewish Matrimonial Law in the Middle Ages* pp 35 ff). Of course, in modern times this document has become a formalized statement which reflects little about the couple. In twentieth century America the Reform and Conservative groups have developed their own *ketubot* to reflect the specific needs of these groups. The decorations on a *ketubah* especially commissioned by the couple may reflect the thoughts and wishes of the couple.

We should note that illuminated marriage documents have survived from the Middle Ages onward. The earliest is from Fostat, Egypt in the eleventh century, and only fragments survived. Among the others is one from Krems, Austria (1392), Ostiano, Italy (1612) and many from Persia (Franz Landsberger *Illuminated Marriage Contracts*; J. Gutmann *Beauty in Holiness* pp 370 ff). As one looks at these illuminations and decorations, one sees that they fall into two categories. A large number contain formalized decorations of plants, Biblical themes like the symbols of the twelve tribes of Israel, or the twelve signs of the Zodiac; they were only rarely personalized. A *ketubah* from Rome in 1818 showed a married couple walking hand in hand while others displayed semi-nude rather formalistic angels (Ferrara, 1719, Reggio, 1774, Bosetto, 1801). The last, in one of the signs of the Zodiac, showed a nude couple (Moses Gaster *The Ketubah* plate 5 ff). As we have looked at the evidence from the text themselves, we must also ask about the attitude of tradition toward such documents.

Although the tradition was hardly puritanical and often dealt very forthright with sex and questions relating to it (L. M. Epstein *Marriage Laws in the Bible and the Talmud*), it did not do so in a way which could be considered as titillating or pornographic. The wedding ceremony and the accompanying festivities are joyous, but kept within limits of decency. Tradition has done its best to encourage restraint. The *sheva berakhot* recites during seven days of festivities again and again added an element of prayer to the festivities of those days. Whatever the couple did privately has always been considered their business and outside the purview of regulations (L. M. Epstein *Sex Laws and Customs in Judaism*). The public ceremony, however, is to be conducted in a decorous fashion with everyone sober and in the presence of the *minyan* (*Shulhan Arukh* Even Haezer 34.4; A. H. Freimann *Seder Qidushin Venisuin* p 16) as well as two witnesses (*Shulhan Arukh* Even Haezer 42.5).

We would therefore indicate to the couple that whatever decorations they have at home is their business, but semi-pornography can not be permitted on the *ketubah*. The *ketubah* is a formal document signed by two witnesses which may be read at the wedding ceremony (*Shulhan Arukh* Even Haezer and Isserles 62.9). We should note that Maharil (*Minhagei Maharil* 64b) in the fourteenth century did not know the custom of publicly reading the *ketubah*. We can not permit the use of such a *ketubah* for a wedding.

March 1990

226. ERROR IN THE HEBREW DATE

QUESTION: A couple has recently reviewed their *ketubah* with someone who knows Hebrew well. He immediately noticed an error in the date of the wedding. The Hebrew year has been given incorrectly. They would like to have a correct *ketubah*, but the original witnesses to their marriage are dead. So, they do not know whether they can simply correct the one which they have, or should they have a new *ketubah* written with different witnesses. (Kathy Hurwitz, Charleston SC)

ANSWER: Although the modern *ketubah* is enforceable as a legal document in some jurisdictions, it remains primarily a religious document symbolic of tradition. The nominal sum of money stipulated bears no relationship to any agreement; it is reminiscent of the ancient dowries. So the figures provided in a *ketubah* are not relevant. The only thing which is important are the two witnesses who must be adults Jews and not related to each other or to the bride or groom. The other data provided by the wedding document especially after a couple has been married for a considerable length of time may be significant to the family, but from a *halakhic* point of view are not important. This is different from a traditional *get*. In that divorce document the names of the parties and the city must be correct, etc., but in a *ketubah* if a name of a town is misspelled or the name of the bride and groom are not quite correct, the couple nevertheless are properly married. The reason for this is that marriage can occur in three different ways:

(a) The most common form featured a deed witnessed by two competent individuals and handed by the groom to the bride (Kid 9a; *Shulhan Arukh*, Even Haezer 32.1-4). This has remained the essential covenant of the modern wedding. The document is the modern *ketubah* signed by two witnesses. (b) In addition, it was possible to effect a marriage through the transfer of an item of value (*kesef*) in the presence of two competent witnesses. This remains as part of the modern wedding in the form of presenting a ring with the formula "*harei at mequdeshet...*" (Kid 2a, b; *Shulhan Arukh*, Even Haezer 27.1). (c) Finally, marriage can be effected through intercourse (*biah*) preceded by a statement indicating the wish to take this woman as wife in the presence of two witnesses who saw the couple leave for a private place (Kid 9b; *Shulhan Arukh*, Even Haezer 33.1). The last method was severely frowned upon by the rabbis, but, *bediavad,* it is valid. Marriage simply through intercourse with proper intent would be akin to "common law" marriage.

The *ketubah*, therefore, represents only one of those possibilities and in this case all the others have also clearly taken place.

Even if the date is wrong, as you have stated, the couple has been married for many years. It may be historically interesting to note that they have been married thirty instead of twenty-nine years as indicated in the Hebrew dating of the document, but for *halakhic* purposes that is not important, especially as you indicated that children were born late in this marriage. Even on their account the Hebrew date would be irrelevant and could be shown as wrong when compared to the English date on the *ketubah* as well as on the secular wedding certificate.

The couple may either change the document itself, add an addendum to it, or leave it as it is. Nothing needs to be done.

January 1991

227. HEBREW OR RUSSIAN NAMES

QUESTION: A middle aged couple who recently emigrated from the Soviet Union have brought their *ketubah*; it is actually closer to a wedding certificate as it simply states that they have been married. It is written in simple Hebrew and signed by two Jewish witnesses. All the names are, however, Russian first names followed by *ben* and the Russian name of the father. All the names are written in Hebrew. Is this an adequate *ketubah* or should they prepare another with a different set of witnesses? They hesitate as they have been married for many years and the document is dear to them. (Boris Krokovsky, Trenton NJ)

ANSWER: The couple can certainly consider themselves Jewishly married even if the document does not follow the standard form. They had a ceremony, two Jewish witnesses, and at some risk prepared a simple *ketubah*. This should be properly appreciated.

Throughout our history we had adopted many foreign names and simply added them to our Hebrew list. In the last centuries numerous Yiddish names have entered our vocabulary and earlier Greek, Arabic, Spanish, and German names. Even some of the Biblical characters had foreign names, possibly even Moses. There is no problem with the Russian names. We wish the couple a long and happy life together in this country.

October 1989

228. TWO SETS OF HEBREW NAMES

QUESTION: A couple who could not find any naming document asked the rabbi to provide them with Hebrew names for the *ketubah*. A few years later the parents moved and they discovered documents which provided the Hebrew names used during Religious School, *Bar Mitzvah* and Confirmation. Which Hebrew names remain valid? (Donald Pearlstein, Providence RI)

ANSWER: A good deal has been written on the choice of names. Among *Ashkenazim*, it is the general practice to name children after a deceased ancestor, while among the *Sephardim* both deceased and living forbearers' names are used. The history of the development of naming in Jewish tradition is long and complex

(Jacob Z. Lauterbach *CCAR Annual* 1932 Vol 42 pp 316 ff and W. Jacob (ed) *American Reform Responsa* #59).

When the above mentioned tradition was not followed, then names were chosen in a number of different ways. Some selected them at random; others through opening a *Torah* scroll and utilizing the name of the first Biblical figure which appeared, excluding names prior to Abraham (Joseph Trani *Responsa* I #189).

In this instance we have a plethora of names. As we sort them out, we shall see that the names provided in the childhood documents have appeared on nothing with any legal implications. The names used on the wedding certificate possess legal standing and should be used in the future. Nothing would keep the couple from incorporating the earlier names and simply adding them through a phrase like *hamekhuneh* (known as) which would indicate that the other names have also been used to designate these individuals. In this fashion the persons honored through the original names will not be forgotten and the potential problems of the use of incorrect names will be avoided.

There is no problem with multiple names. Many individuals possess more than one name and such couplings with Zeev or Aryeh, etc. are very frequent.

December 1988

229. ERROR IN THE *KETUBAH* TEXT

QUESTION: A caligraphy specialist has prepared an illuminated *ketubah*; the text is modified traditional, but several words have been mispelled. This was discovered a number of years after the wedding. Should the *ketubah* be replaced? One of the original witnesses has died? (Karen Levin, San Francisco CA)

ANSWER: In contrast to a *get*, the spelling in a *ketubah* is not critical, even for the Orthodox. The ceremony was witnessed appropriately and the document attests to the wedding. That is quite sufficient especially as the *ketubah* represents only one of three ways through which a marriage can be validated; this matter has been discussed in several of the other responsa.

June 1988

230. THE SIGNATURE ON A *KETUBAH*

QUESTION: At the signing of the *ketubah*, the witnesses are asked to sign in Hebrew or in English. In many instances they do not remember enough Hebrew to sign their name appropriately and must, therefore, copy the writing prepared by the rabbi. Is this an appropriate way of signing the *ketubah*? (Betty Blum, Pittsburgh PA)

ANSWER: The significance of the *ketubah* has changed for us. It is, of course, one of three ways of indicating that a couple has been married: (a) The most common form featured a deed witnessed by two competent individuals and handed by the groom to the bride (Kid 9a; *Shulhan Arukh* Even Haezer 32.1-4). This has remained the essential covenant of the modern wedding. The document is akin to the modern *ketubah* signed by the two witnesses. (b) In addition, it was possible to effect a marriage through the transfer of an item of value (*kesef*) in the presence of two competent witnesses. This remains as part of the modern wedding in the form of giving a ring with the formula *"harei at* *mequdeshet...*" (Kid 2a, b; *Shulhan Arukh* Even Haezer 27.1). (c) Finally, marriage can be effected through intercourse (*biah*) preceded by a statement indicating the wish to take this woman as wife in the presence of two witnesses who saw the couple leave for a private place (Kid 9b; *Shulhan Arukh* Even Haezer 33.1). The last method was, of course, severely frowned upon by the rabbis, but, *bediavad*, it is certainly valid. Consent was, of course, necessary (*Shulhan Arukh* Even Haezer 42.1).

Our *ketubah* details the nature of the relationship and we insist that it be equalitarian; traditionally it stipulated the financial and economic considerations of the marriage. Normally in the modern *ketubah* such matters are omitted. Among us, therefore, the *ketubah* is more symbolic than legal. Our wording has become standard and does not contain special stipulations.

Irrespective of these considerations the signature on the *ketubah* indicates that two witnesses who have signed have been present and acknowledge that the wedding has occurred. If at a later time the wedding is questioned, the signatures attest to the fact that these two people were married. Any form of signature is valid as long as it has been made by an appropriate witness and that person can subsequently attest to the fact that he/she actually signed the document. I do not know of any instance in which the signature has been questioned because it was copied out, in fact in early periods when not all individuals were literate this must have occurred regularly. It would, therefore, be permissible for the witnesses of the wedding to sign their Hebrew name through copying the letters written for them by the officiating rabbi.

February 1989

231. A LOST *KETUBAH*

QUESTION: An elderly couple, who have moved from a house in which they lived for a long time to an apartment, have discovered that their *ketubah* was lost. Do they need to replace it? They have been married for more than four decades. (Stanley Rosenberg, Atlanta GA)

ANSWER: The *ketubah* is one of three ways through which two Jews may enter a marriage; they are: (a) The most common form featured a deed witnessed by two competent individuals and handed by the groom to the bride (Kid 9a; *Shulhan Arukh*, Even Haezer 32.1-4). This has remained the essential covenant of the modern wedding. The document is akin to the modern *ketubah* signed by the two witnesses. (b) In addition, it was possible to effect a marriage through the transfer of an item of value (*kesef*) in the presence of two competent witnesses. This remains as part of the modern wedding in the form of giving a ring with the formula *"harei at mequdeshet..."* (Kid 2a, b; *Shulhan Arukh* Even Haezer 27.1). (c) Finally, marriage can be effected through intercourse (*biah*) preceded by a statement indicating the wish to take this woman as wife in the presence of two witnesses who saw the couple leave for a private place (Kid 9b; *Shulhan Arukh* Even Haezer 33.1). The last method was, of course, severely frowned upon by the rabbis, but, *bediavad,* it is certainly valid. Consent was, of course, necessary (*Shulhan Arukh* Even Haezer 42.1).

The most important aspects of the traditional *ketubah* are the financial and other stipulations. We use a standardized document which emphasizes the equality of both parties. The signatures on the *ketubah* attest to the fact that the conditions stated in the document apply to the couple and to their marriage.

If there is a conflict or the threat of a divorce, it may be necessary to review the *ketubah* and the conditions stipulated therein. When all goes well the *ketubah* may never be read again by the couple or anyone else.

Among some modern couples it has become customary to create an illuminated *ketubah* which occupies a prominent decorative place in the home. However, in most families this document along with others is put away and forgotten. The couple in question has obviously enjoyed many years of happy marriage; they need not worry about their *ketubah* and should simply enjoy the years which lie ahead for them together.

July 1989

232. DESTROYED *KETUBAH* *

QUESTION: The family has lost their decorative *ketubah* in a fire. They wish to know if it is possible to replace it and if this will have the same validity as the earlier document. The document followed the standard form and did not contain any unusual stipulations, financial or otherwise. (Frieda Blumenthal, Cleveland OH)

ANSWER: We should begin by assuring the couple that the marriage remains perfectly valid even without a *ketubah*. The Talmud, after all, cited three ways of effecting a marriage:

(a) The most common form featured a deed witnessed by two competent individuals and handed by the groom to the bride (Kid 9a; *Shulhan Arukh* Even Haezer 32.1-4). This has remained the essential covenant of the modern wedding. The document is akin to the modern *ketubah* signed by the two witnesses.

(b) In addition, it was possible to effect a marriage through the transfer of an item of value (*kesef*) in the presence of two competent witnesses. This remains as part of the modern wedding in the form of giving a ring with the formula *"harei at mekudeshet..."* (Kid 2a, b; *Shulhan Arukh* Even Haezer 27.1).

(c) Finally, marriage can be effected through intercourse (*biah*) preceded by a statement indicating the wish to take this woman as wife in the presence of two witnesses who saw the couple leave for a private place (Kid 9b; *Shulhan Arukh* Even Haezer 33.1) The last method was, of course, severely frowned upon by the rabbis, but, *bediavad*, it is certainly valid.

We are, therefore, dealing more with the aesthetics of the wedding and the desire to have a beautiful *ketubah* on display rather than with the legal implications of this document. As this was a standard document, it can be drawn up again in precisely the same form as before. If it is at all possible, the same witnesses who signed the original document should sign it again. Somewhere on the document, in order to assure that there is no intent of fraud, it should note that the original document was destroyed in a fire and that this is a replacement drawn up much later than the wedding itself.

February 1989

233. A REFORM *GET* *

QUESTION: Should Reform Rabbis issue a formal document of divorce *(get)*? Should we consider the document in the new *Rabbis Manual* to be a *get*? (Morton Cohen, Los Angeles CA; Karen Silverman, New York NY; Michael Smith, Pittsburgh PA)

ANSWER: An earlier responsum entitled; "Reform Judaism and Divorce" (W. Jacob (ed) *American Reform Judaism* #162), provided the historical background of the divorce proceedings. It did not, however, deal with the technical problems of a *get*. This decision should supplement the previous responsum.

The *get* became important traditionally because of the question of *mamzerut*. In other words, the child of a union with a "married" woman or one otherwise forbidden would be placed in jeopardy and it is important for such offsprings to assume the status of their parent's marriage.

As we look at the entire area of divorce in the North American Jewish Community, we must ask ourselves what alternative paths are open to us. We may simply follow the procedure of the past, acknowledge civil divorce. This will continue to be appropriate for a large number of individuals, however, some individuals now desire a religious act to finalize the separation. It is religiously and psychologically satisfying to both parties.

We might seek a uniform solution for all groups, Reform, Conservative and Orthodox, so that the document would be universally recognized. That is a praiseworthy goal but with the current mood of the Orthodox community may not be attainable. Perhaps some liberal Orthodox would be willing to work out a compromise, but it would not satisfy the rest and so it hardly seems worth the enormous effort.

It might be more possible to establish a common basis for divorce with the Conservative movement or a mutual recognition of each others documents. This process would best be initiated in specific communities. That would provide working models and may lead to a greater understanding of the actual needs rather than satisfying the theoretical claims of each movement.

As we return to summarize the history of divorce within the Reform movement, we see that various rabbinical conferences and synods of the last century in Germany and in the United States, tried to deal with the question of divorce alongside other problems. In the Paris Sanhedrin of 1806, the decision of those assembled was that no religious divorce would be granted unless a valid civil divorce had preceded (N. D. Tama (ed) Kirwan (tr) *Transactions of the Parisian Sanhedrin* 1807 pp 152 ff). This decision has been adopted by all groups within Judaism in every modern country. The Liberal synod, which gathered in Leipzig (1869), passed a number of other resolutions on this issue. They were favored by most of the individuals present including Abraham Geiger. It was agreed that the religious divorce needed to be simplified and that (a) it should be given as soon as a civil divorce has been settled; (b) rabbis should make an effort at reconciliation before a civil divorce is filled; (c) the document of the divorce should be brief, in the vernacular and presented to both parties; (d) the religious divorce should be granted even if one of the parties objected; (e) the woman may remarry even if she has no divorce; (f) a divorcee can marry a *kohen* as may a proselyte (*Yearbook, Central Conference of American Rabbis* Vol I pp 106 ff). The question of the equality of the sexes in matters of divorce was to be discussed at a later synod (*Ibid* 108).

EVEN HAEZER

The synod held in Augsburg in 1871 established a committee to deal with divorce. It was to report at a future meeting and one of the concerns expressed was the equal treatment of both sexes. No later meeting was held.

In the United States, divorce was discussed at the Philadelphia Conference of 1869 which declared that divorce was a purely civil matter and needed no religious steps whatsoever. Therefore, a *get* was not necessary. A rabbinic body should, however, investigate the conditions under which a divorce had been given to assure that they also meet the criteria for a Jewish divorce. At that meeting in Philadelphia two rabbis, Sonnenschein and Mielziner, felt that the *get* should be modified rather than completely abolished which was also a point of view expressed somewhat earlier by Geiger.

It has been the general position of the Central Conference of American Rabbis to follow the stand taken by Kaufmann Kohler who recommended that civil divorces be recognized as long as the grounds for such a divorce were in keeping with the rabbinic tradition (*Central Conference of American Rabbis Yearbook* Vol 25 pp 376 ff). The matter, however, never came to an official vote within the Conference.

We should note that the Orthodox rabbinate of France in 1907 suggested that a civil divorce decree annulled the marriage and the woman would be released and free to marry according to Jewish ritual subsequently. This suggestion, which was attacked by Orthodox authorities throughout the world, is very much akin to Reform Jewish practice (A. H. Freiman *Seder Qiddushin Venisuin* p 390).

In 1924 the Orthodox rabbis of Turkey proposed a "conditional marriage" to solve the problems of divorce and a husband's unwillingness to procure a *get*. This was subsequently

371

rejected by Ben Zion Uziel of Israel (A. M. Freiman *Seder Qiddushin Venisuin* pp 391 ff).

The mood both among rabbis and members of our congregations has changed especially as the number of divorces have increased. Some individuals now seek a religious resolution to the end of their marriage. This has led to the creation of the (*Seder Peridah*) "Document of Separation" in the new *Rabbis Manual*. Others have been willing to obtain an Orthodox or Conservative *get* despite the hardships involved and the secondary status given to the woman in those proceedings.

As we look at the problems connected with a Reform *get*, let us look at the traditional *get*. The original requirements connected with it were rather simple, a divorce was easily obtained. The husband prepared for the divorce by asking a *sofer* (scribe) to write the document for him and indicated that he wished to divorce his wife. The specific name of the husband and the wife were given in the document; the city in which it was prepared was also indicated. No reason for the divorce was mentioned in the document itself.

This document was then signed by two adult male Jewish witnesses who were unrelated to either party or to each other. It was then given to two other witnesses or perhaps to the same individuals who delivered it to the woman. Upon her acceptance the divorce became effective. The witnesses to the signature and to the delivery of the document could subsequently attest to the fact that everything had been accomplished to the law.

This document, therefore, depended entirely on the husband and its acceptance by the wife. A rabbinical court (*bet din*) had no real standing in this matter unless a further dispute arose. It may or may not have supervised the various stages of the document, i.e.

the proper composition, witnessing and delivery, but that was not essential. The court did not initiate the procedure nor did it provide any kind of hearings in the matter.

These proceedings were straightforward and uncomplicated until questions of custody and financial control were raised. As such issues are nowadays settled by the civil courts, we need not be troubled by them.

Throughout the centuries, questions have been raised about the names of the individuals in the documents, the fitness of the individuals who were witnesses, the state of mind of the author of the document and the state of mind of the recipient, the qualifications of the scribe, etc. Eventually this simple document became rather complex. Its Hebrew or Aramaic text was fit into precisely thirteen lines. The names of each of the individuals involved had to be spelled absolutely correctly and there were frequent discussions about the precise name of the individuals, nicknames, etc. Furthermore, even the city involved had to be spelled properly, often in order to locate it precisely, a river or stream flowing through the city was also mentioned. If it was the first *get* written in a location, then each subsequent get had to be written in the same manner. The delivery of the *get* had to be properly attested and since the decree of Rabbenu Gershom (1000 C.E.) a *get* could not be given to a woman against her will. Delivery had to be established through the woman's actual acceptance of the document; it could not be deposited with her. There is a vast literature which deals with each of these questions in every century.

Most of the issues involved which troubled previous generations are of no concern to us as the civil court has already dealt with them in its own way and in a manner which is acceptable to us. At this time, therefore, we have accepted civil divorce without a *get* for more than a century. We are not prepared to suggest a formal change in this procedure. The "Document of Separation" (*Seder Peridah, Rabbis Manual 1988*) provides an alternative which may be religiously and psychologically satisfying as it gives the couple the feeling that there has been a religious dissolution of their marriage. This document is not to be considered a *get* as indicated in the note of the *Rabbi's Manual*: "However, it should also be understood by all that such a ritual and the document attesting it do not have the standing of a *get*".

The use of the "Document of Separation" may eventually lead us to reopen the mater of a Reform *get*. At this time we recommend that Reform rabbis use the *Seder Peridah* for those couples who seek a religious dissolution of their marriage within the Reform framework. Those who wish to marry a traditional partner or face other obstacles may obtain an Orthodox *get*. The *Seder Peridah* is not to be considered as such a document.

July 1988

234. AGUNOT

QUESTION: Should we marry women considered *agunot* by Orthodox rabbis? (Martin Cohen, Los Angeles CA)

ANSWER: In the long span of Jewish history, aside from the normal problems and aggravated circumstances surrounding divorce, the chief issue has been that of the *agunah*, a status caused by the disappearance of the husband or by his refusal to provide a religious divorce (*get*) for his wife. The second problem has often been solved through communal pressure which stopped short of actually forcing a *get,* as that would not be legally valid (Solomon ben Aderet *Responsa* IV #40; Simon ben Zemah Duran *Responsa* II #68; *Tur* and *Shulhan Arukh* Even Haezer 134 and 154; *Responsa Reanana* #43; *Responsa Mabit* II #138; *Pisqei Din shel Batei Hadin Harabanim* Vol II pp 300 ff).

Much more difficult is the problem of a husband who disappeared. Usually in the past this condition occurred when the husband had disappeared in time of war or during a long journey to distant lands. Despite a presumption of death, as it could not be proven, the wife continued to be considered as married. During the period of heavy Eastern European emigration to the United States and other western lands, some men were lost at sea or in the wild West, while others slipped away and thus relieved themselves of family responsibilities. In modern times, in addition to these cases of *agunah,* we have thousands of Orthodox women whose husbands simply refuse to provide a *get* and leave their wives with no solution. After civil courts have dissolved the marriage, only moral persuasion can be exercised on the husband and that is frequently difficult because of the hostility which exists between the individuals. Although some states, for example New York, now recognize the obligations of a *ketubah* and would enforce its provision until a *get* had been given, this is only minimally helpful as it is easy to escape its jurisdictions.

The problem of the *agunah* in modern times has been solved in a number of different ways. Our Reform method simply acknowledges civil divorce. For the Orthodox an annulment is possible, but very difficult. Some traditional Jews solve the problem when the original marriage was Reform or Conservative by not accepting the witnesses who signed the *ketubah* and so denying its validity. As no marriage has taken place in their eyes, no *get* is necessary (Moses Feinstein *Igrot Mosheh* Even Haezer #74 #75;

David Hoffmann *Melamed Lehoil* Even Haezer #20).

Although this path may be technically correct from an Orthodox point of view, it is insulting to all Reform and Conservative Jews; it also does not satisfy psychologically. One of the problems with this approach is the Jewish doctrine that Jews who engage in intercourse do so with serious intent; furthermore, individuals, who have lived together for a period of time and are recognized as husband and wife by the community in which they live, are so accepted (Git 81b). The Orthodox authorities who suggested the above mentioned solution claim that this ruling does not apply to sinners (Moses Feinstein *Op Cit* #75; Jehiel Weinberg *Seridei Esh* Even Haezer #28).

A variety of modern proposals have incorporated some statement about divorce, or at least about the jurisdiction of the rabbinic court in the *ketubah* in order to solve the problem. The modern Orthodox scholar, Eliezer Berkovits, made such a proposal and urged the use of a conditional marriage; he subsequently defended it in his book *Tenai Benissuin Vehaget*. The rabbis of Turkey in 1924 made a similar proposal which was later rejected by Ben Zion Uziel of Israel (A. H. Freiman *Seder Qiddushin Venissuin* pp 391 ff).

A most determined effort in this direction was made by Louis Epstein for the Conservative Rabbinical Assembly in 1930; he suggested that a conditional divorce be given at the time of marriage. This approach which is *halakhically* sound was rejected by the Orthodox rabbinate and Epstein's efforts to defend it failed. (I. Epstein *Hatzaah Lemaan Taqanot Agunot*; *Lisheelah Ha-agunot*). Many considered it inappropriate to deal with divorce in the wedding document. The Conservative Rabbinical Assembly has added a clause to its *ketubah* which simply states that the couple places itself under the authority of the Conservative *bet din*. This removes one of the objections to the document of Epstein (*Rabbinic Manual* pp 37 f). The effort of the Conservative Rabbinical Assembly was made under the guidance of Joshua Liebermann and has been incorporated in the *ketubot* used by the Conservative movement.

A more radical suggestion was made by the French Orthodox Rabbinate in 1907, which urged that all *ketubot* include a clause which indicate that a civil divorce decree would annul the marriage and the woman would be released and free to marry according to Jewish ritual subsequently. This suggestion was attacked by Orthodox authorities in other lands (A. H. Freiman *Seder Kiddushin Venisuin* p 390).

These efforts have tried to deal with the problem of *agunot* but largely to no avail, as the complications have usually led individuals who sought a second marriage to use a Reform rabbi who recognizes a civil divorce or a "Document of Separation" (W. Jacob (ed) *American Reform Responsa* #162) or to turn to the civil authorities. We should continue to perform such marriages of *agunot* as a way of helping the Jewish community with a difficult problem. We recognize civil divorce as sufficient. Our solution is within the range of those proposed by some Orthodox authorities and so is part of our effort to unite the Jewish community.

October 1988

Hoshen Mishpat

235. SUING THE RABBI

QUESTION: A rabbi who does a considerable amount of counselling has asked whether it is necessary to purchase malpractice insurance. What, according to tradition, is the range of liability? (Walter Rosenthal, Trenton NJ)

ANSWER: We are going to look at this matter with the understanding that the rabbi in question is not a licensed therapist, and so would do counselling as part of ordinary congregational responsibility and not in the special capacity of a therapist. Such cases would be akin to the responsibility of a physician which has been discussed previously (W. Jacob *Contemporary American Reform Responsa* #75).

This entire area has been treated thoroughly in American secular legal literature; it is the general desire of the courts to remain out of this area, as it is very difficult for them to establish the parameters of training and appropriate religious conduct for so many religious groups and sects (Funston, "Made out of Whole Cloth - A Constitutional Analysis of the Clergy Malpractice Concept" *California Western Law Review* Vol 10 pp 507 ff; McMenamin *The Jurist* Vol 45 pp 275 ff etc).

We are not concerned with the judicial function of the rabbi and possible errors which might take place in the exercise of that function (*Shulhan Arukh* Hoshen Mishpat 25 and commentaries), but rather with the general area of responsibility through counselling. The rabbi would be liable if there was gross neglect, for then he/she would be violating the Biblical statement "Do not place a stumbling block before the blind" (Lev 19.14). However, the later *Talmudic* development of the law of torts is rather confused; we have two concepts, *garmi* which includes those actions directly responsible for damage, and *gerama* matters in which the action is indirect (*Encyclopedia Talmudit* Vol 6; Ramban *Dina Degarmi*; *Shulhan Arukh* Hoshen Mishpat 386). The general rule which we may abstract from the many cases cited in the literature is as follows: If the individual in question is an expert and the advice which is followed is based upon his expertise, then he would be liable. As for example, a coin appraiser has been shown a coin and has declared it as good, but subsequently it was discovered to be bad coinage. If he has been paid for his advice, then he is liable. If he has not been paid, then he is not liable. On the other hand, if he is not an absolute expert, but the individual who came stated that he was relying on this person's opinion alone, then he is also liable (*Yad* Hil Shirut.5). We can see from this that the matters which are involved are: (a) The expert status; (b) the exchange of money for the advice and evaluation; (c) the agreement between the individuals that this person is the only one to be asked for advice.

In the case of counselling ordinarily done by rabbis, there is no exchange of funds. The rabbi makes no pretense to being an expert in the field. In addition to that, a rabbi would and should not permit himself/herself to be placed in a position of being the only person consulted, particularly in a difficult matter. It is our common practice to refer difficult matters onward and even in other counselling situations to provide only tentative advice. Furthermore, following the rabbinic advice is entirely voluntary. This is not like a business transaction in which the paths are much clearer, but involve a great many areas: (a) Theological issues raised;   (b) to what extent was the party being counseled completely forthcoming; (c) was there an opportunity to see other parties or to gather additional information about this matter; (d) the party seeking counselling remains completely independent and may accept or reject the advice. From a traditional point of view, therefore, there is little or no ground for a suit to be brought against a rabbi as the counselling situation leaves so many areas open.

January 1991

236. CONTRADICTORY RESPONSA

QUESTION: Several of the responsa in *Contemporary Reform Responsa* seem to be contradictory. For example, #67 has decided that a Messianic Jew should be refused burial, while #122 and #138 have indicated that apostates along with criminals are buried in a Jewish cemetery, although normally at a distance from other graves. As these answers were written at different times, does this reflect a growing strictness among us or are there other reasons for the disparity? (Rabbi Benno M. Wallach, Crosby TX)

ANSWER: We should note that all responsa address very specific questions and are not intended to provide broad general answers. An entire collection of responsa or several such collections may begin to provide a broader view of Jewish life and may set a pattern for generalizations. However, individual responsa address specific issues as will become apparent in the subsequent discussion.

Tradition has indicated that Jewish criminals were to be buried (Deut 21.23; *M* San 4.5; 47a; *Shulhan Arukh* Yoreh Deah 362.52 and 334.3 and *Tur* Yoreh Deah 334 and commentaries). Furthermore, apostates were similarly buried. We did so not to honor the apostates, but to help the surviving family. For that reason all matters connected with the "honor of the dead" were avoided while normal other burial procedures were followed (Moses Sofer *Responsa* Yoreh Deah 341; *Tur* and *Shulhan Arukh* Yoreh Deah 344, 345 and Commentaries). When an apostate died suddenly it was assumed that he had repented and returned to Judaism before his death (Isserles to *Shulhan Arukh* Yoreh Deah 340.5; Hoshen Mishpat 266.2). However, in #122 the Messianic Jew did not die suddenly nor had he in any way indicated a return to Judaism. Furthermore, his family remain apostates. These grounds are sufficient to refuse the burial of a Messianic Jew or a Jew for Jesus.

We may also refuse burial as these individuals masquerade as Jews and mislead others and they therefore pose a danger to the unsuspecting members of our community. Anyone who endangers the Jewish community in a serious fashion may be refused burial by that community (Nahmanides *Responsa* #224; Jacob Levi *Responsa* #49).

These responsa, therefore, may seem inconsistent on initial reading, however, they answer different questions and the circumstances are sufficiently distinctive to demand different answers.

April 1988

237. FREEING HOSTAGES

QUESTION: A man in my family has been taken as a hostage by bandits in South America. How far may the family and the community go in order to obtain his release? (Daniel Stern, New York NY)

ANSWER: The discussion of hostages and their ransom is ancient; captivity as a hostage was considered a terrible fate. The Talmudic discussion of a verse in Jeremiah came to this conclusion as captivity was the last of a list of horrors (Jer 15.2; B B 8a). The later tradition elaborated further and Maimonides warned that numerous commandments were violated by anyone who ignored the plight of hostages or even slightly delayed their redemption (*Yad* Hil Matnot Aniyim 8.10; *Shulhan Arukh* Yoreh Deah 352). Among charitable obligations the redemption of hostages was primary; it took precedence over feeding the poor or building a synagogue, and funds to be expended for this purpose could be moved from any other obligation (B B 8b). Even the sale of a *Torah* was permitted for the redemption of captives (*Sefer Hahinukh* #613).

The primary obligation rested on the immediate family; yet the obligation was also communal. However, matters were slightly different if the redemption posed a danger to the community. So, for example, Meir of Rothenburg refused to allow himself to be redeemed as that would have impoverished the community and set a precedent for taking communal leaders hostages. He, therefore, died in captivity (H. Graetz *Geschichte der Juden* Vol VII pp 203 ff, 476 ff).

The redemption of a hostage is a major *mitzvah*; all the members of the family and their friends should participate in it. In this instance the community may also be appropriately involved. Your description indicates that the man was taken hostage by bandits; this act does not have broader political implications as for example, the taking of hostages by the Palestinian Liberation Front. Such efforts at blackmail of Western governments or Israel must beresisted and rejected. There the community may be hurt by ransom efforts and that is akin to the problem which Meir of Rothenburg faced. Here, however, everything within reason should be done by the family and the community to obtain the release of the hostage.

December 1988

238. JEWISH LAWYERS AND TERRORISTS

QUESTION: According to Jewish tradition, is a Jewish lawyer obliged to defend Arab terrorists who attempt to kill Jews in Israel if a Jewish lawyer is designated to defend them? Is a Jewish lawyer obliged to defend terrorists who attempt to kill people in general if a Jewish lawyer is designated to defend them? Is a Jewish lawyer obliged to defend a member of the American Nazi Party when he knows that the goal of the American Nazi Party is detrimental to the Jewish people? (Rabbi Jack Segal, Houston TX)

ANSWER: We should begin by making it clear that the current system of appointing a lawyer or the hiring of a lawyer to defend appears late in our tradition. Although a person might have engaged someone to speak for him, this was usually not an individual who made his livelihood as an attorney. A representative akin to the modern attorney was used if the individual could not appear personally due to illness or distance or if one of the parties felt inadequate to the test of presenting a case. Most cases proceeded without an attorney. The traditional Jewish court procedure saw judges engaged in interrogation and so they did much of what attorneys do in the American courts. Various responsa mentioned attorneys and dealt with problems associated with them but not with our problem (Jacob ben Judah Weil *Responsa*; Meir of Rothenburg *Responsa*; Isaac ben Sheshet *Responsa* #235; Moses Isserles *Responsa* and others).

Although there is nothing like a court appointed attorney in the traditional system of Jewish law, nevertheless, the tradition may provide some guidance for Jewish attorneys in the United States and in the State of Israel in which the courts function differently. In these systems an accused individual engages an attorney or has an attorney appointed. What is the duty of a Jewish attorney under those circumstances?

In order to answer this question, we must ask ourselves about the purpose of a trial. Our concern is justice and that was expressed by the Bible which demanded close cross examination of the witnesses (Deut 13.15) as the accused was perceived innocent till proven guilty. The accused must be present during the examination of each of the witnesses who are testifying against her/him (*Yad* Hil Edut 4.1). Furthermore, the defendant must be personally warned by those who saw the crime or by someone else (San 30a; Git 33b; Kid 26b and Codes). The examination must concentrate on precise facts and not wander afield (San 32b; *Yad* Hil Edut 18.2; 22:1 ff; *Shulhan Arukh* Hoshen Mishpat 15.3; *Responsa Rivash* #266).

There are strict rules against self incrimination and no evidence of that kind is permissible (Ex 23.1; San 9b; Yeb 25; San.

6.2; 18.6 and commentaries). The defendant may plead on her/his own behalf in front of the court before the court begins its deliberations (M San 5.4), but he/she is not permitted to say anything which might prejudice the court against him (San 9.4). If the defendant is not capable of speaking for himself/herself, then a judge may do so for her/him (San 29a). If the matter involves a death sentence, then the court remains in session until the individual has been executed so that if any new evidence appears, the execution may be halted (M San 6.1; San 43a and Yad Hil San 13.1 ff).

This is merely a sample of judicial safeguards against injustice, it demonstrates the great care given to the defense of the accused and the efforts made on his behalf by the ancient system of courts. Lawyers or other representatives have not been involved, but the spirit of the law demands that we seek justice. We, in many modern lands, do so through an adversarial procedure.

The spirit of traditional legislation would indicate that lawyers in our system must participate in this effort to seek justice. This would apply to war criminals, terrorists or others who may be tried in the United States or in the State of Israel. Jewish attorneys should consider themselves within the framework of tradition if they are appointed to such tasks or wish to volunteer for them. No one can, of course, be forced into such a position against their will. They will help to assure that justice is done and that the accused has a reasonable opportunity to defend herself/himself within the framework of our judicial system. "Justice, Justice, shall you pursue" (Deut 16.20) or "in righteousness shall you judge your neighbor" (Lev 19.15) will continue to be our guide.

April 1989

239. PREFERENTIAL TREATMENT OF CHILDREN IN ESTATES

QUESTION: What is the Jewish law regarding inheritance? May the distribution be rearranged from the standard recommendation and favor one child over another to compensate for the bad luck of that child or inability to take care of itself properly. What role should love play? (Rabbi Richard M. Litvak, Santa Cruz CA)

ANSWER: The entire matter of inheritance is quite complex. Initially it was based on a verse in the *Torah* which indicated that sons were to inherit and if there were no sons, daughters, and subsequent other kinsman who were specified (Nu 27.8 ff). Daughters were systematically excluded in the early rabbinic period unless no male heirs existed (B B 110a f). Furthermore, the direct descendants of a son also took precedence over any daughters. In this system, lineal descendants took precedence (*M* B B 8.2, 115a, b; *Yad* Hil Nahalot 1.3, 5). Sons also inherited from their mother (*M* B B 8.1), however, the mother's other family members were generally excluded from inheritance. In this entire system it was taken for granted that daughters received a dowry and, therefore, their economic future was guaranteed. If they were permanently single or not yet married, it was the duty of the brothers to provide for them, including a dowry, so no further economic benefits needed to be bestowed. Appropriate provisions were made in wills to assure or force the giving of a dowry.

In accordance with verses from Deuteronomy, the first born son received a double segment of the estate (Deut 21.16-17). This applied to the father's estate and even if the first born was a *mamzer*. This did not apply to daughters. There was a limitation, however, as the first born received a double portion only from the father's estate not from that of the mother (*Yad* Hil Nahalot 2.8; *Shulhan Arukh* Hoshen Mishpat 277.1). The amount to be divided was calculated by the number of sons and the first born received a double portion of that sum. The status of the estate was governed by the time of death. In other words, if a child was born after the death of the father, that child was disregarded for the purpose of calculating this amount (B B 142b). Just as the first born was entitled to a double portion of inheritance of all kinds, he was also responsible for a double portion of the debts of the estate (B B 124a; *Shulhan Arukh* Hoshen Mishpat 278.9).

The right of a husband to inherit from his wife was absolute, although there was a good deal of debate over what rights still existed if divorce procedures had begun (*Yad* Hil Nahalot 1.18; *Shulhan Arukh* Even Haezer 90.1). This right to inherit extended to items which she might inherit from someone else (Maharashdam *Responsa* Even Haezer #98). A wide variety of medieval ordinances dealt with the complex problems of inheritance when sons stemmed from a former marriage. Sometimes the dowry or a portion, thereof, reverted to the wife's family if she died without children. This was especially true if she died within the first or second year of marriage (Isserles to *Shulhan Arukh* Even Haezer, 53.3; 118.8; Asher ben Yehiel *Responsa* 55.1). All of these restrictions were intended to adjust to new circumstances and to treat the heirs family fairly. They protected the inheritance of the wife's family especially.

Although daughters were excluded from all these matters of inheritance, the sons who received the inheritance had to maintain their sisters and also provide them with adequate dowries (*M* Ket 4.6 ff; 53b; 68b; *Shulhan Arukh* Even Haezer 112.10). Of course, if there were no sons, then the daughters received and divided the total estate (*Shulhan Arukh* Even Haezer 112.18). These laws took effect under normal circumstances. A person could, however, make other provisions by giving away his property during his lifetime and thus circumvent the normal laws of inheritance. He had to operate within the principle *ein shetar lahar mitah* (Ket 55 b; B B 152a; *Shulhan Arukh* Hoshen Mishpat 250.9; Moses Sofer *Hatam Sofer* Hoshen Mishpat 142). Moses Feinstein disagreed with this principle (*Igrot Mosheh* Even Haezer 104). Often this was done in such a way that the property was given as a gift while the right of usage remained during the lifetime of the owner (*M* B B 8.7; *Shulhan Arukh* Hoshen Mishpat 257.6 f). Some kind of formal *kinyan* (acquisition) was necessary (B B 149a; San 29b; *Shulhan Arukh* Hoshen Mishpat 250.3; 257.7; 281.7). Depending on how this was worded he could change his mind during his lifetime. In any case it referred only to property then in his possession. He could also stipulate that his property be distributed in accordance with his wishes and that was to be effective one hour before his death (B B 136a; *Tur* and *Shulhan Arukh* Hoshen Mishpat 258). Verbal declarations during a fatal illness were considered valid without *kinyan* (Git 13a; 15a; B B 151a; *Yad* Hil Zehiya Umatanah 7 ff; *Shulhan Arukh* Hoshen Mishpat 250.1).

It was in precisely the same way that a father could favor his daughters. This was done through a special deed which becomes effective one hour before the individual's death (*shetar hatzi zakhar*). Often the deed stipulated that half of a son's share shall go to a daughter (*Nahalat Shivah* #21.1). In order to enforce his wishes, the document could also state that if the gift was not made, an unusually high amount of dowry was to be given to the daughter (Isserles to *Shulhan Arukh* Hoshen Mispat 281.7). This *shetar*, which takes effect just before the individuals death, overcame the problem of the rights of succession. The proper language had to be used to indicate that these gifts were serious and permanent and, of course, there have been innumerable cases of challenges.

In the lengthy discussions of wills and estates, which took place in traditional literature, there is little which deals with the question which you have asked.

Some wills cited in the responsa favored one child over another for the reasons mentioned in your questions. Others overcame the problems, which you raised, through the ethical will, a document which appealed to the conscience of the heirs. Although this avenue is open to anyone, it has become primarily a literary device through which scholars and philosophers address the moral problems of their age. The outward form of a father speaking to his children actually addresses a larger audience.

The tradition gradually permitted greater equality among all children in matters of inheritance through the devices mentioned above. The more recent testamentary documents reflect this clearly. Reform Judaism would encourage it. This would, however, not preclude making special provisions to deal with unusual problems among children. In other words, placing funds in a trust to safeguard them against misspending, etc. Traditional Judaism has permitted and Reform Judaism encouraged the equal treatment of all children so that closeness of family and the love of siblings for each other will continue from generation to generation.

November 1987

240. RESPONSIBILITY TOWARD PETS

QUESTION: An elderly parent died and left, along with household items, a pet cat to which she was very much attached. His children wish to know whether they are responsible for the care of this cat, or whether they can give it away, or perhaps put it to sleep. (Laura Ellman, Kansas City MO)

ANSWER: The prohibition against cruelty to animals goes back to Biblical times and has been reinforced often in our tradition. It was permissible to use animals for work as long as they were not treated cruelly, to sacrifice them, but again in a manner that did not in any way prolong their suffering and, of course, to consume them if the animal was slaughtered in an appropriate way and fit into the system of *kashrut*. Almost nothing has been said of the pets in the Jewish tradition and so virtually all animals which were akin to our pets such as dogs were used as guard or watch animals. Dogs were traditionally considered unclean, mainly through their contact with corpses (Lev 22.4). The dog was seen primarily as a scavenger, as already shown in Exodus. Cattle which had been killed by wild animals were thrown to the dogs. Elsewhere, male pagan religious prostitutes were referred to as "dogs" (Deut 23.18). When the *Talmud* wished to be derogatory about Goliath, it provided him with a genealogy in which he was called the son of a loose woman who had intercourse with dogs (Sotah 42b; Rashi and commentaries).

Only in the post-Biblical book, *Tobit*, were there some favorable references to a dog (5.16, 11.4). The *Mishnaic* and *Talmudic* literature understood the danger from certain kinds of dogs which were indistinguishable from wolves, especially in the evening (*M* Kil 8.6, 1.6; Ber 9b). A dog was considered among the poorest of all creatures and often had to subsist entirely on scraps and as a scavenger (Shab 155b). Dogs used in sheep herding were viewed more favorably (*M* Hul 1.8).

On the other hand, the *Talmud* appreciated the atmosphere of safety created by dogs and suggested that one should not live in a town where the barking of dogs was not heard (Pes 113a; Betza 15a). The potential danger of rabies was also recognized (Hul 58b; Yoma 83b). Dogs were to be chained as they were considered dangerous (B K 79b; *Yad* Hil Nizqei Mamon 5.9; *Shulhan Arukh* Hoshen Mishpat 409). It was considered sinful to maintain a dog that was known to bite people (B K 15b), but one could let a dog run loose in harbor cities, presumably as an additional safeguard against lawless seamen (B K 83a). Enmity between human beings and dogs was mentioned in at least one passage of the *Jerusalem Talmud* (Ber 8.8).

Hunting dogs were not mentioned in the *Talmud* but later by Rashi in his commentary (B K 80a). Dogs were sometimes kept as pets, and the *Talmud* in one place mentioned that if a woman spent her time entirely with lap dogs or on games (possibly chess), this was grounds for divorce (Ket 61b).

Although cats were certainly known to ancient Israelites, after all they were considered sacred animals in Egypt, there was no mention of the domesticated cat in the *Bible*. The single reference in the post-Biblical book of *Baruch* (6.22) may refer to a wild cat. The *Talmud* considered cats as loyal (Hor 13a) in contrast to the dog. The principle purpose of keeping cats was to rid a building of mice (B K 80a) as well as other small animals (San 105a), including snakes (Pes 112b; Shab 128b). They were, of course, dangerous to chickens and domesticated birds, as well as young lambs and goats (Hul 52b, 53a; Ket 41b). Cats also endangered babies (B K 80b). The limited intelligence of cats was blamed on their consumption of mice, which were supposed to decrease memory (Hor 13a). In nineteenth century Russia, a folk myth warned Yeshivah students from playing with cats because that might diminish their memory. Cats were, on the other hand, seen as a model of cleanliness and modesty (Er 100b). Once cats established themselves in a house, they rarely left and remained very loyal (Shab 51b). Sometimes their fur was used as it was particularly soft (B K 80b).

In the *halakhah* there is nothing that deals with the kind of special role which various pets have played in modern Western European and American life. As we can see, the care of animals was always an important part of our tradition. We would, therefore, say that the heirs are duty bound to either care for this animal which was important to their father or to find an appropriate home for it. They may certainly not put it to sleep or abandon it.

February 1991

241. LOST PROPERTY

QUESTION: A Russian Jewish Immigrant family which recently arrived in America has discovered that one of the suitcases brought along did not belong to them. It is a small suitcase which contains family mementos as well as some Hebrew books. Only Hebrew names were given in the volumes with no indication of the rightful owner. They have kept the suitcase for some time with the hope that some inquiries would locate the proper owner. Now they wish to dispose of it and do not know what to do with the contents and especially with the Hebrew books. How long need they wait for the rightful owner to appear? What action should they take? (Karen Ruttenberg, Birmingham AL)

ANSWER: It is understandable that the confusion of immigration may lead to the loss of personal objects. It has always been considered a *mitzvah* to restore a lost object to its owner (Deut 22.1; B B 23b ff; B K 54b ff; San 73a; *Yad* Hil Gezelah Veavedah 11; *Shulhan Arukh* Hoshen Mishpat 259, 263). It was incumbent upon the individual who found a lost animal to keep it and feed it virtually indefinitely until the rightful owner appeared to claim it. He could, of course, at that time ask that proper recompense be made for the care which he provided for the animal (Deut 22:2 and commentaries), but beyond that he had no claim on the property.

In this instance the family feels that the books have become a burden and they do not think that anyone will ever claim them. It would be appropriate to place them in a communal setting, preferably a synagogue. A memorandum should be circulated among the local Russian Jewish community and in other cities in order to discover the rightful owner. If that fails, the synagogue should simply add this suitcase of books and other objects to its *genizah* and leave them there indefinitely. If they have not been claimed within a generation, it would be possible to give them to an archive.

As these objects were considered sufficiently important to be among the few possessions taken from Russia, they will surely be claimed. The items should be stored in a synagogue or public institution with enough publicity, so that they may be claimed by their rightful owner.

February 1991

242. THE TEMPLE GIFT SHOP AND NON-JEWISH CUSTOMERS

QUESTION: Our Temple gift shop is the only source for Judaica in Northern Indiana. Occasionally, non-Jews will purchase items from the shop as gifts for Jewish friends' weddings or *Benei Mitzvah*. What is the responsibility of the Temple gift shop to sell Judaica to Christians who might use these items for religious purposes, and what would be our responsibility for selling such items to Messianic Jews or Jews for Jesus? (Rabbi Morley T. Feinstein, South Bend IN)

ANSWER: Most of the objects which are connected with Jewish ritual that a gift shop is likely to handle have been designed specifically for Jewish use, but there is no special holiness attached with any of them. Ordinary objects can be used for Jewish ritual. For example, any candelabra with two or more candles can be used for *shabbat* or festival eves and any eight branched candelabrum may be used for *Hanukkah*, although it may not have been specifically designed for that purpose. Through the century we have, of course, decorated a large number of ritual items and a specific Jewish artistic expression has been created around them (Joseph Gutmann (ed) *Beauty in Holiness; Jewish Ceremonial Art;* Cecil Roth (ed) *Jewish Art;* Stephen Kayser *Jewish Ceremonial Art;* Abram Kanof *Jewish Ceremonial Art and Religious Observance; Journal of Jewish Art* Vols 1-15). These items may be sold by a gift shop or by another store in the community which need not be under Jewish auspices or ownership. It would be difficult for us in this period, when we continue to seek good relationships with the world around us, to question a non-Jewish purchaser about the final use of any item. In some instances they are purchased for Jewish friends, a thoughtful gift. In others they are intended for display in a church or a denominational school in order to demonstrate some Jewish ritual. So, for example, several churches in this area have purchased *Hanukkah menorahs* and *Seder* plates as part of their museum collection or for their religious school studies of Judaism. This will help the world around us understand Judaism better.

We should remember that the primary task of a gift shop is to supply the congregation itself and beyond that, the larger Jewish community. It is not a business enterprise and any profit which accrues is secondary to its mission of helping local Jews to celebrate festivals, *shabbat*, and Jewish occasions properly. The shop may very well seek to restrict itself somewhat from the larger community, although in the present day setting that is difficult.

We would prefer not to have any contact with Jews for Jesus and would discourage them using our shop and perhaps indicate that their presence in our gift shop is not welcome, but we should not embarrass others whose intentions are good and helpful. If Jews for Jesus are a particular nuisance in a community, then it is perfectly proper for a Temple gift shop to refrain from selling them anything. We should not let this small group stand in the way of developing better relations with the general community.

December 1988

243. CANDY IN THE SISTERHOOD GIFT SHOP

QUESTION: The Sisterhood gift shop regularly sells candy during the holiday period. A group of parents have objected that this practice is contrary to Jewish ethics as such an encouragement of candy consumption aids to the deterioration of teeth not only of children, but also adults. (Larry Dann, New York NY)

ANSWER: There is a strong series of Jewish traditions which prohibit wounding oneself or in any way endangering one's life (Deut 4.9; 4.15; Ber 32b; B K 91b; *Yad* Hil Rotzeah Ushemirat Hanefesh 11.4; Hil Shevuot 5.57; Hil Hovel Umazig 5.1). This concern for health also applies to the health of a neighbor (B K 91b; *Yad* Hil Rotzeah 11.4 ff; *Shulhan Arukh* Hoshen Mishpat 427; Yoreh Deah 116.5 and Isserles). These statements are clear, but here we are dealing with an item of food which is not necessarily injurious. In other words, if candy is consumed in large quantities it may not be healthy, or if individuals who consume candy do not take appropriate care of their teeth, it may also be injurious. The items in question are, however, not dangerous in themselves. This is true of a great many other materials and foods in general use. They may, if improperly used, lead to serious health problems. The problem lies with the user not the seller. This is true of foods with high cholesterol content, alcoholic beverages, etc.

It would be appropriate for the Sisterhood to indicate that candy is only sold to adults or children with adults, thereby removing the objection that children who would normally not be permitted to purchase candy may do so at the Sisterhood Gift Shop. Furthermore, the Sisterhood may also wish to sponsor some specific programs which deal with health care for children not only in connection with the consumption of candy, but other matters as well. This would alleviate the fear of parents that their children are being misled by this important and very useful group within the congregation.

March 1990

244. GIFT SHOP AND GENERAL MERCHANDISE

QUESTION: Our Sisterhood has managed a successful gift shop for many years. It has dealt primarily in Judaica but in an effort to increase revenue and assist special synagogue projects, has expanded its merchandise. Some have complained and felt that this was an improper way to raise funds for the Temple. Are they correct? (Sally Rosenzweig, Los Angeles CA)

ANSWER: Synagogues have used many different methods to raise funds for the congregation. It has always been considered obligatory for everyone in the community to support the synagogue as was done with the ancient Temple (Ex 30.11 ff; W. Jacob *Centomprary American Reform Responsa* # 139, 151). We have avoided methods which were distasteful or interrupted the service like the sale of Torah honors (*Ibid* 150) and gambling (*Ibid* 160).

The expansion of the gift shop into new directions seems like an appropriate way of helping the synagogue. We should be careful that this effort remains in perspective; I have seen gift shops which are too obtrusive and commercialize the synagogue. There are also taxation issues which must be addressed by the appropriate individuals.

This method of fund raising is appropriate and should be helpful to the congregation.

April 1989

245. GIFT SHOP AND ADVERTISING

QUESTION: May a synagogue gift shop advertise in the communal Jewish paper? Is it appropriate to increase income in this manner or does this provide unfair competition to the communal merchants? (Doris Applebaum, New York NY)

ANSWER: Synagogues have used many different methods to raise funds for the congregation. It has always been considered obligatory for everyone in the community to support the synagogue as was done with the ancient Temple (Ex 30.11 ff; W. Jacob *Centomprary American Reform Responsa #* 139, 151). We have avoided methods which were distasteful or interrupted the service like the sale of *Torah* honors (*Ibid* 150) and gambling (*Ibid* 160). A wide variety of other methods have been used in modern times; some bulletins contain advertising; program booklets have regularly been prepared; donor dinners have been used, etc. Most of these methods have addressed themselves to the synagogue community. The advertising proposed would bring the effort into the broader community which would be appropriate if a special need is met.

If the gift shop wishes to make the community aware of its

Judaica items or Jewish books which may not be available elsewhere, then it would serve a broader purpose. If the shop proposes to deal with general merchandise, then it would not be appropriate as the non-profit status of the synagogue provides unfair competion.   This path may endanger the non-proft status of the gift corner. Even if that does not occur, it would not be ethical to compete in this manner.

August 1989

246. THE WEARING OF EARRINGS BY MEN

QUESTION: What is the *halakhic* attitude and our Reform view of wearing earrings by men? This is a practice which has become more common on the college campus.   Should it be prohibited as part of the general restriction against dressing like the opposite sex, or perhaps because of the permanent injury caused by piercing the ear? (Rabbi Charles Arian Charlottesville VA)

ANSWER: You have properly raised some of the issues which need to concern us. The Biblical statement (Deut 22.5) which prohibited a man from wearing women's clothing and vice versa has usually been interpreted strictly and most traditional authorities prohibited the practice entirely. They were dealing with general items of clothing as well as ornamentation (Eliezer Waldenberg *Tzitz Eliezer* II #62; Isaac Jacob Weisz *Minhat Yitzhaq* II #108; Yom Tov Deutsch *Taharat Yom Tov* 9:55, 77-87). Their discussion included types of women's clothing which imitated men's clothing and may have been designed specifically for women, but if it was called by the same name, i.e. slacks or pants; then it was

400

nevertheless considered men's garb. These authorities felt that wearing clothing of the opposite sex not only violated the Biblical commandments cited but was immodest.

As the *Talmud* reported that Rabbi Judah and his wife shared a garment (Ned 49b), which she wore while in the market and he while praying, there were grounds for permissiveness. Furthermore, some authorities stated that clothing normally appropriate for the other sex may be worn as long as another item of clothing clearly identified the sex of the wearer. In other words, a heavy man's coat might be worn for protection against cold as was frequently done in Eastern Europe (*Shulhan Arukh* Yoreh Deah, #182 and commentaries; *Avnei Tzedeq* Yoreh Deah #72). There were other authorities who disagreed with this interpretation (*Tur* Yoreh Deah #182; *Shulhan Arukh* Yoreh Deah #182 with commentaries by Isserles, Taz and Shakh).

There were, however, occasions such as Purim celebrations in which men and women often wore the clothes of the other sex as a humorous disguise and no objection has been raised (*Shulhan Arukh* Orah Hayim 696.8 and Isserles; Judah Mintz *Responsa* #17).

We have realized as fashions change, what was once considered women's dress may now be worn by men and vice versa; one example are women's slacks (Solomon B. Freehof *Contemporary Reform Responsa* #27). Although the traditional authorities prohibited such dress, it has often been adopted, nevertheless.

We need not prohibit the practice of men wearing earrings on the grounds that earrings are primarily worn by women. Pierced ears have an interesting history in Judaism (W. Jacob *Contemporary Reform Responsa* #76). In Biblical times they indicated lifelong slavery and it was the male slave who was so marked (Ex 21.6; Bekh 37a; Kid 21b). In later *Talmudic* times ornaments of various kinds were worn on the ear to mark trades and professions (*Tos Shab* 1.8; Shab 11b). In these instances males wore the ear ornaments, however, the *Mishnah* also knew of women piercing their ears for ornamentation (*M* Shab 6.6). Tradition made no distinction between ear ornaments worn by men or women. In subsequent centuries and in more modern times, at least in the West, earrings have been limited to women. If they now become an item of fashion for men, Reform Judaism would have no objections.

We would, however, add a caution because of the current AIDS epidemic. Piercing the ear is a minor operation which involves instruments used by semi-professionals who may not completely sterilize them. The practice is potentially dangerous. If ears are pierced, it should be done in a sterile setting and every effort should be made to guarantee it.

September 1988

Index

This is an index to the volumes *American Reform Responsa* (I), *Contemporary American Responsa* (II) and *Questions and Reform Jewish Answers - New American Reform Responsa* (III). The index indicates the volume and number, not the page of the responsum.

Fetus kept as a source for organs, III #163
Jewish reaction to epidemics (AIDS), II #82
Responsibility of an AIDS carrier, III #161
ALCOHOLICS ANONYMOUS
Lord's prayer, II # 171
ANTI-SEMITISM
Christian decorations in a business office, II #174
Fighting discrimination, II # 170
APOSTATES
Apostates proselyte, I #71
Burial of apostate, II #100
Burial of "Messianic Jew," II #67
Children of "Messianic Jew," II #66
Drifting apostate, II #65
Marriage with a "Messianic Jew," I #150
Qaddish for a Unitarian sister, I #124
Return to Judaism for apostate, II #64
Return to Judaism for baptized girl, II #62
Status of a "Completed Jew," II #68
    (See also CHRISTIANS, MIXED MARRIAGE, RELIGIOUS STATUS)
ARK
Ark and *Torah* permanently in a Christian Church, II #148
Facing the ark, III #21
Placing of piano in front of ark, I #20
Position of synagogue entrance and ark, I #19
Rooms behind a synagogue ark, II #141
    (See also SYNAGOGUE)
ARTIFICIAL INSEMINATION, I #157, #158
In vitro fertilization, II #19
Test tube baby, II #18
ART
Berit Milah plate, III #107
Decorated coffin, III #175
Form of the *Yad*, III #28

INDEX

INDEX

Preferential treatment of children estates, III #239
Return to Judaism for baptizes girl, II #62
Teenagers and *Gerut*, II #50
Status of children of doubtful religious background, I #61
Status of a Gentile-born child adopted into a Jewish family, I #62
(See also ADOPTION, *BAR/BAT MITZVAH*, CIRCUMCISION, FETUS)
CHRISTIANS
All night vigils, III #17
Ark and *Torah* permanently in a Christian church, II #148
Apostate proselyte, I #71
Baptism and educating a child as a Jew, III #111
Berit for "Messianic Jews" - "Jewish Christians", III #110
Berit and baptism, III #109
Burial in Christian cemetery, II #105
Burial of a prospective convert, I #97
Burial of "Messianic Jews", II #67
Burial of non-Jewish wives in Jewish cemeteries, I #98
Gentile as a *Kevater* at a *Berit Milah*, III #105
Gentile chairman of Confirmation group, II #163
Gentile members on congregational committees, II #164
Child and two religious traditions, III 388
Child raised in two religious traditions, II #61
Children of "Messianic Jews," II #66
Children of mixes marriages, I #60
Christian children in the religious school, III #89
Christian composer of Jewish melodies, III #19
Christian music at Jewish at Jewish wedding, II #195
Church window honoring a Jew, II #166
Congregational membership for a non-Jewish partner, II #162
Conversion of a child with two non-Jewish parents, III #128
Convert with the Christian family, I #70
Convert with the Christian family, II #54
Employment of non-Jews in a Jewish cemetery, I #105

INDEX

INDEX

Elijah and *berit*, III #106
Gentile as a *Kevater* at a *Berit Milah*, III#105
Minyan and *Berit Milah*, III #97
Naming an uncircumcised child, II #29
Nolad Mahul (Born Circumcised), I #58
Pressured *Mohel*, III #100
Prospective convert who fears circumcision, I #69
Rabbi or *Mohel* at a Moslem circumcision, II #31
Role of a godfather in the circumcision ceremony, II #30
Sandeq and *Mohel* at public services, III #104
Soviet Jewish child and *Berit*, III #103
Status of an uncircumcised retarded adult, I #64
Terminated pregnancy and *Berit*,III #96
Tipat Dam, III #108
  (See also RELIGIOUS STATUS)
COHEN
Marriage of *Cohen* to a divorcee, I #139
CONCUBINE
Concubinage as alternative to marriage, I #133
CONFIDENTIALITY
Confidential information, II #5
Informing on others in criminal cases, II #6
Professional ethics, II #4
CONFIRMATION
Confirmation and *Bar Mitzvah*, III #34
CONGREGATION
Advertising and congregational fund raising, III #42
Aliyah to the *Torah* and congregational dues, II #149
Congregational membership at the age of thirteen, II #152
Congregational membership for a non-Jewish spouse, II #162
Expulsion of a member, I #16
Forfeiture of membership by intermarriage, I #12
Gentile chairman of Confirmation group, II #163
Gentile members on congregational committees, II #164
Gentiles in a Jewish congregation, II #161

412

INDEX

EARS
Pierced ears, II #75
ELDERLY
Children support of parents, II #26
CPR and the frail elderly, III #160
Elderly patient who refuses dialysis, III #157
Financial responsibility toward Jew. Homes for the aged, III #91
Responsibility of children to their parents, I #153
(See MEDICAL ETHICS, WILL, PARENTS)
ENVIRONMENT
Judaism and the environment, II #12
EUTHANASIA, I #78, #79
(See also DYING PATIENT, MEDICAL ETHIC)
FALASHAS
Black Jew, Falashas and conversion, III #132
FAUNA
(See PETS)
FERTILITY
In vitro fertilization, II #19
Test tube baby, II #18
FETUS
Fetus kept alive as a source for organs, III #163
Fetus used for experimentation, II #21
Genetic engineering, II #20
In vitro fertilization, II #19
Test tube baby, II #18
FLAGS
Israeli flag on pulpit, I #22
National flags at religious services, I #20
Old Israeli flag, III #195
(See SYNAGOGUE)
FLORA
(See NATURE)
FREEZING OF BODIES
(See CRYOBIOLOGY)

416

INDEX

GET
(See DIVORCE)

GIFT SHOP
Candy in Sisterhood Gift Shop, III #243
Gift Shop advertising, III #245
Gift Shop and general merchandise, III #243
Temple Gift Shop and non-Jewish customers, III #244
GIFTS
Debuts versus gifts, II #8
Gifts to organizations inimical to Reform Judaism, II #25
GOD
Bronze Hebrew tablet, III #49
Erasing the name of God from the computer screen, III #144
Hebrew Bible on computer, III #143
Kissing a Hebrew book, III #142
Name of God, III #145
Shredding services to protect name of God, III #146
GRACE AFTER MEALS, III #79
GRAVE
Direction of grave in the cemetery, I #103, #104
Fallen gravestones, II #115
Names on a tombstone, II #116
Putting small sticks in a hands of deceased when placing in the grave, I #116
Removal of dead body to another grave, I #106
Setting of a tombstone, II #114
Shiva for delayed funeral, II #120
Shema as a tombstone inscription, II #117
Tombstone with Christian marking, II #118
Two coffins in one grave, I #107
(See also CEMETERY, TOMBSTONE)
HAMOTSI
(See BREAD)

Kosher kitchen in military camps, I #50
Red wine and white wine, III #84
Use of Pyrex dishes for meat and milk, I #51
KETUBAH
Decorations on a *Ketubah*, III #225
Destroyed *Ketubah*, III #232
Error in *Hebrew* text, III #226
Error in *Ketubah* text, III #227
Error in the Hebrew date, III #226
Hebrew or Russian text in *Ketubah*, III #227
Lost *Ketubah*, III #231
Signature on a *Ketubah*, III #230
Two sets of Hebrew names, III #228
Virginity and the *Ketubah*, II #187
KIDDUSH
(See WINE, RELIGIOUS PRACTICE)
KIPPAH
Burial with *Kippah*, III #173
Kippot for men and women, III #12
Women with heads covered, III #13
Worshipping with covered heads, I #5
(See also RELIGIOUS PRACTICE)
LESBIANS
(See HOMOSEXUALITY)
LEVI
(See TRIBE OF LEVI)
LOANS
Conditional loan of a *Torah*, III #136
How should a loan in foreign currency be repaid?, I #169
LOST PROPERTY
Lost property, III #241
MARRIAGE
Adultery and marriage, II #192
Anniversary ceremony, III #223
Confidential information, II #5

INDEX

Hanukkah and Christmas decoration in an apartment complex, III #75

Hanukkah and a combustible *Menorah*, II #185

Menorah decoration for a synagogue, II #147

Sequence of lighting *Hanukkah* candles, II #186

MESSIANIC JEWS

Burial of 'Messianic Jews", II #67

Children of "Messianic Jews", II #66

Marriage with a "Messianic Jews", I #150

Status of a "Completed Jew," II #68

(See also APOSTATES, MIXED MARRIAGE, RELIGIOUS STATUS)

MEZUZAH

Casing of a *Mezuzah*, II #71

Mezuzah on trailer, III #141

Paper *Mezuzah*, III #140

Second paragraph of the *Shema*, III #139

MINHAG

(See RELIGIOUS PRACTICE, SERVICES, HOLIDAYS)

MINORS

Punishment of minors, II #3

MINYAN

Less than a *Minyan* of ten at services, I #3

Minyan at wedding ceremony, II #189

Service with less than a *Minyan*, III #4

(See also RELIGIOUS PRACTICE, SERVICES)

MIQVEH

Origin of *Miqveh* for conversion, II #43

Swimming pool as a *Miqveh*, II #45

The *Miqveh* and Reform converts, II #44

MIXED MARRIAGE

Burial of non-Jewish wived in Jewish cemeteries, I #99

A child raised in two religious traditions, II #61

Children of mixed marriages, I #60

Convert with a Christian family, I #70

INDEX

RETARDATION

Dangers of surgery correcting congenital craniofacial malformations, II #77

Parental obligation to severely retarded child, II #202

RUSSIAN JEWS

(See SOVIET IMMIGRANTS)

SABBATH

Blowing the *Shofar* on Sabbath, I #45

Eruv, II #178

Fundraising on *Shabbat*, III #60

Havdalah spice box, III #64

Holiday gift wrapping project and *Shabbat*, II #177a

Jewish studies on *Shabbat* afternoon, III #58

Orthodox Jew as partner in firm keeping open on *Shabbat*, I #44

Poverty project and *Shabbat*, II #176

Renting a portion of a synagogue to a university, III #59

Shabbat commandment against lighting a fire, III #62

Sabbath observance, I #45

Spices for *Havdalah*, III #63

Synagogue tours on *Shabbat*, III #61

White bread for *Halot*, III #57

Why do we kindle the lights on Friday evening? III #56

Work on synagogue on *Shabbat* by non-Jews, I #26

SCHOOL

Dress code for religious school, II #27

SEFER TORAH

Fabric used in *Torah* mantle, I #41

Ownership of a *Sefer Torah*, I #40

Repairing damaged *Sefer Torah*, I #72

Ritual for disposal of damaged *Sefer Torah*, I #73

(See also *TORAH*)

SERMON

(See RABBINATE, SERVICES)

INDEX

SERVICES

INDEX

Tallit at interfaith service, III #11
Women wearing *Tallit*, I #4
  (See also RELIGIOUS PRACTICE)
TEMPLE
  (See CONGREGATIONS, RABBI, RELIGIOUS PRACTICE, SYNAGOGUE)
TERRORISTS
Jewish lawyers and terrorists, III #238
TESTIMONY
Testimony against a family member, I #170
TETRAGRAMATON
  (See NAMES, GOD)
TOMBSTONE
Ashes of a couple in a single urn, III #191
Colored tombstone, III #184
Exchanging a tombstone, I #113
Fallen gravestones, II #115
Insignia on a tombstone, I #110
Isaiah verse on a tombstone, III #187
Lapse of time before setting a tombstone, I #108
Location of tombstone, III #182
Metal tombstone, III #185
Mother's name on son's tombstone, I #114
Name of deceased on two tombstones, II #119
Names on a tombstone, II #116
Responsibility for cemeteries, II #113
Reuse of a grave, III #190
Scattering ashes of the dead, III #192
Shema as a tombstone inscription, II #117
Setting of a tombstone, I #109, II #114
Tombstone for scattered ashes, III #193
Tombstone in absence of a body, I #112
Tombstone with Christian marking, II #118
Unmarked grave, III $189
Unmarked tombstone, III #186

INDEX